SAY IT'S SO

Papa, Dad, Me, and the 2005 White Sox Championship Season

Ben Shapiro
David Shapiro

For Papa, who waited his entire life,
For Dad, who saw the dream fulfilled,
For Gabriel, who won't have to waste three generations
waiting,
And for the 2005 White Sox, who finally made it all
happen.

"Do you think the Sox will ever win a World Series, Dad?"

- *David (age 7) to Nate after the White Sox finish second to the Yankees in 1963*
- *David (age 8) to Nate after the White Sox finish second to the Yankees in 1964*
- *David (age 9) to Nate after the White Sox finish second to the Yankees in 1965*
- *David (age 11) to Nate after the White Sox blow the 1967 pennant*
- *David (age 27) to Nate after the White Sox blow the 1983 playoffs to the Orioles*
- *Ben (age 6) to David after the White Sox finish second in 1990*
- *Ben (age 7) to David after the White Sox finish second in 1991*
- *Ben (age 9) to David after the White Sox blow the 1993 playoffs to Toronto*
- *Ben (age 16) to David after the White Sox blow the 2000 playoffs to Seattle*

"Now they're one out away from their first World Championship in 88 years. Not since 1917 .... Tying run at second, two out ... Palmiero ... over the head of Jenks ... Uribe charges ... throws ..."
- *Joe Buck, October 26, 2005*

DAD:

It is the habit of fathers to wax philosophical. Mothers are rightfully concerned with more prosaic affairs: making sure the children are fed properly, and reluctantly reminding their husbands to take out the garbage. Mothers are sometimes too busy and always too pragmatic to indulge in the navel-gazing that engages men in the Big Questions of Life. One of the beauties of marriage is this dichotomy – men pontificating while their wives sit patiently waiting for them to reach The Big Conclusion. If the truth be told, women generally have better things to do.

Which is why men have sons. Sons, if brought up correctly, have an undying worship of their fathers that enables then to listen ad infinitum while their fathers share the Wisdom of the Ages. This is what makes sons so important to men: they worship the father that the mother knows all too well is fallible.

Of course, there is a fly in the ointment. What does the father do when he knows he's *not* the proper person to offer advice, when he senses that his knowledge of the subject is not sufficient to command his son's attention? What does he do when his position as the All-Knowing father is compromised, when his status atop the marble throne becomes suddenly unstable? To what must he turn?

Baseball.

Baseball is the medium through which the father-son relationship flourishes despite the son's growing comprehension that although his father is wiser than he, his father also possesses the same doubts and fears that plague all men. The father turns to baseball – not news, not politics – because in the end, baseball is a world to itself, and can be detached from the world around it.

1

And in the end, this is what fathers and sons need: a world of their own.

Why, though, should baseball retain the unique position it does as the quintessential father-son mode of discussion? Why not football, basketball, hockey, ping-pong?

Because baseball is the perfect metaphor for life, that's why. I once asked my mother why she preferred for my younger brother (born in 1966) to watch Mr. Rogers instead of "Sesame Street." She answered that Sesame Street had a frenetic feel to it. (Remember the frantic counting clip? "Onetwothreefourfivesixseveneightnine . . . ten!") Mr. Rogers was slower, more reasonably paced, more like school.

That's baseball, too. Baseball moves at the speed of life. Baseball, unlike basketball, where someone scores every 15-20 seconds or so, does not reward the A.D.D. segment of the sports population. Baseball doesn't reward the violence-thirsty fan of football, who gets fired up by the announcer's manic Dick Vitale-esque "What a monster hit! He almost took his head off on that play!" Baseball doesn't reward the frat boy hockey fan, who is disappointed when he goes to see a fight and a hockey game breaks out. As for ping-pong . . . forget it.

Baseball is like life because life itself does not move at an insane rate of speed. True, there are many people who insist on living their lives at that speed, but they only delude themselves. Life will not move any faster no matter how much you put your ambitious pedal to the metal, or how much coffee you chug. And unlike the other aforementioned sports, there is no clock letting you know when time runs out, just as none of us know when our own time clock runs out.

The true baseball fan is not subconsciously eyeing his wristwatch because he has something to do afterward. There is no telling when the game is over, and so the game itself becomes the total focus of the fan. The world does not exist outside of the baseball game, and so a father sitting at the ballpark talking baseball with his son is privileged to command his son's total attention. The world outside has no meaning, then, and the pristine nature of their communication raises their relationship to a greater spiritual height.

Baseball reflects life. So, too, do baseball teams. Teams have lives. Not just the life of one season, but lives over the course of their existence. From their inception to whatever era constitutes the present, their history weaves together with the fathers' and sons' lives to make a rope tough enough to withstand the vicissitudes that all human relationships endure. Some teams experience intermittent success, such as the Los Angeles Dodgers (notice I didn't say Brooklyn), who win the World Series at least once every ten years or so; some experience inordinate success, like the Yankees (sorry, Tommy, the Man in the Sky, does not favor Dodger Blue, but Yankee pinstripes, from all the evidence); some suffer for a lifetime, but romantically, like the Red Sox, who failed so dramatically in various World Series and pennant races that millions of other teams' fans vicariously enjoyed their redemption in 2004.

But none of these teams quite reflect the underlying fashion of life in its meandering way as well as the Chicago White Sox do. Their triumphant scream of infancy, in 1901, at winning the pennant as they joined the land of the living; their giddy success at the age of five, trouncing their older brothers, the seemingly invincible Chicago Cubs, who had set an all-time regular season record that year of 1906; their great adolescence at the age of sixteen, when their 1917 team flexed its growing musculature and soundly defeated the team managed by the living legend John McGraw.

Then, in 1919, at the age of 18, when the young embark on their first steps toward independence, a fatally wrong choice. Catalyzed by the stinginess of their owner, the team lost its way, eight members leading it away from the hopeful journey toward a lifetime of self-discovery and leading it instead down the path of lifelong self-incrimination.

I was four in 1960, and I became a fan of the Chicago White Sox that year when my father took me to my first baseball game at Comiskey Park. They had just won the pennant for the first time in 40 years in 1959, and although they had lost the Series to the Dodgers, Sox fans were confident another chance would soon be at hand. I remember the optimism that pervaded the park that early May evening. If I had known what the next 45 years would bring, I would have understood why the conversations about baseball I had with my father, and those I would have with my own son, would carry the undertones of the ephemeral nature of the joys of life, and why those moments are to be cherished forever.

This book is a record of those conversations – and how our three-generation love of the Chicago White Sox reflects our understanding of what life should be, whether comic, absurd, dramatic, or simply an acceptance of the inevitability of life's capacity to bewilder, annoy, excite, and seduce us into loving it with all we've got.

BEN:

There are two types of people in this world: people who love baseball, and people who don't. It's impossible for people who love baseball to explain to those who don't why they love this non-contact game of long pauses, calculated risk-taking, attention to detail. How can you love a game that often takes four hours to play? How can you love a game that hinges on whether your slugging number three hitter knows how to lay down a bunt? How can you love a game where Tim Wakefield, tossing the ball all of 70 mph, wins games, and Randy Johnson, burning them in at 98, loses them? How can you love a game that depends on the hit-and-run, the squeeze-play, the two-out walk, the passed ball, tagging up, nicking the outside corner, turning two, the infield fly rule, pulling the string with a changeup, and the Texas Leaguer?

Here's the baseball fan's answer: how can you *not* love this game? There's no other way to answer the question. Baseball fans are from Mars, and non-baseball fans are from Venus (or, perhaps, Tampa Bay). Baseball is fluid, beautiful, detailed, and romantic in a way no other sport is. Ray Liotta's tragic Shoeless Joe Jackson sums it up well in *Field of Dreams*: "Man, I did love this game. I'd have played for food money. It was the game. . . . The sounds, the smells. Did you ever hold a ball or a glove to your face?. . . It was the crowd, rising to their feet when the ball was hit deep. Shoot, I'd play for nothing."

It's more than the beauty of the game that keeps me coming back. It's the fact that I share the experience with my dad – or rather, he shares it with me. After all, he was here first. My best memories involve my dad taking me to the park, hitting me pop flies. Or coaching my Little League team, the White Sox; we won the League championship in our second year, overcoming

5

all odds and the Curse of Comiskey (if the Curse applies in Los Angeles to 12-year-olds). Or simply sitting around and talking about the game: the intricacies, the hot stove trade talk, and the White Sox's chances ("Maybe they'll have a better shot next year, after they blow a division lead in the second half of this season and dump [insert name of latest White Sox manager]").

When we talk baseball, we never have to worry about boring each other. A.J. Pierzynski's latest antics and brilliant pitch-calling are fodder for countless hours of conversation (conversation that irks my three younger sisters beyond all reason). Do Juan Uribe's Smith & Wesson arm and underrated range compensate for his inability to hit the outside curveball? (Yes.) Should the White Sox go out and acquire a third baseman at the trading deadline, preferably Joe Randa? (Me: Yes. Dad: Let's wait on Crede.) How much should the Sox give up to get Ken Griffey Jr.? (Both of us: everything.) Sometimes we're right, sometimes we're wrong, and sometimes we disagree; but at the end of the day, we've had a wonderful time talking to each other.

It's those moments that you remember. Talking about other subjects may make your blood boil or your eyes roll, but baseball is always a rich vein for conversation. The game where attention to detail is most crucial provides the most conversational material. Does the pitcher's stutter step toward the plate give away whether he's throwing a breaking ball or a fastball? Is the first baseman holding the runner close enough? Is the left fielder playing off the line, knowing that the pitcher is going to throw one hard and outside?

And one of the great beauties of baseball is this: the game provides you with time to talk. Nobody is going anywhere. There's no two-minute drill, no shot clock. It's time that builds tension in a great game, and it's time that allows you to turn to your dad and ask him whether he'd give Scott Podsednik the green light in this situation. It's time that allows you to ask your dad his advice about women, and time that allows you to moan about classes. It's time that allows you to discuss life.

And often you don't even need conversation. There is nothing finer in life than sitting beside your father on a beautiful summer afternoon, filling out a scorecard, watching your team. That is, unless you're a White Sox fan – in which case every game is tortuously close and maddeningly frustrating.

Every baseball fan has his own special baseball moments. It is strange and amazing that so many of our best baseball memories involve our fathers sitting beside us. I remember the time I caught a foul ball at a Dodgers-Angels game (June 2001) – Adrian Beltre fouled one back. I backhanded it on the fly. My dad was sitting right next to me, ducking, and then laughing and cheering. In 1989, at age 5, I met then-White Sox shortstop Ozzie Guillen, and took a picture with him. My dad was standing about three feet away. About a year later, on July 1, 1990, I attended the first White Sox game I remember in detail – Andy Hawkins of the Yankees pitches a no-hitter and loses, thanks to a ridiculous error by right-fielder Jesse Barfield. My sister and mom, no doubt, were falling asleep. My dad was sitting next to me, explaining what was going on.

Baseball is an adhesive that holds fathers and sons together. It is a balm that salves the scratches of daily life. It is like a member of the family. Perhaps that's why baseball fans are so constant. Thinking about baseball is like coming home from a business trip – you want everything to be where you left it, and how you left it. The last thing you want is to come home and find that your brother has had a sex change. The same applies for the baseball fan. The true baseball fan finds change alarming, unless we've been shown that change will be superior. The true baseball fan hates the designated hitter, doubts whether there should be 30 teams in major league baseball, and wonders about interleague play.

No team is more constant than my Chicago White Sox. Maybe they were constant losers. Maybe they were constant chokers. But they were certainly constant. Unlike other teams (see Yankees, New York), the White Sox roster has never had a revolving door. Their current manager, Ozzie Guillen, their hitting coach, Greg Walker, their first base coach, Tim Raines, their third base coach, Joey Cora, their bench coach, Harold Baines, and their general manager, Kenny Williams, are all former White Sox players. And there's a certain beauty to continuity.

Continuity reminds us that time is passing. Ozzie Guillen once roamed the dirt between second and third; now he roams the dugout. My dad has been waiting 45 seasons to watch the Sox win a Series; I've been waiting 15. By reminding us that time is passing, yet simultaneously providing us with the time to share with our dads, baseball glorifies and enriches life. Perhaps *that* is why baseball is timeless. Maybe Kevin Costner has it right in *Field of Dreams*: maybe sharing baseball with Dad on an autumn afternoon *is* Heaven.

On October 26, 2005, as Bobby Jenks faced Orlando Palmiero with two outs in the bottom of the ninth inning, it sure was.

Part I
Year 88: A New Hope

February 23, 2005
DAD:

Forty-nine years old? Not yet, not yet . . . don't hurry me. I'm still having recurring dreams, as any red-blooded baseball fan has, of waking up to find I can throw the ball with the speed of Steve Dalkowski (the legendary pitcher of the 1950's who was timed by the Army at throwing a baseball 114 miles mph) and the pinpoint control of Sandy Koufax. What the heck, Satchel Paige was still pitching at about my age. There's hope yet.

The girls asked me what I wanted for my birthday, and I couldn't think of anything besides forty or fifty more years to watch them grow up and raise families of their own. But when Ben called from Cambridge, I confessed that seeing the White Sox win the World Series would be pretty high on the priority list, now that it looks like they can make a run. "You say that every year, Dad," Ben reminded me. "You're the eternal optimist." Approaching fifty, what else can I be? It's my nature to think the best is just around the corner, even with the White Sox. I don't live in the real world regarding them, but what White Sox fan truly does? It's not like being a Cubs fan, which has become trendy since celebrities like Bill Murray boasted that they rooted for the "Cubbies." How cute. How nauseating. Nobody called them the "Cubbies" when I was growing up on the North Side. They were the Cubs, and I hated them just as much as I loved the Sox. And although I hated Cubs fans, at least I respected them.

Now it's considered just darling to root for those lovable losers. That's crap. Nobody ever called the White Sox cute (except for the game where they wore shorts and Carlos May could hardly get his legs through them.) The White Sox were never cute; they were a team that sweated for every run and

11

made you develop bleeding ulcers watching them. The teams of the 70s were an aberrant nod to the power game that never looked right for a White Sox team. The rare good teams they had thrived on pitching and defense.

Which is why I love what Ozzie Guillen is doing. He's molding them in the image of the Marlins, pitching and speed, and as a traditionalist, it sounds great to me. Before the brutal advent of the Yankee power era (see 1920-1960), baseball was built around pitching, speed and defense. Ty Cobb, Honus Wagner, and Tris Speaker aren't in the Hall of Fame for tape-measure homers.

I hope the Sox do well, because I want to see Kenny Williams, the general manager, get a break. He took a hit in *Money Ball*, where Billy Beane, the GM in Oakland, tries to make him look stupid with all that computer garbage. I hate the whole Bill James approach to baseball. It's stat after stat after stat of relatively useful material that has been elevated to a holy art. That's garbage, too. It's the same approach to baseball that society has for everything else: the more detail you focus on, the more control you have. Except that there are these things called intangibles. You can cram all the arcane statistics into your brain, but the game is won by players, and sometimes the unlikeliest ones at that. It's more an attitude than anything else. It's no accident Derek Jeter gets into the playoffs every year; he never dogs it, and he's hell-bent for leather every time he's out there.

And Ozzie wants that attitude. He got rid of Carlos Lee and Magglio Ordonez during the off-season, and said yesterday, "If you look around and you're smart enough, you can figure out who is on the team and who is not." He also said, "I think we have a chance and if we stay healthy and stay together and pull for each other like real teammates. We really don't need one leader because everybody is on the same page. I talked to Kenny Williams and said, just give me good players, don't give me leaders. I'm the leader of the team."

He's not messing around. And when they picked up Scott Podsednik (who can fly), Tadihito Iguchi (who was lured from Japan by the presence of Shingo Takatsu - I knew there had to be a reason we kept him), and most of all, A.J Pierzynski, I knew they were serious.

Pierzynski's the key, I think. I've always insisted to Ben that the smartest players in baseball are the catchers, and you don't win a World Series without a good one. And he's my type of catcher, a hard-nosed supposed jerk who irritates the hell out of opponents. When I look at him, I see The Great Hambino.

In the wonderful movie *The Sandlot*, The Great Hambino is the slightly chubby, in-your-face catcher who goads the opposition constantly and forces the elite town team to play the sandlot kids by spitting at their leader, "You play ball like a girl." It's a pure Pierzynski moment. His reputation is of someone who'll do anything to win. I love it.

Of course, there's doing anything to win, A.J. style, as in knocking a second baseman on his butt if he tries to complete the pivot with A.J. coming from first, and then there's doing anything to win Barry Bonds-style, as in steroids. He was quoted today as saying, "All of you lied. All of you have said something wrong. All of you have dirt. All of you. When your closet's clean, then come clean somebody else's." That's the classic cop-out, to say that nobody should ever sit in judgment on anyone else without being squeaky clean.

Bull. Justice never gets done that way. It's bad for baseball. All of these guys, Bonds and Sosa (who now have hat

13

sizes like Shrek), and McGwire, who looked suspiciously ripped when he broke Maris' record, should be stripped of their records. Maris was not perfect, but he played the game honestly.

And that's what Ozzie is doing; playing the game honestly, hard, the old-fashioned way. Waiting for the White Sox to win is like waiting for the Messiah; you wake up every morning hoping it will happen, you go to bed disappointed that it didn't, but you never lose the hope deep in your heart.

February 1961

"Mama, when will Daddy be home?" My mother, perusing *The Joy of Cooking* at the kitchen table in the dwindling sunlight of the late afternoon, answered, "About an hour, David." She turned to look at me as I fidgeted with my new White Sox cap. "Why? Is something wrong?"

"At school somebody told me I should like the Cubs," I said.

"That's probably because we live on the North Side, David."

"So what?"

"Well, the Cubs play on the North Side, where we live, and the White Sox play on the South Side."

"Then why do we like the White Sox?" I asked her.

"You should ask Daddy," she said.

"Okay," I said, and left the kitchen, walking over to the front door of our apartment. I sat on the floor, and waited.

An hour later, I heard my father's heavy tread coming up the steps to our second floor. He opened the door, saw me, and tousled my hair. "Hi, Butch!" he exclaimed. He always called me Butch, not for my crew-cut, but because my mother's mother had lovingly referred to me as the "Butcher Boy."

14

"Daddy," I asked, seizing his attention before he could call for my older and younger sisters or my mother, "Why do we like the White Sox instead of the Cubs?"

He pulled off his earmuffs and heavy overcoat and threw them on his oversized living room chair. Squatting down next to me, he said, "Because I like the man who owns them."

"Who's he, Daddy?"

"A man named Bill Veeck," he answered.

"Why do you like him, Daddy?"

Tired of squatting, he said, "Let me kiss Mommy first and your sisters, okay? Then I'll tell you over dinner."

"Okay, Daddy."

Over dinner, my father, who loved to hold court while we paid rapt attention, first talked about his day at work in the PR department of Illinois Bell Telephone, then asked my mother and my older sister how their days were. I tried to remain patient, and hoped he didn't forget what was really important.

He didn't. "So now let me tell you about Bill Veeck Jr., Butch," he said. Luckily for me, my father had a steel-trap memory, and so he reeled off all sorts of information about the White Sox maverick owner.

How Veeck, a native of Chicago (born in Hinsdale) was the son of William Veeck Sr., a sportswriter, who was the president of the Cubs. When Bill Jr. was young, he had worked for the Cubs as a vendor, ticket seller and junior groundskeeper, so he had seen the club from the fan's perspective. "He wasn't some spoiled brat," my father said. "He never forgot what fans feel. And what a PR man! When he owned the Milwaukee Brewers in the early forties in the old American Association, he gave away live animals, scheduled morning games for night shift workers, and had weddings performed at home plate. And the most famous stunt of all was when he sent up Eddie Gaedel, a midget, to bat for the St. Louis Browns in the fifties. And last year he was the one who put the exploding scoreboard in Comiskey Park to go off when the Sox hit home runs. He makes the game fun for everybody."

He turned to me. "Never forget something, Butch. Baseball is supposed to be fun. If it's not fun, who would be interested? Fun is a very important word."

"I like him, Daddy. Mr. Veeck, I mean," I said.

"I do, too, Butch. I do, too."

There were other, deeper reasons why my father liked and admired Bill Veeck, but I was only five, so he waited until I was older before he told me.

BEN:
Called Dad this morning to wish him a happy birthday. This is his first birthday where I'm more than a few miles from home, and I miss being in Los Angeles. The weather here is brutal – it's been snowing here nonstop. Being from L.A., this was a new and exciting thing for me; those of us from California at the law school annoy all the East Coasters with our naivete (*"Look at this neat white stuff falling from the sky! This is so cool!*). Of course, after a few months of snow, we hot-weather people are simply puzzled (*"What the heck is this? Does God hate Massachusetts?!"*).

But at least baseball season starts soon. I was here last year when the Red Sox won the Series, so it's been a fun offseason to be in Boston. During the playoffs last year, our law professors were livid that at least half the class ditched on mornings after BoSox games. One professor, Mort Horwitz, actually said that he hoped the BoSox would lose already so that people could come back to school.

The Red Sox winning gives me hope for this year. But this is the time for hope. This is the season for optimism. Once the actual season starts, White Sox fans have learned that pessimism is the safest emotional state. That's because usually by about July we're out of it, or at least collapsing. It gets to the point where I can't even stand to watch my beloved Sox – watching as they blow a four-game lead in the middle of summer can't be good for your health.

But at this point, everything looks great. In fact, I'm more optimistic about this year than I have been anytime I can remember, or at least since the slugging White Sox of 1994. That team was great, but it was built around one player – Frank Thomas. Yes, we had Robin Ventura. Yes, Ozzie was still playing shortstop. But Dan Pasqua? The man with the one-handed follow-through after whiffing?

This year, we look *very* solid. For the first time, I really trust both our manager and our general manager. Kenny Williams makes good, solid moves – and this has been an offseason of fantastic moves. I believe that the best pickup of the offseason was Scott Podsednik. Carlos Lee was always dogging it in the outfield, and he was feast or famine at the plate. Off the field, if his weight is any indication, it was feast rather than famine. Ozzie's patterning this team after the 2003 Marlins, and Podsednik adds some much-needed speed. The guy is a steal machine, and if the coaches tell him to boost his OBP and worry less about hitting the ball out of the park, he'll be fantastic.

I'm less optimistic about Jermaine Dye. His stats have been down since 2000; I don't think he'll ever be the same player he was early on with Kansas City. With the loss of Magglio

Ordonez (which may be addition by subtraction, if rumors of Ozzie/Magglio infighting are correct), we lack big boppers. We'll just have to manufacture runs this year, unless Joe Crede and Aaron Rowand step up.

And there's hope for that. Crede has always been a fantastic defender (so has Rowand), but he's never quite been able to put it together for a full season. He's got tremendous power, and he's a good clutch hitter. He's only 26 at this point, so maybe this is the year. Rowand is another story. Last year, he really started to produce, putting up some nice offensive numbers (.310, 24 HR, 69 RBI). He's a potential Gold Glover, and maybe an All-Star. This year is a big test for him.

When I spoke with Dad this morning, he was raving about A.J. Pierzynski, our new catcher. I like everything I've heard about him. All he does is win. He won with the Twins; he won with the Giants. Now let's hope he can bring that here. He has a reputation for shaking things up in the clubhouse, to put it mildly (my favorite Pierzynski story has him telling opposing batters that the Giants' pitching stunk – while he was catching). He seems like just the type of guy the White Sox need. They still have that Jerry Manuel, "let's just go to sleep in the dugout" type of attitude out there. At least he can't be any worse than Ben Davis.

I love the Orlando Hernandez signing as well. I recently commented to one of my friends that if Hernandez can stay healthy, we'll have the best rotation in baseball. Buehrle will win 18, Garcia 16-18, Hernandez 15, Contreras 13, and Garland his usual 12. Our bullpen needs some work – I don't know if Cotts can handle himself out there, even though I like Cliff Politte. Do we even have a closer? Let's just pray we don't play a lot of close games.

As for Tad Iguchi, I'll just have to take Ozzie's word for it. Then again, that's nothing new; living and dying with a team is always taking the team on faith. There's nothing you can do to help the team win (other than making sure that you don't leave the TV during a big rally, of course). When it comes right down to it, you just have to trust the people you believe in, and let things go. That's the only way to make the game fun – if you try to micromanage from the couch, you'll only make yourself nuts. In past years, letting go and having fun has been tough. This year, I'm finding it a bit easier.

Letting go is a tough lesson to learn. I'm finishing up the writing of my new book *Porn Generation: How Social Liberalism Is Corrupting Our Future* at this point, and I have a tough time telling myself that I just have to put it out there and see what happens. Dad's constantly reminding me that God is really in control, and that he has a plan – and that being the case, I need to have fun with this. When I talked to Dad today, he said, "Look, how many 21-year-olds have two books out there? How many get to appear on radio and TV? You need to have fun with this. If it isn't fun, you might as well quit." That's true, but it's still tough to relax emotionally. I'm sure that I'll take a fair bit of heat for what I say, but being right and being popular aren't always the same thing. The tendency is always to grab tighter, though, to see if I can do more, to control things better.

Maybe I'll try to take a lesson from being a Sox fan, and just let things go. At least until Opening Day, when I'll start working on my honorary White Sox ulcer.

April 4, 2005
DAD:

It's Opening Day, and I've got the jitters. I've always wondered: Do the players get the same jitters that fans do? Do they get nervous before they start the season? When I've performed at a concert, I always do better if I'm not feeling nervous, but just a little more aware, a little more of a heightened anticipation. Of course, the significance of the job I have to do is directly proportional to the amount of heightened anticipation; the more important the job, the more I'm mentally awake.

Which makes me wonder; with 162 games to play, do any of them this early in the season feel important to the players, or do they just ease in to the season? For the first time since the Sox moved into the new Comiskey Park/U.S. Cellular Field in 1991, they open at home. That's rather hard to believe, that it's been 14 years since they've opened the season at home. And out of their first 28 games, 22 are against the teams in their own division, so getting off to a fast start is crucial. Yet Ozzie was quoted as saying, "I always believe it's not the way you start, it's the way you finish up." Then, in typical try-to-make-sense-of-this Ozzie style, he said, "A good start would give us a lot of cushion just in case something bad happens in the middle or end of the season." He does make you scratch your head when you listen to him, but his baseball instincts seem to be zoned in on how to win, so I forget what he says and just watch him manage.

Then there's Paul Konerko, who with Frank Thomas out seems to be emerging as a team leader. He said, "You can't win anything the first month or two, but you can lose it, so you just want to start off decent." Sounds a little closer to rational, although just remembering the searing starts of the 1984 Tigers and the 1998 Yankees makes you aware of how important a fast start can be.

I was thinking about Ozzie's instincts for winning while I was listening to talk radio this morning. The host was speaking of Martin Luther King, since 37 years ago today he was assassinated. Ben and I have spoken about what King's dreams were, how truly color-blind he was, how *strong* he was. Of course, we view him through politically conservative lenses, and so what we like about him was that he had bigger goals than just to empower those who had been oppressed; he truly wanted to end racism from *both* sides. Although we differed politically as I grew to adulthood, my father, a strong New Deal Democrat who hated racism with a passion, shared ground with me on that issue.

So I was thinking about how Martin Luther King would have liked this White Sox team. They've got two Japanese guys, Iguchi and Takatsu; nine Hispanics, Marte, Vizcaino, Ozuna, Perez, Uribe, Contreras, Diaz, Garcia and Hernandez; four African-Americans, Thomas, Dye, Everett, and Harris; and ten Caucasian guys, Rowand, Crede, Konerko, Politte, Buehrle, Cotts, Hermanson, Pierzynski, Podsednik, and Garland.

It's a really diverse lineup. Not for the sake of diversity, but for the sake of *winning*. If Ozzie had wanted diversity, he would have kept Carlos Lee, who is African-American, instead of getting Posednik, who is white. But then, Lee teased relief pitcher Damaso Marte for his family's poverty back in the Dominican Republic, as well as ignoring defensive shift instructions from centerfielder Aaron Rowand last year. So not only did the team get rid of a problem socially, but by getting Posednik, they'll try to win in a more tried-and-true way.
Ozzie's all about winning.

Which is why I became a conservative, I guess. Not only because it fits my religious principles better, but because of the bedrock belief that only in a meritocracy is there ultimate fairness. If winning means getting the players who play baseball the best, who want to win the most, shouldn't society function the same way? Shouldn't the best person, regardless of race, creed or color, get the job? No racism, and no *reverse* racism, just the simple proposition that hard work gets results.

I got that hatred of racism from my father.

April 7, 1968

"The car needs gas," my father said to me, as he munched on a malted milk ball. He made a swift left turn to drive south. It was a bright, cool morning and we were on our way home from my piano lesson, which was in Evanston. Normally we headed west until we hit the Edens Expressway to head north for home, so I peered over from my passenger seat to view the gas gauge on the dashboard. Sure enough, the car was half-full.

I grinned. I knew where my father was heading, to the Bulko gas station in Evanston. But not right away: Bulko was promoting their product by offering a free baseball glove with a fill-up, and my father wanted to run off some gas so he could qualify.

"Won't Mama be worried if we're late?" I asked him.

"She's out shopping with the girls," he replied.

I relaxed. We drove around for another half an hour, talking about the White Sox and their chances. (I had still not forgiven them for finishing the '67 season by blowing a doubleheader in Kansas City and a three-game weekend series against the Washington Senators, two of the worst teams in the league; my father said they wouldn't have won anyway, it was the miracle year of the Red Sox.)

Finally we pulled into the Bulko station, where my father bought the gas, then handed me a new baseball glove. I had a glove at home – an old Rawlings Warren Spahn good quality model that was still in pretty good shape. This glove was a cheap glove, but it wasn't about the quality; it was about my father spending extra time with me, getting me something to start the season with that brand-new feeling.

As we pulled out of the station I sniffed it; it had the ambrosial scent of all new baseball gloves. Then my father surprised me by reaching under the newspaper next to him on the seat and handing me a tube of oil for the glove. "Better break it in now," he grinned.

To our surprise, when we got home, my mother was waiting. "The washer broke," she said. "I couldn't reach John so I took out the Yellow Pages to look for a plumber and called someone. He's downstairs now."

My father said, "I'll go see what's up." He headed downstairs and I followed him, smelling the glove. A man about my father's age was bent over the washer, peering into it.

"Hi," my father said to the man's back. "I'm Nate Shapiro."

"Uh-huh," said the man without turning around.

"Do you know what's wrong with it?" my father asked.

"Not yet," the man replied, still peering inside. "But this old thing has taken a beating."

"Well, we've had other things to take care of," my father said defensively.

"This washer's worth about as much as a nigger's," the man muttered under his breath.

But my father heard him.

I never asked him whether his enraged response was because I had heard it too or because he simply hated bigotry, but he grabbed the man by the shoulder, and roared, "*Get out of my house!*"

"What?" said the man stupidly.

"Get out!"

Ten minutes later, my father sat me down, and said, "I want to talk to you about what that man said, Butch."

"Okay, Dad."

"I don't want you ever to associate with anyone who says things like that, Butch. Not ever. That's the kind of thing we've suffered as Jews forever, and we can't let people like that win. You saw what happened to Martin Luther King the other day?"

I nodded.

"That's one of the worst things that ever happened to this country. He was a great man, trying to do great things. To help people when they're down. . . ." He got up and said, "Just remember, if you have a chance to help people who don't have your luck, just do it, and ask questions later."

"Okay, Dad," I answered.

Later that week, after school, I walked outside our house, pounding my glove, looking for someone to play catch with. Two doors down from our house lived the Hirschs. They had three boys, the oldest of whom was a year younger than I. We sometimes played together, when friends my age were unavailable, and after fruitlessly calling some friends, I looked over toward their house.

I saw Mitch, the oldest boy, playing catch with a boy the same age who I knew wasn't from Northbrook. He was black.

I walked over to introduce myself, and soon we were playing Running Bases, with two of us throwing it back and forth while the other attempted to reach the base without being tagged. After a while, Mitch went inside to get a drink.

"That's a nice glove," the black boy said.

"Thanks," I said.

"Is it new?"

"Yeah," I said cautiously.

"I don't have a glove," he said slowly.

I studied him, trying to figure out if he was telling the truth. He sat on the sidewalk with his feet over the curb into the street.

"Where do you live?" I asked, sitting down next to him.

"Chicago," he said. "How about you?"

"Right there," I said, pointing.

"That's a nice house," he said.

I nodded, trying to see it from his perspective. We had a small three-bedroom house; my baby brother and I shared a room and so did my sisters. "What do you live in," I asked curiously.

"'n apartment."

"Where do you play catch?"

He looked at me defiantly. "In the street, same as you . . . just that I don't have a glove, so sometimes I can't play." He looked away.

"Here," I said impulsively, handing him my glove. "You take this one."

"Okay," he said, taking it before I could reconsider.

I was angry with myself. "My new glove," I thought to myself. "And Dad got it for me." I was ready to cry, but he leaped to his feet and raced toward the Hirsch's house. "Lookit this!" he shouted. "I got me a new glove!"

Two hours later, my father got home. After he kissed my mother and hugged my sisters, I shamefacedly told him what I had done with the present he had gotten me.

He never hesitated. "Good for you, Butch," he said.

"But, Dad, I don't know if he *really* needed it," I said.

"There's no way to ever tell for sure how much people need, Butch," he said. "That's what real generosity is – when you give straight from the heart even when you don't know whether they need it. Besides, now one more kid will get to play baseball. That's always a good thing," he grinned, "even if he's a Cub fan." He paused to look at me. "I'm proud of you, Butch," he said.

BEN:

Today was go time. All the speculation up to this point means nothing. And we won't know for at least a few weeks whether the Sox are a good team or a bad one, so this game doesn't mean all that much. Still, like every baseball fan, I'm a bit superstitious. When the White Sox are playing, I like the first pitch we throw to be a strike. When we begin a season, I want the first game to be a victory.

And so it was. This is the kind of game the White Sox would have lost last year. Mark Buehrle pitched a gem in a 1-0 ballgame, outdueling Jake Westbrook of the Cleveland Indians. At this rate, we'll win 162 games!

But this is the kind of game good teams win and bad teams lose. The White Sox won this one on an error by Cleveland's dyslexically-named shortstop, Jhonny Peralta. In the seventh, Konerko doubled to lead off the inning and Dye moved him over to third with a fly ball to right. Up came Aaron

Rowand, my pick to click this year. He didn't *really* click – he hit a bouncer to Peralta – but it was enough. Peralta booted the ball, and Konerko scored.

That was all it took. Buehrle's an innings-eater, a real horse. I'm still not sure how he does it. His fastball doesn't look like it could break a pane of glass, but he has great control. He is like a lefty Greg Maddux, and he could pitch for another decade and a half. He also makes the game fun to watch, since he doesn't take much time between pitches. Takatsu, the little closer who could, got the job done in the ninth. I'm not a big fan of any closer who has a breaking ball for his out pitch, but if Takatsu can pitch like he did last year, I'll take it.

I talked to Dad after the game tonight, and he was excited about how the Sox look. He was also reminiscing about the Martin Luther King Jr. assassination, which happened 37 years ago today. Dad was 12 at the time, and he remembers how stunned Papa was by the news.

In any case, it'll be interesting to see what happens with the Sox. Dad was mentioning the racial diversity on the team tonight, and he's right – it is striking. What's even more striking is that a team so diverse in terms of personality can get things done. You have the fireball: Ozzie. You have the hard-ass: Pierzynski. You have the goofball who slides across the field tarp during rain delays: Buehrle. You have the crafty veteran: Orlando Hernandez. You have the solid clubhouse guy: Konerko. And you have the crazy, anger-management man: Everett. How it all works is a mystery to me. But diversity for the sake of winning is sure looking good right about now.

DAD:
They won, 1-0.

Thank God, it's good to be a White Sox fan.
At least until tomorrow.

April 10, 2005
DAD:

What a week so far; taking two out of three from the Indians at home, and then taking two out of three from the Twins. After the Opening Day win, the two remaining games against the Indians were like Dickens: it was the best of games, it was the worst of games. Game Two against the Indians showed our grit and determination, but Game Three showed theirs. The games were astonishingly similar; in Game Two we stormed back in the ninth from a 3-0 deficit with four runs off of their closer, Bob Wickman, to break their hearts; but in Game Three we had a 5-2 lead in the ninth before Takatu imploded, allowing three runs for them to tie it before they decimated Luis Vizcaino with six runs in the eleventh to win 11-5.

In Game Two, the Indians built a 3-0 lead off of a second inning RBI double by Belliard, a balk by Freddy Garcia with runners on second and third in the third, and an RBI double by Hafner in the ninth. Garcia had tremendous stuff, striking out six in six innings, but he was outdueled by Kevin Millwood, just over from the Phillies, who also pitched six innings but gave us nothing. Matt Miller and Arthur Rhodes held us scorelees for two more innings, and by the bottom of the ninth, we had still not scored an earned run this *year*.

Bob Wickman, the portly right-hand sinkerball closer, entered to face us in the bottom of the ninth, and suddenly, we were the New York Yankees, circa 1927. Everett lined a single to right, and then Konerko took an 0-1 sinker that didn't sink and drove it far over the left-field wall, cutting the lead to 3-2. Dye took *his* 0-1 pitch and drove *that* over the left field wall, and in a wink and a blink, we were tied, 3-3. Rowand followed, and he doubled over Sizemore's head to center. They intentionally walked Hambino, to set up the double play, but Willie Harris, batting for Crede, laid a bunt down that Wickman bobbled, and now there were bases loaded with no one out. All of the preceding took less time than a single pitch by Takatsu, and it was almost anti-climactic when Uribe took Wickman's first pitch and drove a ball to deep right that was caught but scored Rowand with the winning run.

It was an incredible comeback, especially against Wickman, and Game Three looked like we'd sweep the Indians. But then, there's Takatsu, and his famed 75 mph express fastball, and. . . .

Ben has never been a big fan of Shingo, even despite his excellent record last year; he has no idea how he doesn't get hit all over the lot. And in Game Three, he did. We were up 5-2, and he gave up three home runs in the top of the ninth inning. The first was an absolute bomb to Casey Blake on a pitch fatter than Oprah Winfrey circa 1992, a 76 mph softball pitch right down the pipe. The second was another fat pitch, all of 86 mph, on the meaty part of the plate to Coco Crisp. The third dinger, tying up the game, came on yet another 76 mph floater, which Rafael Belliard hit into the corn fields of Iowa. Vizcaino then came in and proceeded to give up 6 runs in a bit over two innings. Brutal bullpen work.

Ben IM'd me after the game:

BEN: I certainly hope this isn't an indication of the White Sox relief corps, because we're in trouble if it is. Will Neal Cotts be the Neal Cotts of last year, or will he finally fulfill his potential? Will Damaso Marte maintain his status as the reliever who escaped from the mental institution? Will Cliff Politte step up? And is Dustin Hermanson really a closer?

It was disappointing to end the Cleveland series that way, and with the Twins in the Metrodome to follow, I hoped that we could bounce back. The Twins seem to win the division every year, and even though they scored 90 runs less than we did last year, they finished nine games ahead of us. I have mixed feelings about them; most of my extended family lives in the Twin Cities, and the Twins are their pride and joy. Still, they won the Series in 1987 and 1991, so their fans have enough rings for a while.

Ozzie said in the off-season he wanted the Sox to be like the Twins, with their great defense, timely hitting, and stellar pitching. So far, he's gotten his wish. The first game Hernandez was outstanding for seven innings, throwing everything from an 89 mph fastball to a 54 mph Eephus pitch. He's the veteran on the club (there's a rumor that Satchel Paige was his illegitimate grandson) and he threw as if he wrote the pitching instructional manual.

There is a car wash in Burbank that I would use for years only because they had a baseball pinball game that I loved and showed Ben how to use. It was a two-player game, and the player pitching used a joystick that not only could curve the ball, but if jerked back, could actually slow the pitch down to a crawl in mid-flight. The batter had to have ridiculous self-control to refrain from swinging as the pitch was thrown, and inevitably he would swing well ahead of the pitch, which started fast but then suddenly traveled at half-speed. I would demonstrate to Ben that unlike real estate, where location was everything, in hitting, timing is everything. If you throw the hitter's timing off, he's finished.

That was Hernandez. He had the Twins off-balance the entire game. And the timely hitting Ozzie spoke of occurred in the sixth inning. Konerko, who was 3 for 39 lifetime against Kyle Lohse, took the count full, fouled of a bunch of pitches, then homered deep to left. He is now 4 for 40 against Lohse, with 2 hrs and 2 RBIs. I'll take those statistics, because the HR came when it mattered. It seemed to unnerve Lohse, because he gave up a single to Dye, and then Rowand hit a HR to left that mirrored Konerko's. After the sixth, it was clear sailing. We won, 5-1. No nail-biting here.

We had to win yesterday, with Santana going today for them. The guy's the best pitcher in baseball, in my opinion (and most everyone else's) – and if we lost yesterday, they'd probably win the series and there we'd go again, chasing them all summer long.

We did win, and impressively, too. Everett crushed one to right in the first, putting us ahead 2-0, and by the fifth we were up 3-0. Then Shannon Stewart came up with two on, smashed one to left, and we were tied 3-3. Jon Garland, (also known as the 26-year-old one-time Phenom with unlimited potential who always goes 12-12 for the season) looked like he might be done in the sixth because a) the Twins had second and third with nobody out, and then bases loaded with one out, and b) he had been sick yesterday. But he got Jacques Jones to line out right at Konerko, and then Cuddyer to hit into a double play, and somehow they seemed like us and we seemed like them. Then in the seventh, the deluge, and for once, we were the ones that rained for forty days and forty nights.

Timo Perez led off and launched a bomb to right. Then Rowand and Crede sandwiched two blistering singles around an A.J. out. Ozzie sent them on a 3-2 pitch to Uribe, who lined a pitch just out of the reach of Punto at second, scoring Rowand and sending Crede to third. And I thought, wait a minute, first Jones lined one right at Konerko and now Uribe lined one just out of their reach? What's going on here?

Then whatever was going on got even wilder. Podsednik flared one in front of Bartlett at short, who bobbled it. Crede, running on contact, scored, and Bartlett could only turn around and throw to Punto for the force on Uribe.

This left Podsednik at first instead of Uribe. I *love* Podsednik. The guy flies like the wind, never flinches when a ball is thrown up and in, and in general is a throwback to the dead ball era, when speed ruled baseball. Sure enough, Romero tried to pick him off, threw wildly, and instead of Scotty P. going to second, he *never even looked*, just rocketed to third, where he scored on a wild pitch. It was 7-3, suddenly, and I wasn't even thinking about Santana, just thinking we're gonna take at least 2 out of 3 from these guys. Unbelievable.

What comes through about this year's team, as Ken Harrelson and D. Williams were saying on the air, is our balance. They're right; we are soooo balanced. Three HRs, by Konerko (in the 8th), Everett, and Perez, speed by Scotty P., a gutty performance by Garland – heck we beat them every which way, and for once, *we* weren't the ones screwing up.

The first two against the Twins under our belt, and then we saw Santana today. Unbelievably enough, we got out to a two-run lead. The trick was, we had three infield hits that we turned into two runs. Buehrle had a 17-inning scoreless streak and looked as though he might be okay. Then, in the third, with

32

two runners on and two out, Matt Lecroy hit a grounder to Uribe that should have been the third out. Instead, Crede tried to cut in front of him to make the play and the ball glanced off his glove for an RBI single. Torii Hunter was next up, and he slammed a shot over the left-field fence, putting them up, 4-2. That was it. Two runs off of Santana is about as good as it gets, and in this case, it wasn't enough, as we lost 5-2. As an indication of how good he is, in the sixth inning he threw *eight* pitches, with two K's. I expect that from Santana, though, so I'm happy we got two out of three from these guys. Four out of six from the Indians and Twins? Don't wake me up.

	W	L	PCT	GB	Home	Away	Div	Streak
Chicago WSox	4	2	.667	---	2-1	2-1	4-2	Lost 1
Cleveland	3	3	.500	1	0-0	3-3	3-3	Won 1
Detroit	3	3	.500	1	3-3	0-0	3-3	Lost 1
Kansas City	3	3	.500	1	0-0	3-3	1-2	Won 1
Minnesota	3	3	.500	1	1-2	2-1	1-2	Won 1

April 15, 2005
BEN:

It's been a bit of a tough week. Spoke with Dad yesterday, and apparently he got hurt while exercising – he's unable to walk or raise his arms without severe pain. Dad's trying to keep his spirits up, but he's feeling very restricted.

It's brutal to watch Dad go through this. He's closing in on 50 at this point, but you don't think of your parents as aging as long as they're able to do what they've always done. I still feel like he and I can go out in the front yard and play catch, just as we did when I was 11 or 12 and he was still 40, and it's hard for me to think of him being unable to do that. Age always feels like just a number until the body starts to wear down. Dad's tough, and he'll tough his way through this with a smile on his face (that's the way he is), but I just wish that he didn't have to.

Mom's making calls, trying to get as much information as possible about this ailment, whatever it is. She and Dad have an incredibly solid relationship; it's wonderful for me to have that model. Friends tell me all the time that my picture of marriage isn't realistic – that it's too pie in the sky – but all I have to do is point to my parents.

At least the Sox are on a roll. It diminishes baseball somewhat when real life intrudes, but it cheered me up to chat with Dad this morning, since he was so optimistic about the Sox. Their record going into tonight's game with Seattle is 6-3; they've won their six games by a combined total of 11 runs. Winning close games is the hallmark of a good ballclub. And these aren't 10-9 games. The scores in their wins have been 1-0, 4-3, 5-1, 8-5, 2-1, and 5-4. That's some serious pitching. The bats haven't been on fire (which could be a problem, since we *did* lose so much power over the offseason), but the new speed and timely hitting formula seems to be working to perfection so far.

We are a front-running team. We have led each game of the season up to this point, and only shoddy relief from Shingo Takatsu (who looks terrible) and Luis Vizcaino (who looks equally terrible) has prevented them from going 7-1 to this point. Takatsu's horrific performance in the climactic game of the first Cleveland series on April 7 has opened the door for Dustin Hermanson, perhaps the most unheralded pickup of the offseason for the White Sox. In the second game of the just-concluded Indians/Sox series, Ozzie called on Hermanson to close out a 10-inning thriller, and Hermanson was great. He pitched one inning, gave up one hit, and shut the Indians down.

While Hermanson looks great, there's a serious problem for the Sox: Scott Podsednik, who is simply fantastic, has a strained adductor muscle, and he hasn't played the last two days. I don't think the Sox can survive for long without Podsednik playing at full speed, since he really catalyzes their lineup. If the Sox are indeed front-runners, it's Podsednik who guarantees them early leads by getting on base, bugging pitchers, and stealing. I love the fact that Ozzie recognizes this, and is giving Podsednik time to heal. Smart move.

But here I am being pessimistic, and my Sox are leading the division at 6-3. They've won all three series they've played; their series win against Cleveland this week was simply beautiful. On Monday, Freddy Garcia showed what he's made of, holding the Indians to four hits through eight innings. If the White Sox do serious damage this year, I truly believe that people will point to the Miguel Olivo-Freddy Garcia trade as a major reason why. Like Buehrle, Garcia is a horse. We've got a lot of horses on this team, but I like a horse with a 95 mph fastball and a good changeup. Control pitchers are nice, but give me someone who can blow smoke every time.

Podsednik made the play of the game here, cutting down a sprinting Rafael Belliard at third base in the third inning. Belliard was trying to take two bases on a single. That's a cardinal sin – don't run your way out of an inning with no outs. It's just silly. And this single was hard-hit and shallow. Podsednik made the throw off of the wrong foot to nail Belliard at third. Podsednik couldn't have been more than 75 feet away from Crede when he threw the ball. It turned out well for us, because the inning ended up being the only inning in which Cleveland scored.

It was Scotty P. who made it a tie ballgame with his baserunning in the sixth. After he put down a bunt single – a terrible bunt single (he popped it just over the head of Kevin Millwood), but a bunt single? For the formerly slugging, Earl Weaver-esque White Sox? Who woulda thunk?! – He promptly stole second, his fourth steal of the season. Carl Everett hit a single into the gap, and Podsednik scored.

And guess who – Scotty P! – did it again in the seventh, singling home Chris Widger with the game-winning run. The ninth provided some heart-pounding White Sox relief (as usual, they can't ever make it easy), as Damaso Marte walked Travis Hafner with one out. Victor Martinez crushed one into deep right, but the wind knocked it down and into Jermaine Dye's glove. Takatsu got the last out on a 62 mph changeup. Didn't change much for me – I'd rather see Hermanson in there.

The second game was another thriller, with the Sox coming out on top yet again. Jose Contreras got himself behind the eight-ball; he was down 3-0 after three innings. Contreras is a mystery to me, just as he was a mystery for the Yankees. He's got unbelievable stuff – his forkball is pure nastiness – but he can't seem to bear down out there. In any case, we were down 3-0 until the fourth inning, when we put together a nice comeback. Pablo Ozuna, a very capable backup for Scotty P, bunted his way on, and Tadahito Iguchi singled him over to third on a hit-and-run (Smart-ball! I love it!). Juan Uribe put down a swinging bunt (apparently we play smart-ball even when we're swinging for the fences, as Uribe is apt to do), and Cliff Lee threw the ball into the left-field stands, scoring Ozuna and sending Uribe to second and Iguchi to third. After an out, Jermaine Dye put down another swinging bunt to the right side, scoring Iguchi. Aaron Rowand singled into left to drive in Uribe, tying the game.

Cut to the top of the tenth inning. Both the White Sox and Indians scored a run in the seventh, and neither one had scored since. A.J. "The Great Hambino" Pierzynski lined a double into the gap in right field. From there on in, it was execution. Joe Crede laid down a bunt in front of the plate, and Indians first baseman Ben Broussard threw to third, missing Pierzynski. Uribe hit a long fly ball to center, and Hambino trotted home for the game winner. This is just great baseball.

I loved Hambino's comment after the game: "I was getting my name chanted by the visiting crowd [because he allowed a run on a passed ball and allowed Jhonny Peralta to score in the third when he couldn't come up with a good throw by Ozuna] . . . I hit a ball hard early in the game and [Grady] Sizemore caught it. It was nice to hit one and have nobody catch it." Yes, it is. Hambino sure loves to break the hearts of opposing fans. I'm glad he's on our side.

We dropped the last game of the series. Orlando Hernandez, who is now 1-1, didn't have his good stuff today, and the Indians knocked him around for six runs in five innings. Neal Cotts also got hit around the yard. Cliff Politte, on the other hand, looked very solid. He's got a hard fastball and a good, hard slider. He's also a veteran, which is good for tough spots.

Despite today's loss, I still feel great about the Sox. That's the difference between this year and last year.

BEN: Last year, every time they lost a game, I thought the Sox were going to head into their patented spiral and lose ten straight. This year, they look somewhat consistent.

DAD: Weird that their consistency should spring from a guy considered by many in baseball to be a hotheaded loon.

BEN: If Ozzie is crazy, he's crazy like a fox. . . .

Ozzie summed it up well: "During the last 10 years, with the 50 and 70 home runs and all that . . . all of a sudden everyone wanted that type of game. . . . Play smart, pitch good and you have a chance to win." The words of a true poet.

Now if only we can get Dad healthy and keep the Sox winning. . . .

April 17, 2005
DAD:

I must be getting greedy. The Sox took the first two from Seattle this weekend and I started tasting a sweep, especially because we had Freddy Garcia going today with his gaudy 1.93 ERA against Gil Meche with his ERA that looked more like Babe Ruth's slugging percentage, 7.88. I should have known better. We lost 5-4, and continued the eerie season long trend of winning the first two games of a series and losing the third.

That being said, the first two games were immensely satisfying, since Jon Garland threw six perfect innings Friday while Juan Uribe drove in four runs (which must have had Ozzie fantasizing about the many multiple RBI games he had as a shortstop; it had to be a very short dream). The ninth inning got interesting, with Vizcaino running out of gas after two innings of relief, Marte coming in and using his AT&T reach-out-and-touch-someone delivery (except that in Marte's version, that *someone* is sitting by the right field foul pole, and it looks like he reaches that far before wildly throwing to the plate) to hit the next batter, and Takatsu enlivening the Mariners by giving up a hit and a walk, leaving the tying runs on base. Finally Hermanson came in and shut the door with a strikeout and a force play on a nice play by Uribe.

But the story was Garland. His sinker was dominating, and he looked strong. After his fifth perfect inning, I flashed back to the only perfect game I ever saw (on TV), Koufax's gem against the Cubs in September 1965. It was an unbelievable performance against a team that included Ernie Banks, Billy Williams, and Ron Santo, and Bob Hendley, pitching for the Cubs, only gave up one hit, and lost 1-0 to Koufax. That night I was not rooting against the Cubs as much as rooting for Koufax.

Every Jewish kid I knew rooted for Koufax just the way I did. Like the great Hank Greenberg before him, he was a gentleman, but he was also dominant in a way that seems hard to believe now. He won the 7th game of the 1965 World Series on two days rest against the powerful Minnesota Twins with essentially one pitch: his fast ball. He had tamed the mighty Yankees in the 1963 series, and in each of the 1965 and 1966 seasons, he had thrown *27 complete games*. Nowadays a team is lucky if it gets 15 by the whole pitching staff.

One year after Koufax's perfect game, on September 25, 1966, my father took my older and younger sisters and me to Wrigley Field to see the Dodgers play the Cubs. But before that, he somehow found out where the Dodgers were staying. He always managed to introduce us to famous people, whether it was Artur Rubenstein when I was 6, Duke Ellington when I was fourteen, or other successful people in the fields in which we were interested.

When we got to the hotel that Sunday morning, the Dodgers were in their suits, waiting to leave for Wrigley Field. My father approached Don Drysdale, the huge Hall of Fame hurler who paired with Koufax as the Ruth-Gehrig of pitching, and asked if he would take a picture with my sisters and me. Drysdale was wonderful, picking us up, laughing, joking, just wonderfully personable, and we got the pictures. Then my dad approached Koufax.

There must be a moment for those who climb Mount Everest when they finally see the summit, and their heart is in their mouth (if they can even breathe up there). That was my Mount Everest moment. The greatest pitcher in the world was talking to my father.

But he seemed reluctant. My dad, never one to take no from anyone, persisted and persisted, and finally Koufax took a picture with the three of us kids, a picture on my wall to this day. I was about as excited as I ever got in my childhood, and the moment lost none of its magic even with Koufax's reluctance. Still, after the Dodgers left the hotel and we walked back to our car to head for Wrigley Field, I asked my father why Mr. Drysdale had been so friendly and Mr. Koufax had been less fun.

"Well, Butch," my father said, "Mr. Drysdale pitched yesterday, and Mr. Koufax is pitching today."

I got the message: when someone has a job to do, the great ones are relentlessly focused on the matter at hand. (Sure enough, in the game, Koufax outdueled Kenny Holtzman, the "Next Koufax" 2-1.)

That was Garland on Friday, totally focused. And Buehrle was just the same on Saturday, only giving up three hits to Ichiro, one of them a HR, and winning a complete game 2-1 on two solo HRs by Konerko. Both Garland and Buehrle looked zoned in, as opposed to Garcia today, who had moments of brilliance amid other moments of here's-my-heater-down-the-middle-see-if-you-can-hit-it. They did, but we almost caught them in the fifth inning when the volatile Everett, with the tying runs on base, was called out on a checked swing that wasn't. He was truly robbed by the ump, and I could see him just-this-far from being thrown out.

But he wasn't. He was focused enough not to get trigger-happy, so perhaps there's a silver lining in this loss. The whole team seems to be more focused, more resolute this year.

I'm trying to glean some of their resolve for myself. Every test they've done on me comes up negative, whether it's a cat-scan, MRI, or simple physical exam. Walking is getting more and more painful, and lifting my arms, too. But I'm taking my hint from the Sox and Koufax – I'm staying focused.

	W	L	PCT	GB	Home	Away	Div	Streak
Chicago WSox	8	4	.667	---	4-2	4-2	6-3	Lost 1
Minnesota	8	4	.667	---	4-2	4-2	6-3	Lost 1
Cleveland	5	7	.417	3	2-4	3-3	5-7	Won 1
Detroit	5	7	.417	3	3-3	2-4	5-7	Won 2
Kansas City	4	8	.333	4	1-5	3-3	2-4	Lost 2

April 20, 2005
BEN:

I'm in the editing process with *Porn Generation* at this point. After you write a book, the temptation is to never look at it again – or at least wait a few days. When you expend so much effort, you want to let the project sit there, completed, before you begin taking it apart again. Unfortunately, the editing process doesn't allow for a lot of time to sit back and take it all in. You just have to keep working, keep moving forward, keep perfecting until printing time. And then, you have to keep pushing, pushing, pushing to get the book sold. It is certainly draining. It's a good thing that the process is fun – otherwise, it would begin to grate.

Maybe that's the difference for the White Sox this year. During the Jerry Manuel tenure, the Sox always looked tense. Manuel, meanwhile, always looked like he was asleep. Now the Sox look loose, and I've never seen a manager more alert than Ozzie. If he were any more energetic, he'd be A.D.D.

Ozzie is smart, though. He makes it a priority to keep the clubhouse loose, but he also makes sure to let everyone know who's boss. Two days ago, the *Chicago Tribune* reported that Ozzie blasted Frank Thomas and some other members of the team for their "bad attitude" in the past. "Frank was a big part of the bad attitude," Ozzie stated. "Now he can see the guys, how we handle stuff, why we're not whining every day, why we're hitting today after a day game. Everybody is happy, and I want Frank to be a part of it. . . . He got better last year. His attitude [before that] was horrible here. Everybody's was. When you're part of the team, that means you too."

It occurs to me that being a good manager must be like being a good dad. You have to have fun with the kids – spend "quality time," in today's idiotic PC parlance – but you also have to set standards. I know that Dad handles me and my sisters like that. He's constantly thinking of fun things for us to do, and he's constantly trying to make everyday events fun; but at the same time, he won't stand for clashes between the kids. At the end of the day, we're family, and we have to stick together.

That's what you need in a team, as well. And the Sox seem to have that kind of chemistry this year. Ozzie won't let any bad eggs ruin this concoction; he's made it very clear that if you talk back, if you point fingers, you're gone. "There's not too many guys left [from past years], [and] that's why, because of the attitude," Ozzie said. "[W]hen you see something wrong, say it. Talk, don't go hide it like a [child]. When you don't like

42

something in the clubhouse, say something. If you want to get together and stay together, communication is the best thing in life."

Ozzie's message seems to be resonating. The Sox keep on rolling. They just finished a two-game series with Minnesota, and they swept them. Two-game series seem like they should benefit the Sox right now, since the Sox have won the first two games of every three-game series they've played to this point, and then lost the last game. If they had nothing but two-game series, the Sox would go undefeated this year.

The first game of the series was another nail-biter, an ulcer-feeder. Once again, the Sox scored first, this time on a solo shot from Carl Everett in the bottom of the first inning. The Twins came back to take the lead pretty quickly. Jose Contreras looked bad all night. His stuff is always decent, but when he can't find the plate, it gets ugly. In this game, he gave up six hits and four walks in four and two-thirds. He threw 104 pitches. Not good.

In the first, he got lucky. He loaded up the bases with one out, and Torii Hunter hit a sharp grounder to Joe Crede, who ate it up. Crede has always been a fantastic defensive third baseman, and he gobbled up the grounder, tossed to Iguchi at second, and Iguchi made a great turn to nail Hunter at first. The Sox will be in this all year if their defense is this good. Defense and pitching win championships, and the contrast between this year's Sox and last year's beer-league softball Sox proves it.

Contreras wasn't so lucky in the second. He was just plain awful. He hit Jacque Jones with a sharp breaking ball, and Jones promptly stole second, despite a good throw from The Great Hambino. Michael Cuddyer hit a single, and it was all tied up.

Contreras wasn't sharp, and in the fifth it bit him again. A leadoff single from Jason Bartlett and a bouncer in the hole to Iguchi put two men on base. Contreras induced a double-play ball, but then he collapsed. He balked home Bartlett, and then walked Torii Hunter. Hunter stole second and the ball ended up in center field. After Hunter took third, Contreras uncorked one to the backstop. 3-1, Minnesota.

The Sox struck back in the bottom of the fifth. Hambino hit a single, and then Crede went down to his ankles and golfed one out of the park. Finally in the sixth, the Sox regained the lead. Carl Everett came through in the sixth with another two-run shot. Everett was the story of this game; he's a real Twins killer. Already this year he has nine RBI against the Twins.

Once again, Takatsu made it interesting by giving up a run, but we had a two-run lead. We definitely need a better closer. Maybe after Dad heals, he can go up there and throw some heat. He certainly can't throw any slower than Takatsu – to do that, you would have to put the ball on a tee.

Game 2 of the series was a magic show from El Duque, who is turning out to be a great pickup. El Duque isn't comfortable unless he's surrounded by opposing baserunners. After all, every magician needs a crowd.

Here was Hernandez's line: six innings, 10 hits, one walk – and no runs. In the top of the second, he got out of a first and third, no outs situation. He got out of it with two strikeouts and a pop-up. In the fourth inning, it was first and second and one out. He got out of it with a double play. The bullpen was great as well, except for Takatsu, who was brutal as usual, giving up the only run of the night to the Twins. His ERA is now up to 12.27. When will Ozzie stop using him? When his ERA hits triple digits?

This was Ozzie's dream small-ball game. After the game, Ozzie said "We have to do the little things. . . . It sounds like little girls' baseball, but that's the way we have to play." Apparently, we play ball like a girl. What say you, Hambino?

Anyway, we scored two runs in the sixth inning to break up the 0-0 tie. Crede doubled home the first run on a low ball (he's like Vladimir Guerrero-lite, a bad ball hitter). Uribe bunted over Crede, and Podsednik hit a fly ball to left field. Crede tagged up and scored, and gave Twins catcher Joe Mauer a bit of a nudge as he did. This is a tougher Sox team than last year. Hambino's Revenge?

Well, things are looking up. We face Detroit now, and I'm sure there will be some Ozzie-Magglio Ordonez fireworks. Detroit is 6-8 going in, and we're 10-4. Let's keep it going.

April 21, 2005
DAD:

The feud between Ozzie and Magglio Ordonez has heated up. Ozzie was quoted today that Magglio was "playing with fire" and he'd better "shut up and play." Ozzie also said of Mags, "He's a piece of [bleep]." This after Mags called Ozzie his "enemy" yesterday, when the Sox completed a two-game sweep of Detroit. Ozzie said he was just "protecting himself."

The whole affair left me sad. The feud between Ozzie and Magglio started when Ordonez accused Ozzie of forcing him to play in 2004 when he was hurt, and then Ozzie convincing the Sox not to re-sign Magglio for this season after they had already offered him a long-term deal.

Mags also expressed his frustration over his latest injury, which is supposed to be some sort of undetermined hernia. I can sympathize with him; this injury I'm struggling with has symptoms like a hernia too, and all my tests show up negative. It's murderous to put on a happy face when you're in constant pain, and if that's what Magglio is enduring, I'm more than willing to forgive his terrible anger. He said, "I don't talk bad about people when people are hurt." He's supposed to be examined by a surgeon in Philadelphia who's a hernia specialist, and I wonder if perhaps that doctor might know what's wrong with me, too, since I've totally struck out here in Los Angeles.

In the meantime, the White Sox aren't striking out at all. They took the first game from the Tigers 9-1, with Jermaine Dye exploding (finally!) with four RBI and Garland dominating for eight innings. The second game was more interesting. Buehrle threw seven innings, scattering three runs; but we trailed 3-1 into the sixth and it looked like the standard-issue loss for the Sox of yore – not enough hitting to overcome a steady but unspectacular effort by the starter.

Then, lo and behold, Everett doubled, and Konerko hit a grounder right at the shortstop; but it took a bad hop past him and Everett scored, cutting the lead to 3-2.

Ever since I was a kid, every time I see a bad-hop single, especially at shortstop, I think of Tony Kubek getting hit in the throat by that bad-hop single in the 1960 Series, giving Pittsburgh the chance to beat the Yankees. As a result, as a lifetime Yankee-hater, I love bad-hop singles. Not to mention you just don't see acts of God like that in other sports, where the fields they play on are identical in make-up.

I should correct myself. I *was* a lifetime Yankee hater until the late 1990s. The team under Joe Torre was impossible for me to hate. They played the game so professionally, so beautifully, especially the 1998 team, of course, that I had to admire them. One other reason I admired them was that although their payroll was huge, the players didn't act like prima donnas, the way the Reggie Jackson Yankees used to.

Our Sox play like that now, no prima donnas, just a workmanlike approach to the game that's easy to love. After that bad-hop single I wondered if we'd take advantage the way Yankees traditionally do.

We did. In the seventh, A.J. and Crede singled, and after they were moved up, Scotty P. rifled a shot into right to score them both. Hermanson almost gave the game back, but Takatsu shut the Tigers down in the ninth.

We're 12-4 now, holding on to first place so tightly that the Twins can't gain any ground. They're still two games out even though they've won their last two games. Now it's on to Kansas City.

Every time we visit Kansas City, I have bad feeling from that doubleheader thirty-eight years ago, when the lowly Athletics took two from us and ruined our chances to win the pennant. I know they're the Royals now, but it doesn't make any difference. That '67 season was a fairy-tale right up to that moment. We were tied for second with Boston, one game behind Minnesota, and it was anyone's pennant to be had. There was a beauty to the fact that there was only one ten-team league, that there weren't three divisions, the wild-card team, that nobody ever won on a fluke. The best team over the course of the season won, and that was that.

The tension built over a 162-game season was inexorable, since only one team went to the post-season. The Sox had great pitching and no hitting as usual, and the pennant was so close you could almost taste it. . . .

September 1967

47

"I can't believe it! How could they do that!" I threw my glove against the wall in a fury, close to tears. The Sox had just lost the second game of the double-header to Kansas City. Joel Horlen, my favorite player, who was 19-6 going into the game, had lost 4-0 to some pitcher named Jim Hunter, after Gary Peters had lost 5-2 in the first game to some guy named Pat Dobson.

"Who are those guys! They stink! How can Peters and Horlen lose to those guys? And we didn't hit one home run all day!"

"The Sox never hit many home runs, Butch. And you can't expect Peters and Horlen to win every time," my dad reminded me, getting up to turn off the TV.

"I hate them! How can they lose to Kansas City? They stink. Did you know that the only team that we have a losing record against this season is Kansas City? They're the worst team in the league!"

"It just looks like they were outpitched."

"Yeah, well who are those other guys? That guy Hunter was twelve and sixteen before today, and Dobson was nine and ten!"

"But they're pitching for a bad team, Butch," my father said patiently, "and Catfish Hunter made the All-Star team this year."

"*Catfish*! What a stupid name!"

"He's only called that because Charlie Finley, the owner, gave him the nickname, Butch. It sells more tickets if the team is colorful."

"I still think he and Dobson stink."

My dad said, "You know, Butch, there's a lesson here for you."

"I don't care!"

48

"But listen, Butch. You can't judge someone in a team sport the same way that you judge a runner or a skater. Statistics don't tell you everything. There might be some very good players whose statistics might be better if they played on better teams."

I looked up at him, as I wiped the tears off my face. "So?"

"So don't be too sure that the other pitchers aren't good. They might be very good, and you just don't know it."

Although I was only eleven, I managed a professional snort. "*Catfish* Hunter. I bet Gary Peters and Joel Horlen win more games than he *ever* does."

"I don't know, Butch," my dad said. "For all you know, he and Dobson may be greater than you think. The great thing about baseball is that quality usually wins in the end. Maybe someday this doubleheader will make more sense."

April 21, 2005
DAD:

Of course, Catfish is in the Hall of Fame now, and Dobson had a great career later, too, so my father was right: cream does rise to the top, and we lost to two great pitchers that day. That doubleheader does make more sense now, and I try to remember my father's wisdom about judging people's ability before I have all the facts.

But I still get nervous for the Sox when they go to Kansas City.

April 28, 2005
BEN:

It was really nice being back in town for the beginning of Passover. Of all the Jewish holidays, Passover is my personal favorite: the story of the exodus from Egypt, the customs associated with the holiday, the food. Most of all, I just love being home. Cambridge can be fun, but it's much richer being with the family over a holiday.

This is the first time I've been home since Dad got hurt, and it was hard to watch him in pain. He's a grin-and-bear-it type of guy, but he was clearly hurting. We're hoping that this thing can heal itself, but in the meantime Mom is working hard to find out from the doctors exactly what's going on. It's amazing that despite the amazing advances in medical technology over the past few decades, a problem that should be relatively simple (pinpointing the source of pain) remains a mystery.

On the upside, looks like Dad didn't have to worry too much about the Royals. We swept them, which was a true pleasure, especially since one of my dad's best friends is a huge KC fan. Last year, he couldn't stop bugging us about how great a manager Tony Pena was. This year he is convinced that with a pitching staff of Zack Greinke (lots of potential), Runelvys Hernandez (who?), Denny Bautista (who? Part II), Jose Lima (born before the invention of baseball), and Brian Anderson (have arm, will travel), the Royals will surprise everyone and win the AL Central division. So far, that vaunted rotation has led the Royals to a 5-17 start. Is it possible to finish triple digits behind the division leader? We should find out this year if Tony Pena keeps his team playing at this level. George Brett once commented that he checked each morning to see who was batting below the "Mendoza Line"; he was referring to the batting average of Mario Mendoza, the starting shortstop for the

Pittsburgh Pirates, Seattle Mariners, and Texas Rangers (lifetime average: .215). Nowadays, my dad's friend has to check the Royals' lineup to see who *isn't* below the Mendoza Line.

It was a fun series to watch. The first game, we took advantage of every opportunity, and Scotty simply was on base all night, with three walks, two hits, and three stolen bases. The bottom of the order was fantastic: Hambino, Crede and Uribe went 8-for-13, with six runs scored and three RBI. Runelvys Hernandez threw for them, and because of the cold temperature, blew on his fingers all night to warm them. Meanwhile, Freddy Garcia dominated their lineup, giving up only four hits in seven innings. It was our fifth win in a row, and it all looked easy. We won, 8-2.

The next two games were not so easy, but the Royals helped us along. In the first of the two, Scotty got an infield single to lead off the game, and advanced on catcher's interference to Iguchi. (Mistake # 1.) Greinke balked them along to second and third (mistake #2), which set up Everett's RBI groundout to first. After the Royals tied it on a solo HR by DeJesus in the first, we scored again when Hambino scored from first on a double into the left-field corner by Uribe. Hambino shouldn't have been sent by Joey Cora, our third-base coach, but their left-fielder Diaz overthrew the cutoff man (mistake #3), handing us another run. Jose Contreras looked unhittable for us, striking out six in the first three innings, but he exited in the fourth when he pulled a hamstring. Our bullpen came through; Politte and Cotts held them scoreless, and despite Vizcaino giving up a run, we managed to hold on, tied 2-2 going into the bottom of the ninth.

Enter Marte. Which means, of course, that high drama had to ensue.

It did. With one out, Diaz singled, and Buck followed with a line shot into the right field corner that should have won the game. But Diaz took a huge turn around second, swinging wide (mistake #4), and even though he ran through the third-base coach's sign to stop, he had to reverse back to third because Dye had relayed it quickly to Konerko, who fired home.

Graffanino was walked intentionally to load the bases for a possible double play, but when Marte threw a fastball way inside on the first pitch to DeJesus, Diaz saw it glance off Hambino's glove and took off for home (mistake #5). Hambino made a terrific play, backhanding the ball a la Derek Jeter to Marte, who caught it and tagged the sliding Diaz out by inches. Marte then struck out Long for the third out, and we went to the tenth.

With Hambino on first and two out, Uribe singled to center, and Hambino surprised everyone by motoring around second and chugging for third. He made it, and Rowand then flared one to center that dropped. We had the lead, 3-2, the Royals went down in order to Marte in their half, and that's how it ended.

The last game we tried to hand to the Royals, since we hadn't swept a three-game series all year. El Duque was wild enough to walk six batters in five innings, but they could only score two runs off of him. That kept them even with us, 2-2, because we scored twice in the first after Scotty and Willie Harris walked, then scored when Gload and Perez singled and grounded out. Ozzie went with his reserves today: Perez for Dye, Widger for A.J., and Gload for Konerko (although Konerko DH'd) and it worked out, especially in the eighth, by which time the Royals were ahead 3-2.

Willie singled with one out, and Konerko broke his bat and flared a single to left. Dye pinch-hit and struck out, but Rowand came through just as he did in yesterday's game, singling to drive in the tying run. Pablo Ozuna then pinch-hit for Perez, and lined one down the right-field line to drive in Konerko to put us ahead, 4-3. Vizcaino and Takatsu held them scoreless for the last two innings, and we had our seventh win in a row, and our first sweep.

BEN: You shouldn't have worried about the Royals, Dad.

DAD: I don't think that '67 series will ever leave me.

If worrying about the Royals was a waste, Dad *should* have worried about Oakland instead. The Athletics *always* kill us. Last year, we went 2-7 against them; the year before, we went 4-5; the year before that, 2-7. Since 2001, the A's are 27-9 against us. Maybe that's because they've generally been constructed the same way we are this year – lots of pitching, sufficient hitting. We *did* give them a tough time in the series, even if we lost two of three. If we can play a team like Oakland close, if we can keep winning at this rate (we're now 16-6), we're going to be tough to beat come playoff time. Let's just hope that the A's don't win the AL West or the Wild Card.

We took the first game in Oakland 6-0 behind a brilliant start by Jon Garland. Garland went all nine innings in the win, and is already 4-0. Unlike last year, this year Garland seems able to control his sinker; in the past, he hasn't been very good about mixing his pitches, but in this game, he was great at keeping Oakland's lineup off balance. Is this the year Garland finally breaks the 12-win barrier?

Garland also got lots of help from a great defensive squad. Jermaine Dye made a very good catch in right field on a sinking liner in the first, Aaron Rowand covered a lot of ground in center field, and Juan Uribe snagged some slow rollers up the middle. Even backup catcher Chris Widger got into the act, backing up a bad throw by Rowand to first and saving the Sox from an error. Widger also hit the two-run bomb in the seventh inning off of a tough Barry Zito to put the Sox ahead in the game.

Unfortunately, the first game in Oakland was the only big highlight. The second game demonstrated the type of defense Sox fans became accustomed to last year: three errors, a balk, and a hit that probably should have been called an error in the ninth inning. This game should have been called "The Ghost of Carlos Lee Returns: Carlos' Revenge." It was a brutal performance all around, despite the fact that the White Sox had 14 hits (3 from my pick, Aaron Rowand, who improved his average to .260 – if he has to *raise* his average to .260, he's going to lose his roster spot to Brian Anderson). Crazyman Damaso Marte got the loss after giving up two runs in just over an inning. Juan Uribe got hurt, and so did capable replacement infielder Pablo Ozuna, leaving us in dire straits for the third game of the series – will Ozzie suit up?

The supposed upside to the second game was Mark Buehrle's 33rd straight outing of six innings or more. Here's my question: so what? It isn't exactly a quality start when you give up 11 hits and seven runs over six innings. Buehrle's lucky he didn't get a loss. This obsession with statistics, the obsession with eating innings even if your pitcher is laboring out there – it seems bizarre to me. I could throw six innings if you give me enough runs to waste. The number of innings pitched isn't important – it's the number of quality innings. I hope Ozzie doesn't get caught up in the hype surrounding this dubious streak, because at some point it will cost him. He'll leave in Buehrle too long trying to get him his six innings, and it'll cost us a game.

The last game of the series was even more of a heartbreaker. Unlike Buehrle, Freddy Garcia pitched a powerhouse of a game, going seven innings, giving up only one run on four hits. It wasn't enough, though, as the bullpen gave up the winning run. Guess who? Damaso Marte did it again, putting the winning run on base in the ninth inning. Dustin Hermanson, who has been amazing all year (his ERA currently stands at 0.00), gave up a walk and the winning hit. Because we were playing shorthanded, Joe Crede started the game at shortstop and catcher Chris Widger started at third. Crede and Ozzie were ejected in the top of the ninth inning after umpire Hunter Wendelstedt disallowed a hit-by-pitch that struck Crede on the upper arm. Wendelstedt said that Crede violated Rule 6.08(b), which states that a hit-by-pitch should be disallowed if the "batter makes no attempt to avoid being touched by the ball." Announcers Hawk Harrelson and Darren Jackson went nuts after the call, saying it was "bull." I happen to think the ump got the call right – I wish umpires would make that call more often. In the age of body armor at the plate (Barry Bonds looks more like a 12th-century English knight than a baseball player at the plate), it's too easy for a hitter to make no effort to get out of the way of the pitch. That prevents pitchers from pitching inside, and gives batters a huge advantage.

Of course, Ozzie and Wendelstedt have an ongoing blood feud continuing from last year – Ozzie was ejected last September for arguing a stolen base call at second base.

Wendelstedt filed a report on Ozzie's argument, and Ozzie was suspended for two games, after which Ozzie called Wendelstedt a liar. Guess who was thrown out at second base last September, prompting the grudge match? You guessed it: The Ghost of Carlos Lee Strikes Again.

Bottom line: we just didn't get the job done in the last two games. But at least we played Oakland tough. That's a good sign. We'll just have to wait and see if this begins the typical Sox losing streak of years past, or if the Sox are *really* this good. We're headed back to Detroit next to find out.

	W	L	PCT	GB	Home	Away	Div	Streak
Chicago WSox	16	6	.727	---	6-2	10-4	13-3	Lost 2
Minnesota	12	8	.600	3	6-2	6-6	10-7	Won 2
Detroit	9	10	.474	5 1/2	5-5	4-5	8-9	Won 3
Cleveland	8	12	.400	7	2-5	6-7	6-9	Lost 2
Kansas City	5	16	.238	10 1/2	2-11	3-5	3-12	Lost 7

May 8, 2005
DAD:

What a week and a half it's been! Unbelievable. They've won eight in a row after losing the opener to Detroit; they beat the Tigers two in a row after that, then swept Kansas City and Toronto. They're up four and a half games on the Twins, and their gaudy 24-7 record is easily the best in baseball. And it all started after that loss to Detroit on April 29. . . .

April 29: a date that will always stand out in my memory, because it was the day in 1996 my older sister Suzie was buried after her year-long battle with breast cancer. She and I were extremely close. Our mother used to say that Suzie, the oldest of the four of us, was either two years early arriving or I was two years late, because we were more like twins: we finished sentences for each other, had exactly the same sense of humor, and thought along parallel lines.

There was only one thing that we harshly disagreed on while growing up.

Suzie was a Cubs fan.

This, was, in my view, an unforgivable sin. Except that this was Suzie, whom I adored and admired. She was probably the most brilliant person I have ever known; growing up winning all sorts of scholastic awards. She always hid her brilliance beneath an earthy, crunchy exterior, and she always looked out for me.

But still, a Cubs fan? How could I truly feel that close to a Cubs fan?

There was a baseball reason why I let her off the hook. . .

.

It was Chanukah, 1967. We didn't have much money, so our presents to each other had to be inexpensive. Traditionally, each member of our family bought one gift for every other person, and we opened them the first night. Usually my parents got each of us a gift, and often Suzie and I pooled our money to buy the others gifts. When it was my turn to open my gift from Suzie, I could tell by the shape of the package that it was a book.

I loved books. We all did. There was the typical Jewish reverence for books in our house; it started, I'm sure, with the reverence for the Bible and other holy books that have preoccupied Jews since time immemorial. My own children have it; they know that books are to be treated with great care, and that the world is theirs if they read, read, and read.

So I was excited as I opened the package. It looked like a sports book. . . .

"Home Run Feud" by Clair Bee,'" I read. "The Chip Hilton Sports Series." I turned to my parents. "Can I read it now?"

"Sure," my dad replied.

"Thanks, Suzie," I exclaimed. She just smiled happily.

That thanks I gave her, no matter how heartfelt it was, wasn't enough for what happened as a result of that book. I became obsessed. I swallowed that book faster than the whale swallowed Jonah, and I fell in love. I saw that *Home Run Feud* was the twenty-second book in the series, and I became driven to buy every one and read them all. Over the next year or so, saving every cent I could earn, I bought every book in the series, and read and read them until I knew their lines from memory. Even now, almost forty years later, if someone fires a line from one of the books, I can still recognize in a heartbeat exactly which book and probably which chapter.

The Chip Hilton books are, for my money, the finest juvenile writing for young teenagers I have ever read. Clair Bee was a basketball genius, an icon in New York, where he coached Long Island University for eighteen years, including a 43-game win streak, two undefeated seasons, and two NIT championships (1939 and 1941). He developed the 1-3-1 zone defense, helped develop the three-second rule and the 24-second rule, and authored more than fifty books, including the Chip Hilton books.

They are highly moral, and as the series traces Chip and his four close friends from high school into college, they impart wonderful life lessons. There is a new incarnation of them that changes the focus to be more overtly religious and politically correct, but the originals are much better, if you can find them at the used bookstores.

By the time I reached high school three years later, I had dreams about becoming an athlete. I didn't have the gift; I was meant to do other things, but I found out where Clair Bee was, and wrote him a letter. His response, which I still have, is vintage Bee.

"Do you work hard at being a good player whatever the sport? Are you really dedicated and determined to succeed – the mental approach to competition is as important as the physical approach – are you mentally tough? Enough questions – Work! Practice! Believe in yourself!"

He was the real deal, a truly honest man, a kind man, and I will be eternally grateful to my sister that she introduced me to his world.

Thus, the loss to Detroit, albeit painful, was put into perspective next to my grief on this date for the loss of my sister. The Sox left sixteen (yes, SIXTEEN!) men on base, and lost in the eleventh after tying it up in the ninth and having a chance to win (Timo Perez struck out and Crede popped out). This made three losses in a row, coming after their two losses to Oakland, but I didn't get horribly steamed about it. I thought of how Chip, the consummate gentleman, would take a loss, and . . .

Came *thiiiiiiiiiiiiiiiiis* close to swearing. (That's my story, and I'm sticking to it.)

The next day, April 30, Hernandez wild-pitched a run home in the first, and I thought, here we go again. Then Nook Logan singled in another run for the Tigers in the third, we were down 2-0, still not hitting, which had killed us over the last three games, and I could feel my blood pressure rising.

But then in the third, Willie Harris drew a walk, stole second, and came around to score late on a ground-out. (Well, at least we were on the board). In the fifth, with two out, the Tigers sandwiched two singles around a walk to score again, and the only reason I didn't get more irritated was the play Scotty P. made on the first single, which was pretty slick. Running to his right, he slightly overran the ball (of course, with his speed I'm always suspicious he has a red "S" underneath his uniform) and reached back *with his bare hand* to catch the ball, which would have gone right by him. I was mulling that one over while the Tigers scored.

By the seventh, I was resigned to the fact that the next time we scored would be the Fourth of July. We needed *something*. Then, lo and behold, Rowand, leading off, got hit by a pitch, A.J lined a single to center, sending Rowand flying to third, and Crede singled Rowand home, making it 3-2.

And I was thinking, *come on . . . come on . . .*

Crede on first, Hambino on second, and Harris came through again, laying down a beautiful bunt to move them over.

Scotty's turn. They weren't going to walk him. *Just get it to the right side.*

He did, chopping a slow roller toward the right side, A.J. scored, and Crede moved to third. We were tied, 3-3.

Two out.

The best guy we have going right now was up: Iguchi. And he came through, bouncing one up the middle to score Crede. We were up 4-3.

Whew. Now hold on. Hold on . . .

Politte gave up a walk to Monroe with two out in the eighth, but when Marte came in, Monroe took off, and the Great Hambino gunned him down.

Blow off that pistol, A.J., it's still smokin'.

In the ninth, Dustin Hermanson, the guy with the 0.00 ERA, gave up a single, but then got a quick 6-4-3 double play and a shot right at Konerko, who blocked it, then ran to first – and we'd broken the three-game skid, broken the Tigers' five-game win streak, and restored Justice to the Universe.

That was just the beginning. Over the next seven games, the Sox have looked like they'll never lose again. Jon Garland pitched his second straight shutout (What? Has the future arrived?), whitewashing the Tigers 8-0, as the Sox tied a major league record held by the 1955 Brooklyn Dodgers by holding a lead for the 25th straight game. That was the only championship Brooklyn ever won, so that's a good omen, I hope. The only interesting moment came when Garland hit Rondell White in apparent retaliation for Konerko getting hit earlier. I like that: protecting your own. It's good, hard-nosed baseball.

Tadahito and Everett saved Buehrle the next night. Buehrle gave up four runs to the Royals, three on HRs; but Iguchi went four for four, with his first career Major League HR, Everett doubled home two to vault us ahead after we were down 4-3 in the eighth, and we won 5-4. And we had another lead, which broke the Dodger record. It's a tribute to Ozzie, really, since we've held the lead every game this year, which means his plan to start scoring early with more speed (read: Scotty P., who singled to start the game-winning rally) has worked out beautifully.

Game four of the streak featured Hambino hitting a two-run shot after Crede had solo-homered earlier, and we had a 4-2 lead in the ninth. If you just looked at a summary of the three outs of the ninth inning, it would look simple, but the ninth was another reason why we could really go places this year: defense.

Iguchi made two consecutive sparkling plays on balls hit up the middle, and then on a flare over third base, Uribe raced over and slid on his knees to snare the ball a heartbeat before it hit the ground to end the game, as Hermanson kept his ERA at 0.00.

Game five was a beauty. Contreras was magnificent, allowing only a Tony Graffanino HR in the seventh. Still, Zack Greinke, the Royals' wunderkind, was better, shutting us out, giving up only two hits in seven innings. But then Konerko, leading off the eighth, drew a walk, moved to second on Rowand's perfect bunt, and then came a key play: Greinke hit Dye, placing the go-ahead runner on. I was delighted to see Tony Pena, the Royals' manager, remove Greinke and bring in Andrew Sisco from the bullpen; Greinke was killing us. Jamie Burke moved the runners up with a dribbler to third, leaving them at second and third with two outs.

Sisco then threw five very close pitches to Crede, four of which were called balls, loading the bases. It had to upset Sisco; he had done his job, but now there was no margin for error. On four straight pitches, he walked Uribe, forcing in the tying run.

1-1, bases loaded, two out, and Scotty P. was up. I'm thinking, make the guy throw a strike – don't swing, for cryin' out loud. Sisco threw the first pitch outside, and then Pena must have figured Sisco had lost it; he brought in Burgos, who proceeded to walk a very patient Scotty and force in the go-ahead run. We won, 2-1, and Ben started IM'ing me after the games.

BEN: It had to be heartbreaking for Greinke, but hey, these are the kinds of games great teams win, and we did. Hmmm. . . .

Game six: a 5-3 come-from-behind victory notable for Dye lofting his first HR in 12 games to left, and Hambino blooping a two-run single to left to drive in the winning runs in the eighth. Oh, and Hermanson got another save. He's still at 0.00.

Game seven: a highly unusual game for us, we won our second straight from Toronto 10-7 by slugging five HRs, Konerko with two, and Iguchi, Rowand, and Uribe chiming in to help Garland run his record to 6-0, despite giving up six runs. And, I am happy to report, Scotty P. had four stolen bases, and now leads the league with 16 steals.

BEN: Four stolen bases? That's more than Frank Thomas had in his career.

Game eight: completing a sweep of the Jays, 5-4, we had an early 5-0 lead, and then held on as Buehrle ignored a couple of errors by Uribe that led to runs and kept his cool beautifully. The only sour note was a terrible collision between the Jays' catcher Gregg Zaun and our Pedro Lopez at second. Zaun was out cold, and everyone was scared, but further tests showed he was okay. Everyone, and I mean everyone, was worried out there.

But thank God, he came out of it okay, and tonight the Sox can enjoy their eight-game win streak.

I know I will.

	W	L	PCT	GB	Home	Away	Div	Streak
Chicago WSox	23	7	.767	---	11-3	12-4	18-4	Won 7
Minnesota	18	11	.621	4 1/2	9-5	9-6	12-9	Won 3
Detroit	13	16	.448	9 1/2	6-8	7-8	10-11	Won 1
Cleveland	12	17	.414	10 1/2	3-8	9-9	9-13	Lost 1

May 16, 2005
BEN:

And then we hit Tampa Bay. "Tampa Bay?" you ask incredulously. Yes, Tampa Bay. That forgotten powerhouse down there in Florida, entering the Sox series with an astounding 11-21 record, cleaned our clock. Okay, so taking out Toronto, Kansas City, and Detroit wasn't exactly burning through the Yankees, Red Sox, and Angels. Still, you would figure that a team standing at 24-7 would beat a team that gets fewer fans than a "Yanni In The Park" concert.

Ah, but the fates abhor such predictability, in sports as in life. A Lou Piniella-led team is always a fighting team, but in recent years it's rarely a winning team. Maybe we were due for a letdown. By the way, is it just me, or does Dad get to write about all the good winning streaks here? Maybe I should delay my writings as long as possible – in the fashion of all true baseball fans, I am quite superstitious that it is *my* writing that causes the Sox to lose ballgames.

The first game against Tampa Bay started in typical White Sox fashion: we grabbed the lead early (that was 32 straight games, ladies and gentlemen). Once again, Scotty P. was the catalyst – walking, stealing second base, and scoring. Podsednik is turning out to be just what the White Sox wanted when they traded for him – a true table-setter. It's a good thing he is, too, because the man we traded for him, chunky Carlos Lee, is tearing up the National League (6 HR, 28 RBI going into tonight's game). You can bet your last dollar that the media would be all over Kenny Williams if the Sox weren't winning right now.

64

In any case, the lead didn't hold up. Garcia blew it in the sixth inning with a couple of mistakes, and we lost, 4-2. But the real story of the game was the fact that the Sox got eight hits and scored two runs. That's stupid baseball, and Ozzie was not happy about it after the game. But we couldn't get that kind of effort twice in a row after ending an eight-game winning streak, could we?

You bet we could. Game two was a heartbreaker, a true travesty made even worse than usual by the fact that Ozzie brought in Shingo Takatsu in the ninth. As I've made clear, I don't like Takatsu's stuff very much. In fact, if I could choose between putting a tee-ball stand on the plate or putting Takatsu out there, I'd be stuck between a rock and hard place.

The situation was this: we took a 4-1 lead (what else is new? That's 33 straight). Jose Contreras blew the lead. What else is new? He's had six starts and his record is 1-0; Contreras is prone to giving up the big inning, a trait that drove the Yankees bonkers last year. He's just lucky that we're *really* good, otherwise his record would look like Jeremy Bonderman's last year. This game, Contreras gave up the big inning in the fourth, when Toby Hall tattooed a bad breaking ball for a three-run bomb that barely cleared the left field wall (Contreras had walked the previous two batters).

In the sixth inning, we took a 6-4 lead on a beautiful suicide squeeze play executed to perfection by Iguchi. Iguchi is a solid ballplayer – he doesn't show a lot of power, but he does hit it where they ain't, and he plays a pretty good second base (earlier in the game he made a nifty catch on a pop to short right field).

It wasn't enough. In the seventh, Luis Vizcaino, who should have stayed with Milwaukee, got wild and let home two to tie it at 6-6. But it was the ninth that was heartbreaking. With one out, Takatsu grooved an 81-mph grapefruit to Jorge Cantu. Cantu's eyes lit up like a Doberman at the sight of red meat.

Good afternoon, good evening, and good night. Watching the game via laptop, I could feel my blood begin to boil. Only one reaction could salvage tonight's dismal effort: dump Takatsu and use Hermanson.

Apparently my direct line with Ozzie was working. In the final game of the series, we once again took the lead, this time in the fifth inning, when we scored four runs. Two of those runs came thanks to Paul Konerko, who went the other way with a double. Konerko is hitting .202 but has 25 RBI. Dave Kingman, anyone?

Meanwhile, Orlando Hernandez was spectacular, pitching into the seventh and exiting with a 5-1 lead. El Duque is fun to watch simply because you never know what he's going to throw next – will it be 60 mph or 88? Will he go three-quarters with arm angle, or sidearm? The batters didn't seem to know what to expect up there. Then the bullpen came in and shut the door.

Guess who closed it out? You guessed it: The Goateed One, Dustin Hermanson. 1 2/3 innings, 0 hits. Easy as 1-2-3. You listening, Shingo?

Meanwhile, the White Sox website was reporting that Frank Thomas, the Big (and Often) Hurt, is rehabbing his ankle. Is this good news?

DAD: I'm not thrilled to death about Thomas returning. Frank Thomas is to the White Sox what Nomar Garciaparra was to the Red Sox: big numbers, no clutch hitting. Last time the Sox were in the playoffs, Thomas went 0-for the playoffs.

Both Dad and I have thought for years that the Sox should trade Thomas; the list has varied in terms of who we wanted in return, but it was usually pitching. This year we have the pitching, so just let him ride the Pine Pony until we can buy him out at the end of the year. Harsh? You bet. But the Red Sox didn't win until Theo Epstein had the guts to dump Nomar in favor of little-known shortstop Orlando Cabrera. Badabing, badaboom, World Series Champion Red Sox for the first time since 1918.

DAD: To lose two out of three to Tampa Bay is like losing at singing to William Hung.

The series in Baltimore was another scratch-and-claw affair. We split with them, winning the first two and losing the last two, which puts us back in early season form (win a couple, lose one). I like Baltimore's team a couple years from now – one of my friends, Dani, is a huge Baltimore fan, and he's high on Eric Bedard, who does have great stuff. And Baltimore (despite the egregiously bad signing of Sammy Sosa) *is* competing in the stocked-up AL East. So perhaps I shouldn't take it too hard that they stuck with us.

Still, I do. The first game was a nail-biter; the Sox's usual "take the lead, hold on" formula worked to perfection. The "holding on" in this case was done by newly-blossoming stud pitcher Jon Garland (7-0). Garland struck out superstar Miguel Tejada with men on first and third in the seventh and two outs; Hermanson put the game in the freezer with a perfect ninth inning. Garland's sinker has been working wonders this year; he's also working faster this year, more in the Buehrle mold, which means that the defense is awake out there. For the record, the game-winning run came off the bat of none other than Aaron Rowand, who is redeeming himself for a horrific April with an excellent May.

Game two was another tough win; we came from behind to take it 5-3. Mark Buehrle got the win to make our starters' collective record an astonishing 22-4 (can we split the Cy Young three ways?). The man with the pinpoint control and the average stuff went eight strong innings against a monster lineup. The Sox's comeback took place in the seventh inning, led by – yup! – Scotty Podsednik, who doubled to right (one of three hits on the night). Pods' double was almost a home run, and the O's got lucky – Podsednik was motoring, and the ball bounced into the seats for a ground-rule double. Scotty moved to third on an error, and scored the tying run on a single by Konerko. Iguchi scored right behind him to take the lead.

Hermanson, the man with the golden arm and the perfect ERA, got the save yet again. How does he do it? Sheer smarts. His stuff is pretty good, but he's no Billy Wagner in terms of velocity. Yet he has pitched 18 1/3 scoreless innings this year, and given up only 11 hits. Can we *please* make this guy our permanent closer already?

Unfortunately, Ozzie still seems to be flirting with the idea of using Takatsu in late-game situations. "I still believe in Shingo, and I've told him that," Ozzie said. "He has good stuff, but needs better command and needs to throw more strikes. The main thing coming out of the bullpen is to throw the ball over the plate." No, see, that's the problem: when Takatsu throws the ball over the plate, it ends up in the bleachers. Perhaps we can use him strategically – like when we need an intentional walk.

So, after three straight wins, I began to think that my writing wouldn't hurt the Sox. How wrong I was. Game three saw Freddy Garcia lose his second straight start, with the O's absolutely trashing him. Game four saw the Sox's major league record 37-game lead streak come to an end; Erik Bedard shut us down, as Dani said he would. Despite the two losses, we remain 27-11.

My favorite story from the Orioles series wasn't the split, or even the emergence of Hermanson. In the third game of the series, Scotty P. stole four bases. In the first inning, he stole second and third; in the fourth, he stole second and third. That's the second time this season he has stolen four bases, and he now has 23 swipes on the year after Monday's game (already topping last year's team leader, Willie Harris, at 19). It is no coincidence that Podsednik leads the league in steals and that the White Sox lead the league in winning percentage. This gives the lie to all that Billy Beane nonsense about stolen bases being useless. Michael Lewis' homage to Beane includes the following statement: "Billy Beane's total lack of interest in the stolen base – which has served the team so well for the previous 162 games – is regarded, in the postseason, as sheer folly." Beane talks derisively about the "atavistic need to run." And then he pulls out his stat sheets and demonstrates just how teams run themselves out of innings. Well, Billy, that's only if you suck at running. Scotty P. doesn't. And the White Sox, who are batting slightly above .250 as a team, have the best record in baseball.

I love Scotty's take on the stolen base: prepare, prepare, prepare, and then let 'er fly. Scotty watches tons of tape: "For the majority, I'm just watching starters," Podsednik says. "With relievers, I pay attention when guys get on base, to see their delivery and times and so forth. The more you know, the better chance you have." When it comes time to steal, Podsednik goes for it: "It's about confidence and getting out there and trusting you have done your preparation and know your opponent and that you will get off on the right mark. . . . You can't be afraid to be thrown out."

I tend to be of the same philosophy as Scotty with regard to finals. Harvard Law isn't generally the sweatshop it's made out to be in movies like *The Paper Chase*, but it does get rather competitive during finals time. Many students compete to see how long they can study without having an aneurism. The library is open until all hours, probably so that people can say that they fell asleep on their desks. Everyone here is very smart, and studying does matter, but at some point you just have to let it go and trust your brain. With finals this week, I tried to do that – heck, even finals can't stop me from watching Sox games. Priorities are priorities.

And I don't think that studying is all it's cracked up to be beyond a certain point. These grueling marathon studying sessions are more about students intimidating each other – "Hey, who here knows which provision of the U.C.C. (Uniform Commercial Code) deals with this issue?" – than they are about learning the stuff. All the finals are open book and open notes, so memorizing everything is an exercise in freaking everyone else out.

As soon as I get back to L.A., I'm going to have to start preparing for the premiere of the book. It's a month until go time on *Porn Generation*, and my publicity schedule is still in flux. I had to get used to the last-minute rushing last time with my first book, *Brainwashed: How Universities Indoctrinate America's Youth*, but it's still annoying to me. I like to have all my ducks in a row before the hunt begins. I guess I still have to learn to live with the unpredictability of publicity, just as the White Sox have.

But they're better at it than I am. These last couple series have been up and down. Ozzie remarked after the White Sox lost their second straight game to the pathetic Rays, "The ball is not bouncing our way right now, and that is going to happen to the best teams." Jose Contreras, who pitched rather wildly and unpredictably himself in the second game of the Tampa Bay series, remarked, "I don't think the team or anyone should worry about getting beat or winning tomorrow. We are going to try to win every game."

They had better try to. The series after next is Go Time. It's almost time to turn our wrath against the embodiment of all evil in the universe: the Cubs.

	W	L	PCT	GB	Home	Away	Div	Streak
Chicago WSox	27	11	.711	---	13-5	14-6	18-4	Lost 2
Minnesota	21	15	.583	5	10-7	11-8	12-9	Won 1
Detroit	17	19	.472	9	7-10	10-9	10-11	Lost 1
Cleveland	16	20	.444	10	5-9	11-11	9-13	Lost 1
Kansas City	11	27	.289	16	5-13	6-14	5-17	Won 2

May 19, 2005
DAD:

It's two days before our twenty-eighth anniversary. The White Sox have a day off after taking two out of three from the Rangers, and I'm thinking how proud I am of my kids, that I'm a tremendously lucky guy. I look at my kids, and I look at my wife, who's still the love of my life, and I'm grateful to God for what he's given me.

I have been more than happy to see Ozzie's feelings about family. His priorities are right, too. In early May, Willie Harris left the team for a couple of days, and Ozzie excused him, saying, "He wanted to stay and play this game, but to me family is more important than baseball. Baseball will kick your butt out of here, they don't care about you when you leave. Your family is going to be there, and it's important my players think about family more than baseball."

Beautiful. Makes me even prouder to be a White Sox fan. And the fact that Ozzie has his son beside him in the dugout is beautiful, too. Ben and I are as close as a father and son can be, and it would be my dream to work with him beside me, too.

As a free-lance composer, I was home with the kids, and when Ben was a baby, I used to love taking Ben with me when I went on interviews. He used to ride on my chest in the snugli, and whenever women interviewed me they were charmed by the fact that a daddy could be so nuts about his own kid. As a result of me being home, Ben and I were having discussions from the time he could talk, and they quickly grew into philosophical discussions about everything, always with a highly idealistic perspective. There was never any cynicism; I'm a romantic at heart.

Of course, none of that would have been possible without my wife, who made all my romantic dreams a reality. I met my wife when we were eighteen, three weeks into our freshman year at Northwestern University, and proposed to her two days after we met. She likes to kid me and remind me that it took her five days to say yes, and that the only reason she said yes was to shut me up, since I kept asking her every day. It doesn't matter to me; I had always believed in romance; that one day I'd meet the love of my life and we'd raise a family together. I was right, and it didn't hurt that my father always wrote love notes to my mother and was smitten with her, too.

With our anniversary, the upcoming release of Ben's book, and the series against the Cubs around the corner, I almost took the series against the Rangers for granted. Stupid me. They can really hit, and after Garcia and Contreras got hammered by the Orioles, I should have been more concerned.

The first game was a heartbreaker. El Duque got knocked around and only went 2 2/3 innings while giving up six runs. We had a 4-1 lead after A.J. hit a grand slam, but they chased us, caught us, and passed us right away. Still, we tied it up in the eighth when our best hitter, Iguchi, pinch-hit and homered to left. We hadn't lost three in a row all year, and I didn't see it happening now.

Wrong. In the ninth, Kevin Mench hit his second HR of the game, a rocket off Marte, and the Sox went down meekly in the bottom half of the inning. There was a report that after this game, the clubhouse, which always has music playing after the game win or lose, was dead silent. It was a hugely depressing game to lose. I just hoped they could bounce back.

The next day, Frank Thomas made his debut for the year with the Triple-A Charlotte Knights of the International League, going two for three. The Sox made the question of Thomas irrelevant, at least for the moment. Hambino hit his fourth HR in the last five games, Scotty P. stole his league-leading 24th base, and Konerko, whose average is way too low but always seems to get the clutch hits that Thomas never did, got another RBI. We won, 5-2.

I love to watch Podsednik fly, and another thing I love to watch is A.J. get intense. He's always intense, but sometimes he ratchets it up. He did in the sixth, when the Rangers cut the lead to 3-2, and had runners on second and third with nobody out. Hambino trudged to the mound, and the conversation between him and Garland looked pretty one-sided. I'd guess that some of what Hambino said was rougher than "you're throwing like a girl." Bingo.   Whatever he said, Garland struck out Hank Blalock and Alfonso Soriano on two hellacious sinkers, then got a fly-out from Mench. Garland is now 8-0, and I smelled an All-Star start.

But the next day, Buehrle made that a question worthy of discussion. He shut out the Rangers for 7 1/3 innings, running his record to 7-1. He scattered nine hits, and it's possible *he* might start the All-Star game. Rowand extended his hitting streak to twelve games, Konerko went 3-for-4 and hit his 10th HR, Dye went 3-for-4, (finally! if he starts hitting, look out) and we won 7-0. Oh, and A.J hit *another* HR, his fifth in six games. After the game, Konerko, in his typically modest style, said he's "not out of the woods yet." He and Dye are very quiet, professional guys, and I think they balance nicely the intensity of A.J. and Rowand, and the goofiness of Buehrle.

This series roughly concluded the first quarter of the season, with the Sox at 29-12, and in first place by 5 ½ games. It's been great. They look great, they sound quietly confident, and now they get the Cubs to start the second leg of the race. As a purist, I still hate the idea of interleague play, but under the old rules the only time we could beat those losers would be in the World Series, and they ain't *never* going to get there; so we might as well beat them now and shut their fans up.

Of course, nothing would be worse than to lead our division and then lose to the Cubs, but I don't see that happening. We ought to be able to use them for a springboard to further glory.

Part II
Springboard to Glory

December 12, 1975

"How were classes today?" Cindy asked me. We were in our sophomore year at Northwestern University, and I had decided to switch my major from piano to liberal arts, since I was entertaining ideas about becoming a psychologist. Small wonder, since as a White Sox fan the tremendous vicissitudes in emotion could easily send you to a psychiatrist's couch. Thus, if I became a psychologist I could try to help others suffering from the same syndrome.

"I don't know," I grumbled. "There's something else that's more important right now."

"More important than classes?' she asked, surprised.

"The White Sox might leave Chicago. There's talk that they might move to *Florida*, for crying out loud. *Florida!* What do they know about baseball in *Florida*!"

Cindy said hesitantly, "Don't a lot of the teams play spring training down there?"

"They can't leave Chicago!" I snapped. "If this town becomes a town with only the Cubs, I'm out of here."

"Come on, David. It's only baseball."

I gave her a heated look that could have melted glass.

"Maybe you should call your dad, if you're that upset," she said.

"Good idea."

Two minutes later, I spoke to my father, who was still at work.

"I don't know, Butch," he said. "They've been losing a lot of money for a while. That guy Bud Selig tried to buy them and move them to Milwaukee five or six years ago, remember? Ever since he bought the Seattle team and moved them to

Milwaukee, the folks in Seattle have been trying to buy the Sox. If no one steps up. . . ."

"Dad, they *can't* move. They're one of the original American League teams. Remember, we won the first American league pennant. We've *got* to stay."

"I don't know, Butch," he sighed. "It's a long shot. It'll take a miracle, or at least a magician."

"Can you think of anybody? Who'd take on the team when they're losing so much money?"

"I'm as depressed about it as you are, Butch."

We both forgot there was one magician left.

December 16, 1975

"Yeeeeeessssssss!!!!!!! He did it! He did it!" I shouted, as I grabbed a newspaper from the newsstand and stood there staring at it flap in the bitterly cold wind.

"Who did what?" Cindy asked me, poking me in the side, as she held her hood close around her face.

"The guy's the greatest!" I yelled. "He's the greatest!"

"Who is?" Cindy asked, bemused.

Wordlessly, I handed her the paper. Splashed all across the front page of the *Chicago Sun Times* was the headline that Bill Veeck had bought the Sox, and better yet, would keep them in Chicago.

"I love that guy," I told her.

"Should I feel threatened?" she asked with a grin.

"You're number one, two, three, forever," I told her. "But he's my hero."

"After your dad, of course."

"I've got to call him right away!"

"But you've got a class right now," she protested.

"Class can wait," I said. "This is important! I'll meet you after class, okay?" I jubilantly squeezed her in a bear hug.

"Ouch!" she said, but she was smiling.

Five minutes later, back at the dorm, I called my father at work.

"Hey, Butch, isn't that great? I heard the news on the radio this morning."

"Veeck is the greatest, Dad, just the greatest!"

"I always thought so."

I remembered now that my father had thought highly of Veeck since I was little. "Now the Cubs won't be the only game in town, Dad."

"That's for sure. And you can bet he'll spice up the team and bring them back, too, Butch. You're not the only one who's excited."

"Dad, when did you start liking him so much?"

"I always liked him, Butch. But it was his friendship with Hank Greenberg that sold me." Hank Greenberg, the Hall of Famer who almost broke Ruth's single-season HR record, was a hero to most Jews who grew up before World War II, including my dad. Greenberg was known as a class act, handling the vicious anti-semitism of the day with quiet grace.

"He hired Greenberg as his assistant when he owned the Cleveland Indians, and later Greenberg became the general manager. Then when he bought the Sox in 1959, Greenberg was one of his partners, and became the vice-president. Anyone who sticks with Greenberg is okay in my book." There was a pause. "Hey, don't you have a class right now?"

"Uh, yeah . . ."

He laughed. "Don't miss any more, Butch, but I understand. This doesn't happen every day. When a great moment in your life comes along, don't march through it. Stop and let the feeling wash over you. You'll remember it better that way."

May 20, 2005
DAD:

Oh, boy, would my father have enjoyed this game. If this series against the Cubs is going to be our springboard to glory, this game was a seamless launch into the atmosphere. Great, great pitching from Freddy Garcia, who went seven innings, scattering five hits, and only gave up an unearned run in the seventh after we already led 4-0. He looked absolutely huge out there. He's a big guy anyway, but he has gotten lost this year behind the great starts of Garland and Buehrle.

Not today, though. After giving up 11 earned runs and 18 hits in his last two starts, he only gave up five measly singles. And he looked tough, determined. Greg Maddux hit Iguchi in the top of the first, and in the bottom of the inning, Freddy hit Derrek Lee. Everyone knows Maddux hardly throws hard enough to bruise a grape, so hitting Iguchi wasn't really a threat, but Garcia wasn't messing around. Lee seemed to take it in good humor, though, no staring, or pointing fingers. Just part of the game. I liked that; it had the feel of a game forty years ago, where players knew retaliation was part of the game and they didn't showboat after being nailed.

Lee's generosity didn't help him in the field, though. In the third, Crede singled off his chest, and after Garcia bunted Crede to second, Crede scored on Scotty's shot that caromed off Hairston's glove at second base. That 1-0 lead stood until the fifth, when Crede launched one over the left field wall. Scotty, Iguchi, Konerko and A.J. all singled, and just like that, it was 4-

0, and the way Freddy was pitching, it looked like it was all over. And it was, with mop-up by Vizcaino, Marte, and Politte, plus a rocket Dye hit over the left-field wall that took a nanosecond to leave the field. We won, 5-1.

Not much tension to the game, just another relaxing afternoon beating the Cubs like a drum. Ho-hum.

May 21, 2005
BEN:

And so the joyride continues. I logged onto the computer Saturday night, and lo and behold, the wonderful, wonderful White Sox had beaten Carlos Zambrano and the pitiful Cubs, 5-3. This victory felt so good I went back and watched the entire game on tape.

Jose Contreras pitched brilliantly, going seven but throwing only 78 pitches. Contreras had his good fastball working today. He has so many tools, and it's good to see him finally beginning to put things together this season.

As good as Contreras was, though, Zambrano was better through 5 2/3 innings – he had a no-hitter going. He can bring the heat up above 95 mph on a consistent basis. He also has great off-speed stuff, including a curve that really breaks, and he can pull the string almost at will.

The beanball wars continued in the fourth inning. Zambrano nailed Aaron Rowand, bizarrely batting in the third slot, in the back on a 2-2 pitch. Nobody hits a batter on a 2-2 pitch, so this was obviously a ball that got away from Zambrano. After Konerko grounded out to shortstop, A.J. "Hambino" Pierzynski strode to the plate. On the first pitch, Zambrano nicked Hambino on the elbow with a fastball. Or did he? Hambino immediately took off for first base and stared down

Zambrano as he strode down the line. The umpire issued warnings to both dugouts. Replays were inconclusive. Would I put it past Hambino to take a phantom beanball for the team? Not on your life. It sure hurts less than taking a real Zambrano fastball on the elbow.

The Cubs went ahead in the bottom of the inning on a Neifi Perez single, a stolen base, and a single by beer-bellied Jeremy Burnitz. In the eighth, the Sox made their big comeback – after the exit of Zambrano, of course. The reliever, Mike Wurtz, was somewhat worse than Carlos. As usual, Scotty P. got things started with one out by beating out a grounder to second for his league-leading fifteenth infield hit of the season. He promptly stole second base – everyone knew it was coming, including the announcers, who spent the entire time after Scotty's single talking up the coming theft (26 on the year, sports fans). Willie Harris proceeded to ground to short, leaving Scotty at second. Aaron Rowand hit one into the hole behind shortstop, but Neifi Perez kept it on the infield.

And up came Big Paul Konerko. Wurtz fed Konerko a steady diet of breaking balls, seven in a row. On the seventh pitch, Konerko came through with a blooper into center field, which bounced off the glove of a diving Corey Patterson. A religious man can observe God in anything. On that play, God was very clearly present, turning Corey Patterson's mitt to stone.

Out came Mike Wurtz. In came Will Ohman. And oh, man, did he stink. Hambino slapped one into right field, proving that his Olivier-like abilities are not his only positive attribute. Then switch-hitting Carl Everett, batting righty, hit a double to right-center, scoring both Konerko and Hambino. 4-1. It was largely cake from there, as Cliff Politte and Damaso Marte paved the way for Dustin Hermanson and his platinum 0.00 ERA. Game over.

And there was Friday, and there was Saturday: two wins. And God saw that it was good.

It was great to watch a game where the crowd was so up all the time. At one point late in the game, the Sox fans and Cubs fans started rival chants, and the announcers described the atmosphere as playoff or World Series-like. Attendance for the day was well over 38,000.

The way the Sox are playing, they should be getting big crowds every night. There's no excuse for sitting home while your team starts the season 19 games over .500. The Sox as of May 15 were 26th in the league in attendance, averaging 26,643 per night. Yes, the Cubs get better press (they should – they're owned by the *Chicago Tribune*). Yes, they have a cuter, cuddlier image. Yes, their fans are more upscale and their ballpark is more historic. But their team is *terrible*. There's no way a team with an 18-22 record should outdraw one with a 31-12 record.

Sox fans have a reputation for being unruly, a reputation stemming largely from two shirtless, tattooed thugs using Kansas City first base coach Tom Gamboa as a punching bag a couple years ago. Cubs fans have a reputation for being knowledgeable and good-natured. I'm not a big one for generalities about fans – sitting in the bleachers at a park is very different than sitting behind third base.

For example, Red Sox fans are generally regarded as passionate, knowledgeable, into the game (if a bit looney). But when my family went to Fenway last year to see a game against the Angels, we sat in the bleachers. I've never seen a worse group of fans. A 45-year-old woman who thought she was 19 got dead drunk and started dancing seductively in the sixth inning. The crowd stood up and watched her dance, many of them with their backs to the field. This went on for half an hour. Finally, as the police hauled her away, the bleacher crowd (remember, these fans are supposed to be there for the *baseball*) began booing.

Conversely, I went with my cousin to another BoSox game late in the season. We sat behind first base. Great conversation, wonderful people, all very much into the game. It seems that the cheaper the seats, the higher the alcohol consumption. The higher the alcohol consumption, the more jack-assery. Fenway is a good argument for instituting a beer limit at ballparks.

Everything in moderation, as my mom always says. Beer, too.

Which reminds me of a particular Little League story from about ten years ago.

I played in a Jewish Little League at Fairfax High School in Los Angeles; my dad coached the team, aptly named the "White Sox." My cousin Joel (12, and huge) was on the team, and his older brother Jon (14) was my dad's assistant. That year we had a great team. I played second and hit second, Joel batted cleanup and played first, and our catcher, Joey, was the greatest hitter in league history. You could not strike Joey out. Ever. Our usual pitcher was a guy named Yitzi, who was solid if unspectacular; later in the season, we unleashed our Secret Weapon (but that's another story).

For years, one team had dominated the league: the Dodgers. Their coach boasted constantly about how he had once pitched at USC. His kid thought he was the second coming of Sandy Koufax, and acted that way. The two years before that season, I had played on the Dodgers – one of my greatest pleasures was proving to the coach's son that his curveball was indeed hittable. He had been bragging about his incredible curve, so I told him I could take him deep. He threw it; I smoked it. A wonderful moment. Ain't nothing that feels better than hitting a baseball right on the sweet spot, especially after the pitcher has just mouthed off.

Anyway, the Dodgers weren't just good – their coach was a bit nasty. When we played the Dodgers earlier in the season, we beat them on a bomb by Joey. That is, until the coach of the Dodgers convinced the umpire that Joey had missed first base while rounding the bags. In a Little League game, that kind of nonsense is unconscionable. My dad is a stickler for honesty and sportsmanship (his rule was that everybody played in the games, win or lose), so that incident alone gave him incentive to dislike the Dodgers.

The Dodgers' coach also loved to play mind games with former players. He would come over to our bench and chat with members of the team who had played for him; then when we were batting, he'd tell his son (Young Koufax) that we couldn't hit the curve down and away, just to distract us. One of our players (who would later become the Secret Weapon) had played on the Dodgers the year before, and Dad specifically refused to use him when we played against the Dodgers because the coach would get into his head.

So when we met the Dodgers in the semi-final round of the Little League playoffs, my cousins and I were pretty nervous. We honestly didn't think we could beat the Dodgers, just because the coach was such a manipulative jerk. We all wanted to cream them – Dad as much as anyone. So, to loosen us up, Dad said, "Listen up, guys. I'm making you a deal. If we beat these guys,

I'm going to take you out for a beer." Naturally, my cousins and I laughed. Dad is a virtual teetotaler.

It was a brutally hot day, a typical summer Los Angeles day. Smoggy, 90 degrees. There was no water on the bench. And none of us had eaten breakfast that morning. By the end of the game, everyone was dehydrated. It was a tense contest, but the Sox emerged victorious, 8-5, led by Joey, who clouted a couple of home runs. Triumphant, we headed back to the car, a beat-up two-door red Toyota Corolla, sans air conditioning.

On the way home, Dad pulled into the parking lot of a Sav-On drugstore. "Let's go, guys," he told us, "we're going to go get something to drink." We followed him inside. Dad headed directly for the alcoholic beverages section.

"Is Uncle David serious?" Jon asked Joel.

"Is your dad *serious*?" Joel asked me.

"Um, I think so, guys," I said.

We stopped in front of the beer section. "All right, Jon," Dad said. "You like any particular brand?"

Jon, who was a history nut, thought for a moment. "Well, I don't know anything about beer, but how about Sam Adams?"

"Excellent choice," Dad said. We checked out of the store and headed for home.

On the way, we detoured onto a lonely sidestreet off of the 101 Hollywood Freeway.

"All right, guys. Here's one for you" – Dad handed a beer to Jon. "One for you" – one for Joel. "And here's one for you, Ben."

Dad, naturally, didn't drink. Jon took one sip, and didn't like it. I took a couple of sips, and didn't like it. Joel, however, was thirsty. He downed the entire bottle.

"Okay, guys," said Dad. "Now keep those bottles down. Obviously, I haven't been drinking, but if they find open bottles and minors in the car, we could have a bit of a problem." We all nodded our assurances.

There was only one problem. Joel, who had gone hours without food or drink, had downed a full Sam Adams on an empty stomach. He was quite buzzed. As we pulled back onto the freeway, he happily thrust his fist out the window, clutching the empty bottle. "Hey, look at me!" he gleefully slurred.

"Joel, get the bottle down!" Jon and I yelled, tackling him.

Thankfully, we reached home without further incident. But the moral of the story was clear: if you're going to celebrate with beer, use limited quantities and do it at home. The same holds true for ballparks. I believe Angel Stadium has both limits on beer consumption as well as family sections where beer will not be sold. That's good policy. Beer can enhance baseball – especially after a big win – but it can also ruin it. Some bleacher bums should take note.

Speaking of Angel Stadium, we're going there to see the Sox play next Thursday. It's a great park, and it should be a tough series. But hey, we're pasting the Cubs, we're playing .720 ball, and we're on pace to win 117 games. Clearly, God is on our side. One more win against the Cubs and I'll begin thinking Ozzie has a direct line Upstairs.

May 22, 2005
DAD:

Two in a row and counting. Boy, would three in a row have been nice. But I knew that this would be like climbing a mountain; we were facing Mark Prior, and he pitches like a diamond cutter, precisely and methodically carving games into beautiful gems.

To make matters even more interesting, we were throwing our own Daniel into the lion's den: Brandon McCarthy, our twenty-one-year-old phenom who stands a narrow six-foot-seven and had monster control in the minors, where he had 406 strikeouts and only 60 walks.

For five innings, the Phenom was ahead. The only mistake he made was on a solo HR that Blanco hammered to left in the second that put the Cubs up 1-0. The wind was blowing out, and it looked as though all a batter had to do was loft the ball and the wind would do the rest. Sure enough, in the fourth, Iguchi, who constantly impresses me by going the other way, lofted a ball to right that barely cleared the wall and landed in the basket. One inning later, Dye, who has really started to come alive, didn't waste time with lofting the ball; he drilled a HR over the center field wall, and suddenly the Phenom was beating the diamond-cutter, 2-1. Could this last?

No, but it wasn't the Phenom's fault. After he hit Lee in the sixth, Ozzie pulled the kid out, and brought in Vizcaino, who proceeded to give up a hit to Patterson and then a three-run-blast by Dubois. Despite a HR in the ninth by Konerko, Prior held on and won the game. He made three mistakes: the solo HRs by Iguchi, Dye, and Konerko, but he was smart enough to do it when no one was on base. That's why he wins the way he does; he doesn't beat himself.

After the game, Ozzie was asked why he pulled McCarthy when he did. He said, "I want this kid to leave the mound with his head up and a chance to win the game." I think Ozzie made the perfect decision. He's thinking of the future, and he wants the kid to go out thinking positively, especially since he was actually beating one of the premier pitchers in baseball.

I had a similar situation when I coached Ben's Little League team his last year. We had a lanky kid called Yoni. He was twelve, and during a practice at the beginning of the year, he was playing catch with our catcher, Joey, and Joey was teasing him about throwing harder. It was a morning practice, and I was a bit drowsy. All of a sudden, Yoni started to cut loose, and I woke up with a bang. This kid could *throw*. He didn't have a wind-up, but he must have been throwing close to 70 mph.

So, naturally, I asked him about pitching. He seemed nervous about it, and said he was worried about hitting someone, which was a rational response, since the kid was throwing BB's. The whole year, I kept him in the back of my mind as we played, trying to find a time when I could cajole him into pitching. Meanwhile we had a good pitcher named Yitzi, and my nephew Joel and Ben helped him to hold the fort. The quarter-final game came, and since I had been practicing warming up Yoni that week and Yitzi had staked us to a 5-2 lead (he had to stop pitching after four innings, because of league rules), I turned to Yoni and told him to take over. He did, and shut the other team out.

But there was a problem. The semi-final game was against a team called the Dodgers, a team we had tied earlier in the season. Their coach would bend the rules any which way to win, including playing mind games with kids on the opponent's team, which I despised. To make matters worse, Yoni had been on that coach's team the previous year, and since the coach's son was fawned over as the next coming of Koufax, Yoni had been ignored. I just knew that if I pitched Yoni against the Dodgers, that coach would mess with his head.

So, in order to protect Yoni's still-new confidence, I didn't pitch him that day. I held my breath, threw Yitzi, Joel, and Ben at the Dodgers, and we won 8-5. We proceeded to celebrate on the way home with a beer (the boys, anyway) and we were close to delirious.

The funniest part of the story was its conclusion. The next week, we were playing the Indians for the championship. They had a record of six wins and one tie (against us) and we had won four games and tied three others. *Everyone* expected them to cream us. I had been an assistant coach for the four previous years, and since we lived in the San Fernando Valley and not Los Angeles city proper (where virtually all the other families lived), people didn't really know who I was. The other coach lived in the city, and so everyone expected his team to beat us decisively.

There was only one flaw in their thinking: we had the Secret Weapon. The Secret Weapon, of course, was Yoni, since hardly anyone had seen him pitch. The Indians' coach, who was roughly my age, had a brother who was his first base coach. I was standing about ten feet behind him as he swaggered into the first-base coaching box as our team took the field.

Then Yoni threw his first warm-up pitch. It hit Joey's glove with a *whap!*

"Oh, *shit*," the brother blurted out.

The game was anti-climactic. Yoni was unhittable. They were so intimidated that I don't think they had the heart to even try to compete. Joey hit two HRs, we won, 13-1, and I don't know if I have ever enjoyed a ballgame more than that day. Ben and I still relish that moment. And, in part, it's because I was savvy enough to protect Yoni's confidence, just as Ozzie did today with McCarthy.

I didn't even get too upset with the Sox's loss today, because now we – the Sox, I mean – may have our own Secret Weapon.

	W	L	PCT	GB	Home	Away	Div	Streak
Chicago WSox	31	12	.721	---	15-6	16-6	18-4	Won 4
Minnesota	24	17	.585	6	13-9	11-8	12-9	Lost 1
Detroit	20	21	.488	10	10-12	10-9	10-11	Won 1
Cleveland	18	23	.439	12	6-11	12-12	9-13	Won 1
Kansas City	12	31	.279	19	6-17	6-14	5-17	Lost 2

May 26, 2005
BEN:

On to Anaheim we went. And there we stalled. As usual. Going into the series, we had a .254 winning percentage against the Angels since 1994. That's ten points *lower* than Ozzie's career batting average. The first game of the series should have told me something was wrong. We had Jon Garland, 8-0, 2.41 ERA, going against Ervin Santana, 22 years old, one start, creamed by the Indians. And we were shut out for the first time this season. That, in and of itself, is amazing – we're over a quarter-way done with the season, and we hadn't been shut out until Tuesday night. We're doing exactly what Ozzie and Kenny Williams had in mind when they constructed the team: we're getting a consistent output of runs, even if that output might be lower on average than last year.

But the story of the first game was Ervin Santana. The White Sox have always had trouble with no-name pitchers anyway. For as long as I can remember, we'd beat Chuck Nagy of the Indians 6-5 and lose to some minor leaguer on the Royals with only one career start. I wonder how much of hitting well is seeing a lot of the pitcher. It's easy enough to call a pitch a hanging change-up when it's smashed into the seats, but it's usually a blurry line between a hanging change-up and pulling the string. And that line might be exposure to the pitcher.

Unless that pitcher is Johan Santana of the Twins, who is lights out. He's the league sensation after winning the Cy Young last year. He's got 95-mph stuff and a change-up that falls off of the table, and he's got the exact same motion for both pitches. You try to sit on the fastball, he throws the change. You try to sit on the change, you aren't catching up to the fastball.

Well, Ervin looked a lot like Johan on Tuesday evening. He struck out seven batters, including Scotty P. to lead off the game on a nasty tight curveball, in on the hands. He popped up Iguchi into the first base dugout, with Darin Erstad making an excellent over-the-railing catch. An inauspicious start.

The rest of the game remained just as bad. We lost 4-0. Jon Garland pitched well, but gave up 11 hits over seven innings and surrendered three runs, two in the second inning. Tad Iguchi had two hits. Those were the highlights. The lowlights were more interesting. In the first inning, we got only one out on a 5-4-3 put-out at first base; Joe Crede picked one up at third, tossed it to Iguchi, and Iguchi tossed to first. Only one problem: Iguchi was standing about ten feet away from second base. In terms of distance, he was closer to Tokyo than to second base. In the second, Crede dropped a throw at third that would have nailed Orlando Cabrera – that kept the inning going. It was just a bad game all around for us, and Luis Vizcaino, who is quickly approaching Damaso Marte status as a useless reliever, gave up a bomb to Bengie Molina in the eighth to add insult to injury.

But the White Sox rebounded nicely in the second game. This one was a nail-biter, going 11 innings, with Mark Buehrle getting the no-decision despite handing over only one run on four hits over nine innings. Bartolo Colon, however, was just as tough. His velocity is back up a bit this year and he was brutal on Wednesday. He was painting the corners at 92-93. Buehrle, meanwhile, painted the corners at 88 all night long, with his changeup clocking in at a mere 73 mph. Wednesday constituted Buehrle's 38th straight start of six innings or more. I don't hold stock in that streak, as I've said before, but he certainly deserves credit for this outing.

Our only run in the first 10 innings came on a second-inning blast by Carl Everett, who is an RBI machine, with 30 RBI despite batting .243 for the season. He's a low-ball hitter, and he crunched a low inside pitch into the right field bleachers. That's his wheelhouse. Pitching him up in the zone is the way to get him out.

Their only run came in the fourth on a double by Garrett Anderson, scoring speedy Chone (pronounced Shaun) Figgens from second base. It was Buehrle all the way until the tenth inning, when Ozzie made a call to the bullpen. A horrible call. A disastrous call. A call for Damaso Marte, who has a deceptively low ERA but a heightened tendency toward mound insanity.

But shockingly, Marte came through. He got through the tenth.

Meanwhile, they had us shut down until the 11th, when we finally broke loose. Joe Crede singled to center. Juan Uribe put down a beautiful bunt to advance Crede to second, which made up for booting a ball in the fourth that allowed the Angels to get on the board. Scotty P. grounded out, advancing Crede to third. Tad made 'em pay with a double into the left-field gap.

After we took the lead, I figured that was it for the wild-eyed lefty. Time to bring in the man with the Golden ERA,

Dustin Hermanson. But Ozzie left Marte in to face Adam Kennedy (lefty), Darin Erstand (lefty), and Chone Figgens (switch hitter, better lefty). And Marte was perfect.

Unlike Ozzie, I'm not much for the strategic managerial moves setting up lefty-lefty or righty-righty matchups. I believe that if a pitcher is hot enough, he can get anyone out (you don't pull Mariano Rivera, whether he's facing a righty or a lefty). And Hermanson is as hot as any pitcher I've ever seen. I'm just glad it worked out for Ozzie.

I had to IM Dad.

BEN: In a night that provided all that was expected and more, Marte provided the dose of insanity so common in baseball.

DAD: I'm telling you, some alien took over his body.

And then, game three. Could the White Sox, unbelievably, take two of the first three from the fallen Angels? Yep. We had a veritable offensive outburst, scoring four runs on two home runs, one from Paul Konerko, which was not unexpected, and one from Chris Widger, which was. Chris Widger? He's a catcher, a non-roster invitee who made the team during spring training. Over his last four games, he's 10-19 at the plate. He's not Mickey Mantle, but he isn't Josh Paul either.

Big Freddy Garcia got the win, his fifth. He went eight strong innings, surrendering only two runs, as we won, 4-2. Garcia is an Angels killer; he's beaten them 11 times over the course of his career. Of course, he faced them more often with Seattle than he does with the White Sox, but that could come in very handy come playoff time.

So, going into game four on Thursday night, things were looking up. The worst we could do was split, and we had Contreras on the hill, who seems to be finding his groove. Not only that, my family and I were all going to the game. I've been back in town for about a week now, and it is definitely nice to be back to California weather. It's also nice to be away from school for awhile. Finals always bring out the worst in everyone, so Cambridge becomes rather oppressive. Not to mention that we've almost reached go-time with *Porn Generation*, so being back home has made for a really nice break.

There's nothing like going to a ballgame. When you come out of the tunnel to the field, everything is bright: the grass, the foul poles, the seats. Angel Stadium is quite beautiful, and the crowd is always a nice one. We had seats behind the left field foul pole. About an inning into the game, Dad got into a conversation with a guy sitting behind us. Turned out the guy was a die-hard Cubs fan.

DAD: What is the greatest year in White Sox history?
FAN: I don't know, what?
DAD: 1969.
FAN: You're an (bleep).

Of course, 1969 was the year the Cubs blew a nine-game lead in August to the New York Mets, finishing an astonishing eight games back.

Everyone brought gloves, as usual. There's nothing in the world like catching a foul ball. At an Angels-Dodgers game a couple of years ago, I was up above the first base line, almost directly behind the plate, in the Stadium Club level, which is about two levels up from the field (we had gotten the tickets

95

from a season-ticket holder). At the beginning of the game, I looked over to Dad and said, "I'm going to get a ball today."

Now, I bring my glove no matter what – I've brought my glove to Fenway even though my seat was literally in the last row in center field, meaning that the batter would have to hit the ball about 550 ft. on the fly. Still, I felt I had a good shot.

Adrian Beltre, then with the Dodgers, was batting in the bottom of the seventh inning. Sure enough, he fouled one back, hard. I was eating a hot dog at the time. As the ball rocketed back, I leaped up and to my right – and backhanded the ball on the fly. Dad, who had ducked his head to avoid being decapitated, still managed to twist his head in time to see the play. An old woman in the row behind us was quite grateful, since she was likely headed to the morgue had I not snagged the ball. The crowd around us gave me a big hand.

And I went ballistic. I'm usually a pretty level-headed guy, but something snapped when I caught the ball. Perhaps it's because every kid dreams of catching a ball at the stadium.

There's something special about it. For some reason, catching a foul ball makes you feel as though you've participated in the game, as though some scout is going to spot you making the catch and ask you if you'll sign a $100,000 bonus to play Class A ball. That didn't happen, but I still have the ball, streaked with black paint from the bat of Adrian Beltre. It's worth about $10, but I know that the ball will always be sitting on my desk.

Anyway, the Sox/Angels game went beautifully for the first few innings. Contreras gave up a run in the first on a Chone Figgens triple and a subsequent groundout (he probably should have scored on the triple, with his speed). But aside from the Figgens triple, Contreras was virtually unhittable – his forkball was magic. In person, the ball drops further faster than on TV.

In the fourth, we finally struck back. Scotty P., who is perhaps the one player in baseball I would pay to see on a daily basis (he isn't juiced and he plays every day), led off with a double down the left field line. Iguchi then hit one down the right field line, inside-outing the swing. 1-1. Aaron Rowand, again strangely batting third, hit a single to center, putting men on first and second. Lackey bounced one off his catcher, and Rowand and Iguchi moved up a base.

Then, in one of the weirdest plays I have ever seen, Lackey flung one to the backstop, and Iguchi took off for home. But the ball bounced *right back to Molina*, who threw high to Lackey as Iguchi slid. The tag looked a bit late, but the ump called Iguchi out. Out in the left field stands, we went crazy. Truth is, the ump probably has a better perspective, being about a foot away from the play. But *we* got it right, I think. Konerko then struck out. From first and third, no outs, to man on first and two outs. Inning virtually over. Blown opportunities like that always bode ill.

In the seventh we got another chance, when Pablo Ozuna singled with two outs. He stole second on a bobbled pitchout by Molina, and Scotty P. blooped one down the line in left to score Ozuna, who was running on the play with two down. Scotty got thrown out at second on a bang-bang play, and he argued the call, which he usually doesn't on the rare times he's called out.

Contreras kept on cruising, forkball dropping off the table. Then, the seventh inning. After Contreras' strong six innings, both Dad and I wanted Ozzie to pull him. Contreras has a bad habit of giving up the big inning. But we understood Ozzie's decision to leave him in, since he was really throwing well. Garrett Anderson led off with a single. Okay, no big deal. Jeff Devanon bunted Anderson over, and Molina grounded out to short. Okay, we thought, he's going to get out of it. So did Konerko, apparently, who nodded encouragingly after the groundout. Why worry? After all, it's just Dallas McPherson, the highly-touted but sub-.220 hitter.

Oy. A fastball, down and in, and McPherson turned on it. He's a big fellow, and he hit the ball about 15,439 feet to center. 3-2 Angels. From there on in, it was lights-out Angels relief. And so triumph turns to tragedy with one swing of the bat. Dallas Freaking McPherson. Dallas Freaking McPherson. Dallas Freaking McPherson. Unbelievable.

Lackey got the win, and he deserved it. He pitched well. I always fear Lackey; he was so brilliant in Game 7 of the 2002 World Series against the Giants. He lived up to his billing here.

At least we came out with a split. It's a bit disturbing that despite our 33-15 record leaving Orange County, we're up only five games on Minnesota. We can't keep this pace up forever, can we? And if we don't, isn't Minnesota going to be right there? I'm already starting to think playoffs, too. There's really only one team I don't want to see come playoff time: Oakland. For some reason, they really have our number. The good news is that following the Anaheim series, Oakland has fallen 9.5 games back. Let's hope they don't climb back in it.

DAD:

Ya spends ya' money, and ya takes ya chances. We spent the money, we took our chances, had a great time, and the Sox won. It was perfect.

Well, no. It actually was less than perfect. Rotten? Disheartening? Catastrophic?

Or, as my eleven-year-old daughter would say, "Sucky?" Sucky.

May 30, 2005
BEN:

One team that is in the thick of the AL West race is Texas. They showed us why in this series. The rap on Texas has always been, "all hat, no cattle," or rather, all hit, no pitching. Their offense is simply spectacular. Their lineup includes Michael Young, Mark Teixeira, Hank Blalock, Alfonso Soriano, and Kevin Mench. That's a lot of power. Their pitching staff, on the other hand, leaves something to be desired.

Well, all hit was enough to beat us senseless for two games. Thank goodness the middle game was rained out. In the first game, our young sensation, Brendan McCarthy, came undone, giving up four home runs and 6 earned runs in five innings. He wasn't painting the corners; he was catching too much of the plate. Our offense, meanwhile, was stifled by Chris Young, a young no-name who has been on a hot streak lately. Yuck.

After game two was rained out, Jon Garland took the mound looking to save us a split in Texas. No such luck. He got the treatment worse than McCarthy did. After pitching well through five innings, the wheels fell of the truck in the sixth. It was really Kevin Mench who broke things open with a three-run shot putting the Rangers ahead 5-3. It just barely stayed fair, despite my prayers. Two runs later, out came Garland. I don't understand Ozzie's logic here. You can't leave in your starter to give up seven runs in a tight ballgame, especially when you need the game to come away with a series split. Final score: 12-4, Rangers. Now the lead's only 3.5 games, and we're looking at a tough series with the Angels. Not good.

The only good news in game two was a gargantuan blast by A.J. Pierzynski in the fourth inning, reaching the upper deck in right field. That's eight on the season for him, meaning that he's on pace to hit 26 HRs, which would blow away his current career high of 11 in 2003 and 2004. One other note: Shingo Takatsu made his grand reappearance in game two. He gave up four runs in an inning. When is enough finally enough for the man with the spaghetti arm?

	W	L	PCT	GB	Home	Away	Div	Streak
Chicago WSox	33	17	.660	---	15-6	18-11	18-4	Lost 3
Minnesota	29	20	.592	3 1/2	14-9	15-11	14-11	Lost 1
Cleveland	24	25	.490	8 1/2	11-13	13-12	11-15	Won 3
Detroit	23	25	.479	9	10-13	13-12	10-11	Won 3
Kansas City	13	37	.260	20	7-17	6-20	5-17	Lost 6

June 5, 2005
DAD:

The spaghetti arm has been missing in action lately, and not surprisingly, it's been a productive six games at home. We've reverted to our old ways, the way we started the season – winning the first two games of each series and dropping the finale. And everything, including the two losses, can be construed as a positive sign. I wonder if it's because I took out my lucky baseball . . .

Spring 1965

"Do you have the *Daily News*, Dad? Did you get it?" My father had just opened the front door, and I leaped off the couch and rushed to the door.

"Got it, Butch," he grinned, and waved it at me as he pulled it out from his briefcase.

"Did you look, Dad?" I queried, as I found the sports section. I was one of thousands of boys across the Chicago Metropolitan area who scanned the *Chicago Daily News* that day, anxiously checking the results of the annual competition they held to determine the next White Sox batboy. Every year boys sent in an essay of 25 words or less asserting why they should be selected as the White Sox batboy. Not just for a game, but for the *season*. The runners up got various prizes, but no boy would have been satisfied with anything less than the top prize.

I scanned the list in ascending order of importance, from the bottom toward the top, where the winner was listed. To simply start with the winner would have been too hasty after waiting for weeks for the response. The suspense was delicious, and terrible, too. But in the bottom paragraph, my name wasn't listed, and I breathed easier. The next, more select group omitted my name too, and although that meant I still had a chance at the top prize, a sense of unease started to grow inside me: perhaps I hadn't won anything at all?

I didn't know what to wish for.

The next group was a small group of honorable mentions. There it was; my name was listed as one of those who had won a ball signed by the entire team. I was happy to win something, but cruelly disappointed that I hadn't won the big prize.

My dad saw the look of disappointment, and said kindly, "I did see it, Butch. I saw it on the way home."

"How could you look before me?" I asked. "Why didn't you tell me that you looked first?"

"I didn't have a chance, Butch. You were moving pretty fast there."

"I don't want the ball!"

"I think you should take it, Butch. It's something special. And you came pretty darn close to being the batboy. You might want to keep the newspaper for posterity."

"I hate the whole thing."

"Are you sorry that you tried or sorry you didn't win?" he asked.

I hadn't thought about the distinction. "I guess I'm sorry I didn't win," I admitted.

"Good. I'm glad it's that," he said, "because that's human, and normal. If you had been sorry you tried, that would mean you'd never try things because you were afraid of failing. If you can keep trying, even if you don't get what you want, you can still be proud of yourself for making the effort, no matter the result. You know, that's really the story of life. Nobody gets everything they want, but if they can make the effort, there's every reason to be proud of the attempt. And you *should* be proud, Butch."

I thought for a second. "Maybe I'll keep the ball, Dad."

"That's good," he said. "It'll remind you to keep trying no matter what."

I don't take the ball out much, but after the Sox went on their losing streak it seemed like an opportune time, so I did, and lo and behold, good things started to happen:
1. The emergence of Jermaine Dye
2. The continued clutch hitting of Carl Everett
3. The intelligent choices Ozzie has made, including signing a contract extension now, and not waiting until later in the season and distracting from the pennant chase
4. The return of El Duque
5. Cliff Politte becoming Tonto to Hermanson's Lone Ranger
6. We have started to HIT.

Let's start with the Angels series. The first game was a game we needed badly, having lost three in a row and our lead over Minnesota having shrunk from 6 games down to 3 ½. The game featured two subplots to the main story line: Frank Thomas' return and Ozzie's signing.

Yet those subplots paled next to the drama of the game itself. Buehrle worked 8 1/3 innings, giving up three runs and scattering nine hits, and had a 3-2 lead entering the ninth. Then the Angels got two men on base through an error and a single, and Ben's favorite pitcher entered. Marte proceeded to do the job, though, inducing an easy double play ball right to Iguchi. End of game, right?

Wrong. Iguchi uncharacteristically bobbled it on the toss to Uribe, loading the bases. Not the kind of thing that would relax Marte. Sure enough, the next batter, Robb Quinlan, singled in a run, and only the threat of Dye's arm kept the bases loaded. I had trouble seeing what followed, because the steam from Marte's ears was clouding the picture. He walked in a run, and now it was 4-3 Angels, still bases loaded, and the steam was coming out of *my* ears. Marte managed to recover and strike out Steve Finley, who had already homered, doubled and singled, and then Politte entered to face Orlando Cabrera, who is a good clutch hitter. Politte got us out of the inning on an easy fly ball to Dye, and I wondered if our losing streak would continue.

But then Ozzie Ball saved the day. Scot Shields came in for the Angels. He throws lightning, but Harris pinch-hit for Uribe and walked, then stole second. Crede walked, and Scotty P. laid down a beautiful bunt to advance the runners. Everett, who has been in a slump, struck out, leaving the winning runs in scoring position with two out. The unlikely Timo Perez then took a tough 1-1 pitch that was down-and-in, and slapped it into left. Harris scored followed by Crede, who was off with the

103

pitch, and the Sox had pulled out a major comeback against what I happen to think is the toughest team in the league.

Game one: win attributed to intestinal fortitude and Ozzie ball.

Game two was even more dramatic. The Angels took a quick 1-0 lead off of Garcia in the first, but we answered with two in the bottom half, when Scotty singled, Iguchi tripled, and Rowand blooped a single to right. Rowand is getting hotter and hotter. On Iguchi's triple, Scotty had to hold up because the ball went to the top of the right field wall, and it might have been caught. But once it hit the wall, he assumed the role of Mercury, the God of Speed, and flashed around the bases so fast it reminded me of the end of the movie *Superman,* where Superman flies so fast around the earth that he turns back time.

The big story of this game could have been the wind. It swirled so strongly that Figgins lost an Everett fly ball in right, leading to a double and an eventual run. In the fifth, Dye took over for the rest of the day. He dove for a flare to right, snared it just before it hit the ground, then clambered to his feet and lobbed the ball to first to double off the runner, who was so sure the ball would drop that he was halfway to *third* before he realized what Dye had done. True to form, after Crede had extended our lead to 4-2 with a HR to left in the fifth, Marte gave up three hits and the tying run in the eighth, and Tonto had to ride to the rescue. Politte threw one pitch and got a double play, then shut the Angels down in the ninth.

In the ninth, Dye led off and launched a typical Dye line shot over the wall in left to win the game. At the beginning of the season, I was worried about him, because he just wasn't hitting. But Ozzie has consistently defended him, and he was right. Dye is like a silent assassin; he doesn't make a fuss, nothing spectacular, just kills the opponent quietly and professionally. I like him more and more. He's almost gentlemanly the way he plays.

Game two: win attributed to Tonto and the Silent Assassin.

Game three; a 10-7 loss that was as wild an affair as it sounds. We kept clawing back with HRs by Rowand, Everett, and Crede. We were up 2-0, down 4-2, up 5-4, down 8-5, then 8-6 after Crede hit another HR, and then, the ninth.

Finally, Hermanson gave up a run. Two, actually, his first two runs of the *season*. I think I'll forgive him. Still, we had bases loaded and 10-7 after Thomas walked to drive a run in, and Uribe swatted a ball headed for the left field foul pole for a grand slam. I stood up in front of the TV and did my Carlton Fisk 1975 World Series move, waving the ball toward center, but the ball curved just outside the pole. I think you have to be the one who hit the ball for that move to work. Uribe struck out on the next pitch, ending the game.

Game three: moral victory, since our bats came alive and we came within an eyelash of a ridiculous comeback.

Game four featured the Indians coming to town, a team loaded with young talent.

BEN: We haven't seen them since we took four out of six from them at the start of the season. I'm curious to see if we can master them again.

The first game of the series featured the return of the ageless El Duque, and aside from one bad inning, he threw quite well. After the Sox had scored four runs in the bottom of the first on five singles, El Duque held the Indians off until the third, when a Coco Crisp three-run-shot after a run had scored tied it at 4-4. In the fifth, Jake Westbrook gave up two more singles, to Rowand and Konerko, and Carl Everett's sacrifice fly scored Rowand, putting us ahead. Then Westbrook threw a wild pitch, sending Konerko to second, and the Silent Assassin struck again, singling Konerko home. Neal Cotts did yeoman work, shutting the Tribe down for two innings, and then Hermanson finished it, although he gave up a deep fly ball that Scotty P. caught at the wall with a runner on that ended the game.

Th first Indians game: Aside from one bad inning, good news from El Duque, and the tag-team of Everett and Dye strike again.

The second Indians game was a 6-5 win that featured two turning points and the pregame antics of Mark Buehrle, which only endear him to fans and show why his loosey-goosey style makes him a team leader, even at the ripe old age of twenty-six. While the tarp covered the field because of a rain delay, Buehrle did several belly-flops along with Man Soo Lee, the bullpen catcher. The fans were delighted, but Ozzie wasn't thrilled. He said, "I don't want to take fun away from players, but they don't realize how dangerous that is. I don't want any of my players to get hurt. I just told him he was crazy."

Yet Ozzie also knows how valuable Buehrle is on and off the field. He said, "You take a poll and ask players who's the best teammate out there, and Buehrle should be in the top two. He's rooting for everyone. I wish we had more of him, not just here but in baseball." Ben and I have decided that Buehrle should be called Mr. Slip'N'Slide. It not only describes his antics on the field, but also the way he slips and slides around batters with his great control.

In the game, the first turning point came when we were up 3-2 in the fifth. The Tribe had runners at first and second, nobody out, and Crisp at the plate. Jon Garland, who had good stuff and battled hard, went full on the count, then struck Crisp out looking on a 3-2 change that dropped off the table. It was beautiful pitching, and he followed that by getting the very dangerous Travis Hafner to hit a bullet toward the middle. Uribe was playing Hafner to pull, and he stepped on second and fired to first to end the inning.

The second turning point occurred in the fifth. Konerko went to two strikes, then fouled off at least six consecutive pitches. Davis, who had thrown 100 pitches by then, finally grooved one, and Konerko hit a shot over the left-field wall.

Konerko consistently impresses the heck out of me. He's patient, like Dye, and I haven't seen him lose his temper once, even though his average has been in the basement. He has still managed to lead the league in HRs, and his ability to get the clutch hit is something I've missed for a long time. He's the kind of guy I'd hope was in the foxhole with me if the going got tough, the kind of guy who reminds you of the captain who'd go down with the ship. I think that's what I'll call him: Captain Konerko (or Captain, for short.)

The second Indians game: Garland looks like a pro, holding a good team down, and the Captain steers the ship past the iceberg.

The last game of the series, which they played today, was reminiscent of the loss in the third game to the Angels. Buehrle did his typical scatter-nine-hits-give-up-three-runs game, and we kept battling back; down 3-1, tied 3-3, down 4-3, tied 4-4, then finally losing in the tenth 6-4. Iguchi launched a moon shot to left in the seventh to get us to 3-3, and after the Tribe took the lead in the tenth, Thomas led off the bottom half and smoked one that couldn't have cleared the left-field wall by more than six feet to tie it. It was a *bullet*.

But in the twelfth, Hermanson, who was pitching in his fourth straight game, walked the first two batters, then fired the sacrifice bunt of Victor Martinez past Crede to let one run score. An ensuing sac fly let an additional run score. We went down meekly after that, and Hermanson got his first loss. First he gave up those earned runs the other day, and now a loss? What in the world is going on?

I'm kidding, of course. Hermanson has been a rock all season, and I think he's just finally gotten a bit tired. I've also been thinking Garland may be tired, too. He won yesterday, but he didn't have his best stuff, and I wonder if he's just a bit pooped. But hey, 4-2 on the homestand (and it could easily have been 6-0) against the Angels and Indians? I'll take it.

	W	L	PCT	GB	Home	Away	Div	Streak
Chicago WSox	37	19	.661	---	19-8	18-11	20-5	Lost 1
Minnesota	33	22	.600	3 1/2	18-11	15-11	16-12	Won 1
Detroit	26	28	.481	10	13-16	13-12	10-11	Lost 2
Cleveland	26	29	.473	10 1/2	11-13	15-16	13-19	Won 1
Kansas City	17	39	.304	20	11-19	6-20	5-17	Lost 2

June 12, 2005
BEN:

The swagger … is … *back!* Yeah, baby! Forgive me for going Dick Vitale, but we're on a roll. On our swing around the NL West, we steamrolled the Rockies and the Padres, winning 5 of 6. Yeah, they're the Rockies and the Padres, but so what? Good teams beat bad teams. And we beat both teams to a bloody pulp.

I love Colorado when we're hitting. Playing in Colorado is like hitting on the moon. There's a reason that Todd Helton is a good player on the road but a statistical monster at home. There's a reason the same held true for Andres Galarraga and Vinnie Castilla when they played here. If Paulie hit here on a regular basis, he'd be Barry Bonds (yes, Bonds on steroids, not the 175-lb. Pirates guy).

The first game showcased Freddy Garcia, who was tremendous. He struck out 10 batters over eight innings, surrendering only three earned runs on a bomb by Helton in the first. He then proceeded to retire 22 Rockies in a row before being pulled in the ninth in favor of Shingo Takatsu, making one of his several magical reappearances this year. Thankfully, he pitched better this time than he did against Texas, and got out of the inning with no damage done.

We scored our runs in bunches. After Aaron Rowand singled in the first, Konerko powered a hanging curveball out of the yard, giving us a 2-0 lead. Helton made it 3-2 Rockies, but we came back with one in the second, three in the fifth, two in the sixth, and one in the seventh. 9-3. The heart of the order did most of the damage. Our 4-5-6-7 hitters went a combined 11-17 in the game. Juan Uribe uncharacteristically batted in the six-hole. I'm sure Ozzie put him in an RBI slot because Uribe started off with the Rockies. In any case, after watching the Sox battle to win so many this season, it's nice to watch a laugher once in a while.

The second game was much more typical White Sox. Despite the fact that we were playing in Colorado, we pulled this one out 2-1. A pitchers' duel in Denver? Sort of like a home run derby in Kansas City. But these Sox are anything but predictable. Credit for this win went to Jose Contreras, who went six innings, giving up only one run. Contreras is an odd fish – his stuff is always spectacular, and his stats are great as well, but he seems mentally unprepared sometimes. When he's ahead in the count, Contreras holds batters to a miniscule .149 batting average; when he's behind, he holds them to .204. But he has that penchant for giving up the big inning. Perhaps that's why Ozzie pulled him after six. He did throw 103 pitches, but Ozzie has to know that no matter how many pitches the big guy has thrown, nursing Contreras through six is about as good as it's going to get.

We got our runs in the fourth. We were being no-hit to that point. But Paulie drove one into the gap, his 1,000 hit of his career. Congrats, PK. More importantly, he scored our first run when Jermaine Dye sliced one down the right field line. He, too, ended up on second, and he scored when Hambino singled him home. That was enough for our staff. After Contreras gave up a run in the fourth; it should have been two, but the ump made a bad call, saying that a home run was actually a double when it rather clearly bounced above the yellow HR line.

DAD: Give that ump a free deep-dish pizza.

Contreras exited in the sixth. In came Cotts, our non-psychotic lefty, and pitched two scoreless innings. Then, on to Hermanson and his now flawed 1.04 ERA, who picked up the save.

The sweep game against Colorado was another nail-biter.
Not. If the first game was a laugher, this one was a leave-em-in-the-aisles-gasping-for-breath ballgame.

Actually, that's not entirely true. For the first four innings, we were actually *down*, 4-3. But we picked up two in the fifth, and then absolutely opened the floodgates in the eighth and ninth innings, when we scored six and four runs respectively. Our offense's final line: 15 runs, 22 hits. Ouch. That should inflate some ERAs.

Leading 8-4 in the eighth, one of the funniest plays I've ever seen occurred. Cliff Politte, our *reliever*, faked a bunt, drawing in the first and third basemen, and proceeded to draw back the bat and slap the ball through the hole on the right side of the infield, scoring Chris Widger. The throw to third smacked the second-base umpire, who went tumbling down as Politte advanced to second. 9-4, men on second and third, no outs. Finally, Tad Iguchi flied out to right, scoring Widger. 10-4, one out. The Rockies' pain would soon end, right? Wrong. Aaron Rowand singled home Cliff Politte, making the score 11-4.

We didn't stop there; the final score was 15-5. Crede and Thomas both went deep. I could certainly turn off the computer happy after watching that one.

Then we went to San Diego, and I was prepared for the California fans and their antics, aka beach balls. California has brought America plenty of good ideas, but the beach ball at the baseball game isn't one of them. In LA, it isn't uncommon to see 10 or 11 beach balls bouncing around the bleachers at any time during the game. (Don't even get me started on The Wave!)

One time at Comiskey Park, some bleacher bum began batting around a beach ball. My cousin Jason, a Chicago boy born and bred, grabbed the ball when it came his way. He then proceeded to whip out a pen and stab the ball to death, yelling "Take this back to LA!" I was in complete agreement. There's nothing more embarrassing as a fan than helplessly watching as a

111

beach ball bounces out onto the field after some moron hits it too hard. It delays the game, and can even affect the outcome, depending on when it enters the field of play. It's just another way for fake fans to pretend they're actual fans.

San Diego was a bit tougher than the Rockies had been. They should be: their record as of today is 36-27. We still took two of three, and we should have swept. In the first game, Jon Garland came through with a sterling performance to win his league-leading tenth game of the season – he went seven innings and gave up only six hits and one run. His good sinker was working, and he racked up four strikeouts. His only mistake came in the seventh to Brian Giles, who took Garland deep to right on a hanging breaking ball. In the same inning, Garland got some help from Rowand, who dove to snag a sinking liner to center field, saving Garland two runs.

Rowand sure has a glove. If he uses it, that is – in the ninth, Rowand booted a similar sinking liner off of his spikes, allowing Ryan Klesko to take an extra base. I love Rowand's athleticism in center, but sometimes he's asleep out there. He should have simply pulled up and let Klesko have his single. Dustin Hermanson was able to get the save and overcome the error by Rowand, despite giving up a run.

DAD: Do you think Ozzie is overusing Hermanson? His ERA is 1.00, but he's giving up runs here and there.

We scored two in the top of the second on singles by Crede and Garland(!), and we tacked on another in the seventh on a bomb by Hambino. What is always surprising about Hambino's HR swing is the fact that he doesn't have a long follow-through. Once he hits the ball, he just stops dead in the

112

middle of the swing. I guess when you hit the ball that hard, a long follow-through is just posing for the papers.

Game two was a heartbreaker. We were going for five in a row at this point, and Mark Buehrle clearly wanted the win here, especially considering he hasn't had a win since May 18. He went seven and two-thirds, shutting out the Padres, which was imperative, since some guy named Tim Stauffer was busy holding us to one run over seven innings. Buehrle has a habit of allowing lots of hits and then getting out of jams, a habit that bugs Dad to no end. But it worked out for him in this one, since the Padres were unable to translate seven hits off of him into a single run.

We got our run in the first when Scotty P, who must have a rocket booster in his cleats, beat out a slow roller to shortstop. Tad knocked one into the left field gap, and Podsednik motored around third to score standing up. He is absolutely beautiful to watch – it's as though he can kick it into another gear when he needs to, and he glides when he runs.

DAD: I'm calling Scotty Superman from now on.

BEN: I like your other reference better – Mercury, with wings on his feet. It makes better sense, especially because Mercury is the god of thieves, and who steals better than Scotty?

We blew an important opportunity in the eighth, when we got men on first and third with no outs. Three strikeouts later, the score was still 1-0. When that sort of misfortunate occurs, the game is *not* going to end well. It should have, when Konerko scored on a double into the left-field corner by Hambino in the ninth, but the ump called him out; Ramon Hernandez tagged

113

Paulie high, and Paulie got his left foot to the plate. More bad omens.

Old baseball superstitions never fail. Dustin Hermanson, who has been working harder than Donald Trump's accountant during tax season, finally collapsed. He hung a breaking ball to Ramon Hernandez (the scandalous mis-tagging Padres catcher), and Hernandez crushed it. Tie ballgame. But it wasn't over yet. With the bases loaded, Darren Jackson (former Red Sox) stepped to the plate. The infield was playing in, for some strange reason – to prevent a squeeze, perhaps? If they wanted a double play, they should have been playing deep. Jackson made them pay by hitting a hard ground ball through the left side. Game over. Good night. Drive home safely. Time to throw up. Blech.

Buehrle must have been feeling awful. Here he goes 7 2/3 shutout innings, leaves with a 1-0 lead, and Hermanson blows it. But Buehrle is a class act. "Everyone is allowed to have a bad day and today was (Hermanson's) day," he said after the game. "He's done the job for us all year, with it being two months or 2 1/2 months in, and it's his first blown save. It's a tough loss, but with Freddy out there tomorrow, I like our chances to win the series."

The third game was yet another down-to-the-wire, clench-your-teeth, bite-your-nails-down-to-the-bone type. Carl Everett started us off with a dinger into the right field seats, his eighth of the season. I like how Everett has become part of the team here, after all of the bad talk about him in Texas and Boston. Perhaps it's because Kenny Williams re-acquired him after trading him a season ago. That shows good faith.

Things began poorly for Freddy Garcia, who was so great last time out in Colorado. Robert Fick opened with a single, and Klesko followed with another. On a 1-1 count, Phil Nevin, who looks as though he's about 7'9", crushed one into the left field stands. No doubt about it. 3-1 Padres.

In the top of the fourth, Joe Crede knocked a HR to left. He *just* got enough of it to send it over the wall. Perhaps it's because he's now growing his hair longer – the Samson effect? In the fifth, Mercury led off with a double into the gap, and he scored on a single to right-field by Everett. There is no way Scotty should have been able to score on that hit; the right fielder picked it up in short right, and pegged it to the plate. But Mercury turned it on and slid in under Hernandez's tag. Billy Beane, what was that you were saying about speedsters?

By the ninth it was 5-5. We had an opportunity after we loaded the bases with two outs. Then they brought in their guy, Trevor Hoffman. In recent years, Hoffman's velocity has been down, which makes him more hittable, but he's still dangerous. His out pitch is the change, and he fooled Dye on one to protect the tie.

Cliff Politte came on in the ninth and shut the door. Finally, in the tenth, we began to put it all together. Tad singled up the middle, and Scotty followed with a single to right. Up came Aaron Rowand, whose 13-game hitting streak ended the day before. He revenged himself by taking a low outside fastball and yanking it to left, into the warehouse beyond the wall. 8-5 Sox. Politte nailed it down for the victory.

A good road trip. Yea, verily, an excellent road trip. Now, if only that kind of good luck can rub off on me – *Porn Generation* comes out this Thursday, beginning with an appearance on Fox News. And it's back home for the Sox, who take on Arizona next. If we keep playing like this, and if Minnesota would lose once in a while, who knows? Maybe we

115

could even go into the All-Star break with a real lead. Goodness knows we need one, after last year's second-half collapse.

	W	L	PCT	GB	Home	Away	Div	Streak
Chicago WSox	42	20	.677	---	19-8	23-12	20-5	Won 1
Minnesota	36	25	.590	5 1/2	18-11	18-14	16-12	Lost 1
Cleveland	31	30	.508	10 1/2	11-13	20-17	13-19	Won 3
Detroit	28	32	.467	13	13-16	15-16	10-11	Lost 1
Kansas City	21	41	.339	21	11-19	10-22	5-17	Won 2

June 15, 2005
DAD:

Today is a big game. We've gotten absolutely hammered by Arizona in the first two games of this series, 8-1 and 10-4, which marks the first time all year we've lost a series at home. Contreras got mauled in the first game, giving up four HRs, with three coming in the second, but he did a truly noble thing; he stayed in the game, throwing 118 pitches, because Ozzie decided that the bullpen needed the rest. Vizcaino and Takatsu got mop-up time, but by that time it was 8-1 and the game was over.

The only worrisome note was a play by Dye that underlined the man's professionalism. In the eighth, Chris Snyder lofted a ball to deep right. Down 8-1, Dye could have taken the easy way out, playing the ball off the fence, but instead, he ran into the fence to catch it, injuring his wrist, which didn't look good. It reminded me of a game Ben and I saw on TV many years ago, when Lance Johnson played center field for the Sox. There was a ball hit over his head when the Sox were losing lopsidedly, and he loafed after it, which infuriated me no end. Not Dye. In a game that was essentially over, he never let up.

Then, in the second game, El Duque got mauled, as well. He gave up six runs in 4 2/3 innings, taking his first loss since April 14. We actually led 2-0, after three innings, but then the roof fell in, as Glaus homered and Clayton doubled two runs home. One inning later Glaus had an RBI single followed by Shawn Green's HR. Javier Vasquez shut us down after that, but there was some good news; our initial two-run lead was supplied by Dye, who not only muscled a first-pitch fastball for a HR going the other way, but then did a high-ten with Konerko when he reached the plate. I guess his wrist is all right, after all.

With our lead over Minnesota cut to four games, someone asked the Captain what he thought. Konerko responded, "This is going to go down to the end. I expect that, and I hope this team does. It would be nice to walk away with the division, be up by 10 games two months from now, but realistically it's not going to happen." He *is* a realist.

The losses slowed the express train that the Sox have been riding long enough for me to think about the release of Ben's book. His first book, *Brainwashed*, was a huge success, and launched him into the public eye beyond what his national column had already done. He got reviewed by the *Wall Street Journal* (which loved it), an AP column, and tons of tremendous press for comprehensively revealing the leftist bias in the University system across the country.

The second book is tougher. And in some ways, more important.

There's one image that both Ben and I want to erase: the idea that Judaism is socially liberal. Since my parents' generation was largely in love with FDR, most of them swore by the Democratic Party, which has become more and more tolerant of what was once taboo. Many non-religious Jews have remained within that mindset. But among religious Jews, the very strong tendency is to be quite conservative, since Jewish law is very strict about issues such as personal modesty. Thus Ben and I feel it is imperative for religious Jews like us to stand up and be counted among those who would preserve the innocence of future generations.

That's why I love the innocence of baseball, and become incensed when anything endangers it. Three days ago, Major League Baseball told Rafael Palmeiro he was going to be suspended for steroid use and he asked the players' association to file a grievance. I'm sure I'm not the only one who's looking forward to whatever excuse he throws out. I can only imagine what my father would have said. . . .

Summer 1966

"Will you be able to see any of the practice, Dad?" I asked, as our station wagon pulled up to the baseball field where my Little League was practicing.

He pulled the car to a stop. "Maybe, Butch. It depends on how long our practice lasts." He was the coach of the minor league team, while I had moved up to the major league level. "I'll be on the other field, over there," he said, pointing to a field a few hundred yards away.

"Okay." I jumped out of the car, and ran around to the back of the car to help him unload the bag of bats and balls. "Do you want me to carry the bag for you?"

"Sure," he grinned. I grabbed the bag, threw it over my shoulder, and started to walk toward the minor-league field – when the coach of the major league team, who was already on the major-league field with some of the players, saw us and yelled over to us.

"Hey, Shapiro, get over here!"

"Sorry, Dad," I said

"No problem, Butch."

I unloaded the bag, handed it to my father, and ran as best I could toward the coach. Unfortunately, I was going through my eleven-year-old chubby stage, and I didn't move too fast. By the time I reached him, I was out of breath.

The coach was a pretty big guy. "You're a catcher, right?"

"Uh-huh," I nodded.

"You'll have to lose some of that blubber if you want to get on base, Fatso," he said. The other players snickered, which he saw. My face got hot, and I could feel tears start to form behind my eyes, but I wasn't going to give him *that* satisfaction. He turned back to me. "Well, put the equipment on," he ordered, handing me the chest protector. I started to put the loop over my head when he continued, ". . . if it'll reach that far around you." I quickly turned away and knelt to put the face mask over my face.

That whole practice, the players called me Fatso. I didn't tell my father what had happened, and the next practice it continued. But at the third practice, my father finished his practice early, and unbeknownst to the major league team, wandered over to see how the practice was going. When he heard what they called me, he went ballistic.

He accosted the coach. "What the hell is going on here?"

"Hey, Nate, it'll make him tougher. Stay out of it. It's good for him."

"And why is that?" my father demanded angrily.

The other players had stopped throwing the ball, and stood frozen as the two men started to get heated.

"He's a fat kid, Nate, and if he sees the other kids make fun of him, he might decide he doesn't want to be that way."

"You stop that crap right now," my father said coldly. "Who ever told you that you could work with kids?"

"We went to the championship last year. I think I know how to work with kids. You're the one who doesn't have a clue. Everyone laughed at you at the league meeting when you said that the fielders shouldn't yell 'Hey, Batter!' when the other team is hitting. Do you want them to all be sissies?" he snapped.

"No, just gentlemen," my father snapped back. He got in the coach's face. "You call my son by his name and you make *damn* sure everyone else does, too." He turned toward the players, who had heard every word. "Is that clear?"

They were cowed, and nodded. I fully expected that the next practice I would take some heat, but the harassment stopped, and baseball became fun again. But the lesson was clear: if innocence is to be protected, someone has to step up to the plate.

My Dad did.

June 15, 2005
DAD:

If this third game against Arizona has any cosmic connection to the release of Ben's book, he'll sell more copies than *The Da Vinci Code*. It was, simply put, the first time I have forgotten about my own physical pain. It was unbelievable.

In the first, Rowand made a catch that triggered my new nickname for him. Luis Gonzales hit a deep shot toward center, and Rowand had to turn around and *fly*, just as Mays had done in '54, and he flagged the ball over his head just before he hit the wall. He is absolutely reckless with wild-eyed abandon, to use the cliché, in the way he covers ground. As a result, I've taken to calling him Evel Knievel, after the famous daredevil. The nickname fits especially well since Rowand was almost killed on his dirt-bike in November 2002.

In the second, Dye launched a missile over the left-field fence, and we enjoyed a 1-0 lead. But in the third, Tracy answered with a solo shot, and in the fifth, Stinnett homered, Tony Clark hit one deep to right, and after the dust had cleared, we were down 6-1, and looking not only to lose our first series at home, but being swept. Aaarrrrrrgh. Garland was getting hammered.

We picked up a run in the fifth when Uribe's hard shot handcuffed Glaus at third after Crede had doubled, and we were down 6-2.

Then came the sixth inning.

I remember my favorite Sox game as a kid. I was seven years old. September 24, 1963. They were playing the Baltimore Orioles, and Ray Herbert was pitching. It was a Tuesday, and I had my ear pressed to the radio in our huge Magnovox stereo unit, hoping to listen to as much of the game as I could before my mom sent me to bed, since it was a school night. After the bottom of the fourth, it was my bedtime, and I begged my mom to let me listen to one more Sox at-bat. I finally cajoled her into letting me listen just as the commercials between innings ended.

"One more Sox time at bat," she warned me. "No more, okay?"

"Okay, Mom."

They scored eight runs.

And there weren't any homers, either. The inning must have taken thirty minutes, at least, and my mother kept poking her head out from the kitchen to ask me incredulously if the inning was *still* going on. I have cherished that inning ever since, and never thought I'd enjoy an inning more.

Wrong I was.

In the sixth today, down 6-2, facing a sweep, Thomas started the barrage with another bullet over the left field wall. 6-3. The Captain walked, Rowand singled, and after Dye singled Konerko home, it was 6-4, and Dye was at first and Rowand at second. Hambino, who somehow seems to be in the middle of everything, hit a double play ball to Clayton at short. Inexplicably, Clayton threw it right past the second baseman, and Rowand flew around to score, which left Dye at third and A.J at second. Now we were down 6-5. Crede then hit a slow grounder that crept past Glaus toward the hole, where Clayton, who saw Dye running home, figured he couldn't get him, and then decided to throw to first. But Crede can run, and so Clayton wound up holding the ball while A.J. stayed at second. It was tied, 6-6 now, with men on first and second.

Then suddenly Juan Uribe reached out for an outside pitch and lofted it just over the left-field fence, we were ahead 9-6, and I was delirious. Seven runs! This was as good as 1963.

But it got better.

After Ortiz was relieved by Vargas, Scotty grounded out to the pitcher, but Iguchi tripled to left-center, Thomas walked, and Konerko crushed one to left; and just like that, it was 12-6, and the 1963 inning was knocked off the throne. Ten runs!

Arizona never recovered. Cotts and Politte shut them down the last three innings, and that was the way it ended, 12-6.

My favorite inning ever.

June 19, 2005
DAD:

When we play the Dodgers, I can't help but flash back to 1959, and the only chance my father ever had to see the Sox win the World Series. If there were no other reason to want to beat them badly, that would be enough, especially since they deserted Brooklyn when the fan base dwindled, while the Sox never left Chicago when things got tough.

This Dodgers team is pretty weak, so I hoped the Sox would take advantage of it. They did.

The first game, Buehrle threw beautifully, scattering eight hits and shutting them out. Ozzie loves Buehrle, too. After the game, he said, "No matter how bad he is, we know that he will throw at least six innings." This was the forty-second consecutive start that Buehrle has pitched at least six innings.

There were other stars, too, notably Mercury, who walked in the first, stole second and third, with Iguchi behind him, then scored with Tad when the Captain, as usual, delivered in the clutch with a two-run single. In the third, Scotty doubled into the left-center gap, then scored when Iguchi singled to right. Dye and Thomas each homered for the third consecutive game, and it all looked easy, 6-0.

The second game was a fantastic finish. I mean, *fantastic*.

The game was actually boring for the first eight innings. The only interesting characters in the drama were Freddy Garcia and Jeff Kent. Freddy couldn't find the plate in the first inning, walking four batters. In the middle of that, Kent hit a 2-run shot to left, and after he gave us a run back on an error in the second inning, the game stayed 2-1 until the eighth, when the Dodgers picked up an insurance run after Kent doubled, advanced to third on a groundout, and scored on a Garcia wild pitch to make it 3-1. Cliff Politte entered with a scoreless ninth, and it was comeback time.

The inning started with Tad Iguchi facing Yhency Brazoban, who was throwing smoke. He worked Brazoban to a 3-2 count, then stayed motionless as the pay-off pitch bulleted just outside. Great self-control. Thomas then hit one in the hole, and their only play was to rifle it to first because Iguchi had the throw to second beaten. Konerko flied out to center, just missing the pitch, and gently rapped his helmet with his bat in frustration. Then came the first of two incredibly clutch at bats.

Carl Everett, who leads the league with 16 RBI to give his team the lead, had a chance to either narrow the lead with a base hit, or tie it with a blast. Before you could blink, he was down 0-2, and we were down to our last strike. But he has been a warrior in the clutch, and so I held out a slim hope that he could fight off what seemed inevitable defeat.

Meanwhile, Brazoban was throwing 96 mph. The next pitch was just high and outside, but Carl didn't bite. The pitch after that was slightly higher and more outside, and now it was 2-2. I'm thinking, look fastball. He's throwing nothing but fastballs.

But that's why Carl Everett is who *he* is, and I am who I am. He looked for a curve ball, got one down and in, and laced it into right for a single to score Iguchi. "You're the *man!*" I yelled. Willie Harris took his place immediately as the tying run, and on the first pitch to Rowand, Harris, who had a monster jump, stole second base *without even drawing a throw*.

Now it was up to Rowand. I didn't know until the announcers mentioned it that Rowand was 11 for 23 with men in scoring position and two outs this year. He saw a strike, then patiently waited as Brazoban threw three straight balls. Ozzie showed enormous confidence in him, giving him the green light on the 3-1 pitch, but Evel Knievel flailed at a pitch, missing it, and now it was a full count. The agony continued as he fouled off the next pitch. Then he hit a bouncer up the middle . . .

I don't know if baseballs truly have eyes ("The ball had eyes! Right between the infielders, you couldn't cue a billiard ball better than that!" etc.) but if this ball didn't have eyes, it had *something*. It managed to get past Brazoban and the middle infielders, and Harris flew home in a wink and a blink, and it was 3-3. All of the scoring had taken place with two outs and *two strikes*.

Hambino up now. I think this guy absolutely lives for moments like this. He, to paraphrase the real Hambino in *The Sandlot*, does *not* play ball like a girl. He ran the count full, then fouled off three pitches, before lifting a high pop foul over by the first base dugout. He flung his bat away from him with real disgust. No, it was more than disgust. It was loathing.

Hee-Seop Choi, the Dodgers' huge first baseman, floated toward the dugout without much zeal. But it cost him. By the time he got there, he hadn't reached the railing, and the ball landed four feet from his glove. *Another chance, A.J.* Hawk Harrelson, our announcer, former general manager of the team and the most clearly partisan announcer this side of the late Johnny Most of the Boston Celtics, was pleading for A.J. to hit a "tweener," something that could get between the outfielders and score Rowand.

And Hambino obliged him. But not only did he hit it to left-center, he rifled the pitch *over* the left-center field wall for a walk-off two run HR. I think Hawk might have lost his voice bellowing his famous, "You can put it on the boarrrrrrrrrrrrrrrd, YES!!

BEN: I love when Hawk does that.

DAD: I loved to watch him as a player. I got a kick out of him with his great talent at golf. Did you know that he might have been able to make the Tour?

BEN: Nope, I didn't. I love the fact that he's such an unabashed rooter for the Sox on the broadcasts, like when he says, "And now the score is 2-0, Good Guys."

DAD: The whole pretense of announcers playing non-partisan is a bunch of horsebleep. They're paid by the team, they become friends with the players, why shouldn't they root for the team?

BEN: And the Hawk will tell it like it is. If a Sox player screws up, he'll tell you. I like Darrin Jackson, too. As former players, and articulate ones, too, I truly enjoy listening to them.

DAD: Every time a Sox player strikes out an opponent, and Hawk intones, "He gone," I crack up.

I got my Father's Day gift today. It was a close game, with us down 3-0 going into the sixth. Then, for the Dodgers, as they say, speed kills. Mercury singled, then had Jeff Weaver so worried that he tried to pick him off. Weaver's knee buckled as he threw over, and the ball went sailing past first base, sending the Man of Winged Feet to third. Harris doubled him home, and after Rowand moved Harris over with a sac fly, the Captain grounded Harris home.

But we were still trailing 3-2 in the eighth. Ozzie sent up Frank Thomas to pinch-hit, hoping with his great eye he could draw a walk, which he did. Then I got my gift.

Scotty bunted directly in front of the plate. Hee-Seop Choi, not finished displaying his fielding skill, managed to stumble directly in the path of the catcher's throw to Kent, who was covering first. As a result, the catcher double-clutched and then threw low and wide to first. Kent did a great job of stretching to get it, but Scotty's foot hit the bag and the umpire called him safe, ruling Kent's foot went off the bag. Kent went reasonably ballistic, with Jim Tracy leaping out of the dugout to protest, but to no avail, and I got my gift. The replay was unclear, but in either case, I'm thinking Hee-Seop Choi's gift to me must be because we're related (although I'm 6'0" and he's 6'7", but besides that there's no problem). Willie Harris laid down our second sacrifice bunt of the inning, and now we had second and third, one out. The broadcasters informed us that 74% of the innings that we've used the sacrifice bunt, we've scored. Sounded good to me.

Up stepped Rowand, with his second chance in two games to be a hero. He didn't hit a seeing-eye grounder this time. He ripped a pitch into the left-field corner, scoring two, and we had the lead, one inning from a sweep. Revenge over the Dodgers was beginning to taste sweet. We got it too, with Hermanson allowing a couple of walks but emerging unscathed in the ninth, for his sixteenth save out of seventeen chances.

I think resentment at the Dodgers for 1959 can be put on the shelf for the moment, especially since the Twins have gone cold, and our lead has grown to 7 ½ games. Mercury had a summation of the team that sounded pretty apt: "There's a lot of heart and character walking around this clubhouse . . . we go at teams until the last out is recorded."

	W	L	PCT	GB	Home	Away	Div	Streak
Chicago WSox	45	22	.672	---	22-10	23-12	20-5	Won 3
Minnesota	38	28	.576	6 1/2	20-14	18-14	16-12	Lost 1
Cleveland	36	30	.545	8 1/2	16-13	20-17	13-19	Won 8
Detroit	32	33	.492	12	17-17	15-16	10-11	Won 1
Kansas City	24	43	.358	21	14-21	10-22	5-17	Lost 2

June 23, 2005
BEN:

We took the Royals apart rather easily. The first game was a back and forth scoring see-saw. Apparently our starter, young McCarthy, forgot his arm back in AAA. He didn't know he was starting until the night before the game, but that's no excuse – his control was just terrible, and his velocity isn't high enough to make up for lack of accuracy. The good news was that Jose Lima, who reportedly celebrated his 197th birthday recently, was even worse. So was their bullpen.

We demonstrated some serious power. In the first, Konerko hit a prodigious three-run shot to left, driving in Scotty P. and Iguchi. Thomas clouted one to deep center field off of Lima in the third. That was Thomas' sixth home run in 13 games since returning from the DL. I've always been skeptical that Thomas is a vital cog, but if he hits like this, look out.

I think my unease with Thomas goes back to a game Dad and I went to about nine years ago, when Thomas was in his prime. It was Sox-Angels, and it was a nailbiter. The score was 6-5 in the top of the ninth, with Thomas coming to bat and a man on. Thomas had already hit a two-run shot in the seventh, after Dad and I put the "hex" on the pitcher's back leg. (You put the

128

"hex" on a pitcher, we learned from one of Dad's friends, by touching together your index finger and pinky above your middle fingers, then aiming them at the pitcher.) Now Thomas was up in a clutch situation, facing Troy Percival. At the time, Percival was a relative nobody – Lee Smith had been the closer for the Angels for years. But Percival came in, and went up 2-0 on Thomas. The hex was on, the count was 2-0 – what could go wrong? Three tailing fastballs later, Thomas was out on strikes, and the Sox were done.

Ever since, I've believed Thomas is anything but clutch. He confirmed my suspicion during the 2000 playoffs, when he went 0 for the playoffs. Dad has always thought of him as a latter-day, better-hitting Jim Rice: 140 RBI, few when the game was on the line. Maybe he can change our minds this year. I'm not betting on it.

Anyway, the Royals game got exciting in the top of the sixth. We were up 8-6 when catcher John Buck (who sounds as though he should be a member of the Texas Rangers – "Ranger John Buck") knocked a Luis Vizcaino pitch into the right field seats. Ruben Gotay followed with a bomb into the right field stands. Ah, good old Luis Vizcaino. Way to shut the door, there. 8-8.

Then, in came Neal Cotts. Cotts has had a great season, and came into the game with an ERA of 2.10. This year has been a real change for him; he's spent most of it being used as our non-psychotic situational lefty. For a couple years, he had been touted as the next sure thing in the rotation, but had never lived up to the billing. If he can develop the right mentality coming out of the bullpen, we'll be very tough all year – Politte or Cotts to Hermanson is solid stuff. And who knows? Maybe in the future he'll make it all the way back into the rotation (though that would be a couple of years down the road, since our current rotation is fantastic, and we have McCarthy banging on the door).

Anyway, Cotts finally shut the Royals down. He went 2 1/3 innings, surrendering a single hit and striking out three. After the game, Ozzie had high praise for him, describing him as "our MVP over the last two or three weeks. . . . This kid is great. We have a lot of confidence in him, and that's why he will continue to be on the mound in tough situations." That's good news – up until now, we had to rely on the Michael Myers of lefthanded setup men, Damaso Marte.

We finally grabbed the lead for good in the bottom of the sixth inning. Iguchi singled, and so did Konerko; Dye walked. Hambino strode to the plate and fisted one to center field, just over the outstretched glove of Gotay, scoring Iguchi and Konerko. Crede drove Dye home with a fister into left to finish it off, 11-8. Spaghetti-Arm Takatsu came in for a single out, and then it was on to Hermanson, who was in good form, striking out one in a perfect inning.

Games two and three of the series were almost identical: 5-1 victories with brilliant starting pitching from Jon Garland and Mark Buehrle. Garland (12-2) didn't allow a run until the ninth, and went 8 1/3, allowing only four hits. Buehrle (9-1) went eight innings, giving up only five hits and one run (which differs widely from his usual 19 hits and 2 runs). Even the relief situation was almost identical: my two favorite relievers actually pitched decently. Damaso "Wild Man" Marte went 2/3 of an inning in the Garland game, and Spaghetti-Arm went a full inning with two strikeouts in cleaning up for Buehrle. I guess the Royals can make anyone seem like Cy Young.

Buehrle's performance in particular was sensational. He stretched his scoreless innings streak to 25 1/3 in the eighth inning; he hasn't lost in 12 starts, and his six inning per game streak is now at 43. His ERA is now 2.48. The big question is whether Garland or Buehrle should start the All-Star Game (though Roy Halliday is still an option). Buehrle only gave up a run because of a misplay by Konerko. As he always does, Buehrle took the run in stride, remarking, "It would have been nice to keep it going, but we won the game. I'll just start another [streak]."

Buehrle, meanwhile, was supported by strong performances near the top of the order. After a walk to Ozuna in the third, a double by Iguchi, and another double by Thomas, we were up 2-0. In the fifth, Thomas walked, Konerko doubled, and Everett, batting righty, drove one up and out to left. 5-0. The series was almost too easy, and our sweep made it seven straight wins. Our lead over Minnesota stretched from 7.5 games to 10.

We've got the Cubs next. Let's keep this ball rolling.

June 27, 2005
BEN:

Fail.

Bring me the head of Dusty Baker.

The Cubs. The miserable, horrible, terrible, awful Cubs. The first game was a breeze, and I began to think that we might be able to push our winning streak up to nine or ten games. On the strength of Freddy Garcia's arm (7 innings, 3 hits, 1 ER), Scotty's legs (1 hit, 3 walks, 2 runs, 2 stolen bases – that put him at 38 on the year,), and the bats of Thomas (HR #7, 2 RBI), Pierzynski (HR #11, 3 RBI, 2 runs), and Crede (HR #10, 3 RBI), we took it 12-2. Of course, we *were* facing some no-name pitcher, Sergio Mitre. Not exactly Prior, Wood or Maddux. Still, this had to be a good sign.

All the focus after the game was on Scotty P., who was just dynamite. Pierzynski credited Podsednik with the win, stating bluntly, "He's the story . . . When you're on our team you can see it, the pitchers, as soon as he gets on base, they start pitching out, they start quickening up their delivery. . . . He's been the biggest thing for us right now, especially offensively." Ozzie was similarly enthused: "We need a type of player like Podsednik. . . . We did not have a leadoff player last year, not any speed. This guy brings a lot of motion, a lot of excitement to the ballgame every day." And as for Podsednik, he was typically modest, explaining that getting on base and disrupting pitchers was "my job. . . . [It's] to try to sway the pitcher's concentration a little bit and get myself into scoring position. I reached all four times tonight, but that's the leadoff hitter's job to get on base in any way you can."

I'm not sure we could have gotten three stronger starts consecutively than we had from Garland, Buehrle, and Garcia. In the playoffs, all it really takes is two – remember Randy and Curt, circa 2001. Three is even better – last year's tandem of Schilling, Pedro and Lowe was fantastic. We already have three; now the only question is who number four will be. Come playoff time, I'm betting on the Magical Mr. El Duque.

Looks like we should have saved some of that scoring for the second game against the Cubs. Greg Maddux looked like the Greg Maddux of old, shutting us down. Meanwhile, Jose Contreras, the mystery man, stumbled out of the gate, surrendering four runs in the first inning. After Corey Patterson bunted his way on, Contreras hit Neifi Perez on a pitch up and in. Ouch. After inducing an out from Derek Lee, Contreras walked

Jeremy Burnitz. A forkball that didn't break, and Aramis Ramirez had four RBI on a massive grand slam to left.

The first for us was problematic. Scotty P. hit a double, but on an Aaron Rowand chopper to third, Scotty broke for home. Bad move. Out at the plate, standing up.

That was the way the game went all day long. They were hitting Contreras all over the lot, and without some great defensive play by Tad Iguchi, he surely would have given up eight or nine runs instead of six. Our big chance came in the bottom of the second, when Carl Everett unloaded to right. He has turned out to be a boon thus far (11 HR, 46 RBI). A few seconds later, Jermaine Dye (the Silent Assassin, as Dad has taken to calling him) followed Everett to the right field stands. Hambino chopped one up the middle, and we had a rally going. But that ended with Joe Crede, who smoked a long line drive to left. Did it have enough? Hawk Harrelson was clearly ready to "put it on the board, yes!" but not so fast. Todd Hollandsworth, the former Dodger rookie of the year, leaped up and snagged the ball from the fans. And instead of a 4-4 game and zero outs, it was 4-2 and one out. That was all we got the rest of the ballgame. Where's Bartman when we need him?

At least our relief was good. Cotts continued his stellar run, as did Cliff Politte, and the Norman Bates of our bullpen (Marte) pitched a good inning. I'm just glad Ozzie put him in when it didn't matter.

Game three was more of the same for our offense, which was shut out for just the second time all year. Of course, Mark Prior was pitching. In his return from the DL, he one-hit us for six innings. His stuff is simply electric. His fastball was hitting 94, and he was really snapping his curve, into the dirt in several cases. We had some chances against the Cubs' relief corps (we got our leadoff men on in the seventh, eighth, and ninth), but we really never got started.

Jon Garland was almost as good as Prior, pitching 7 1/3, giving up only two runs. That was the final score: 2-0. We haven't scored in 16 innings. We dropped two of three to the *Cubs*. Grr.

Altogether, though, we're riding high. Our AL Central lead has ballooned to 9 games, though we were up 10.5 after winning the first game against the Bruin Messengers of Lucifer. Torii Hunter of the Twins was quoted as stating that if the Twins have to keep up with us, "then we've got no chance." It's good to see them finally drop behind after sticking with us for so long – they're always dangerous. I thought they'd *never* lose. Then again, I'm starting to think *we'll* never lose, so it won't matter. On the book front, things are moving ahead. Last week, Dr. Laura made *Porn Generation* her Book Give-away, which was fantastic. Today, a wonderful review by Dr. Judith Reisman appeared in *Human Events*. She wrote, "Shapiro's Judeo-Christian advocacy is sane, compassionate, documented and easy to take, although he has drawn the wrath of many suffering the pains of amorality."

Dad, meanwhile, is still in pain from the injury he suffered a couple months ago. Mom is looking into some surgical procedures, and he's doing physical therapy. It's pretty brutal, since he can't walk without pain at this point. Still, we're optimistic that we'll find a solution to this – if Mark Prior can come back from a non-displaced fracture on his pitching elbow to pitch a one-hitter a month later, Dad will be able to heal.

The Sox get Detroit next, which is a recipe for recovery, anyway. Detroit should provide a soothing balm after suffering the lacerations of a Cubs bite. At least we won't see the Cubs again; there's no chance they'll make it to the Series. As for us, however, if we continue the way we're playing . . . we should be able to hold the fort.

	W	L	PCT	GB	Home	Away	Div	Streak
Chicago WSox	50	24	.676	---	27-12	23-12	23-5	Lost 2
Minnesota	40	33	.548	9 1/2	21-17	19-16	17-14	Won 1
Cleveland	39	34	.534	10 1/2	19-17	20-17	13-19	Won 2
Detroit	36	36	.500	13	18-17	18-19	12-12	Lost 1
Kansas City	25	49	.338	25	15-21	10-28	5-20	Lost 6

Part III
Holding the Fort

June 30, 2005
DAD:

Today would have been my father's seventy-ninth birthday. He died four years ago, June 8, 2001, just short of his seventy-fifth. He had been fighting diabetes for years, but what ultimately killed him was pancreatic cancer, which was discovered in January 2000, and staved off by a procedure called the Whipple. That enabled him to hang on long enough, weak as he was, to celebrate his fiftieth anniversary with my mother in December 2000. Our family took them to dinner, and the glow on my father's face was the first time I had seen him happy since my sister died in 1996. He never really recovered from that (what parent ever recovers from the loss of a child?) but if there was one moment that made him glad to have held on, that dinner was it. At the dinner I told him how no one could ever take away from him the pride he felt at having such a long marriage, and tears came to his eyes as he told me for the umpteenth time how proud he was of my own family. But knowing how close he was to the precipice made that the kind of moment that will be burned into my memory forever.

He was an amateur drummer, and as a young teenager had a trio with Lou Levy, the well-known jazz pianist who went on to play for Ella Fitzgerald and Lena Horne, among others. He knew the big band arrangements backward and forward, and jazz was the great love of his life after my mother and his children. But the Sox were also a tremendous kick for him, and although he wasn't the wild-eyed fanatic about them that I became, whenever I was away at camp or a job playing at some resort, he never failed to send me every day's box score in the mail. I used to gobble up the box scores, and read them over and over to try to get the feel of what that game had been like.

139

Memories of my childhood always flood back when the Sox play in Detroit. It seemed that the Sox were on TV playing there more often than any other team when I was growing up, and I loved old Tigers Park, knowing that Ty Cobb had once played there. I always held a special place for Cobb, because he lived and breathed baseball, and was probably one of the smartest, if not *the* smartest, players to ever live. When I got older, and read that he was a racist, I lost respect for him as a man, but nothing could entirely extinguish my respect for the fact that he left everything on the field. Besides, I had memorized all the batting averages of every Hall of Famer, and the fact that he was so far ahead of everyone and had the most lifetime hits made him stand out. (Rose has passed him, but what's Rose's lifetime average? Did you say .303? Cobb's was .366. 'Nuf said.)
Tigers Stadium was the only park in addition to Fenway that had my complete respect, because of its history. The Sox had played in Comiskey Park from 1911, and Fenway and Tigers Stadium came in 1912, making them the oldest parks still in use up until the 1990's. Only Fenway is left now, but Tigers Stadium held on until 2000, and I think of it when the Sox play there.

Detroit, Detroit, it's a helluva town, the Sox just fly there, they never come down.

I know, I know, the song is really about New York, but this year I'm substituting Detroit, because the Sox just swept them, and now have won all five games there this year.

The first game, Mr. Slip'N'Slide was masterful. Buehrle gave up eight hits, but really scattered them well over almost seven innings, walking no one, and only allowing a run in the third when Monroe singled, stole second and reached third on a bad throw by A.J., then scored on a single by Shelton. We got it back in the fifth, when Uribe hit one into the right-center gap with one out, and raced around to third. Scotty, facing Nate Robertson, a left-hander who struck out nine and looked very tough, was smart. He poked a couple of foul balls to left, not trying to pull it, and then reached out and lofted a fly ball to left, scoring Uribe easily. In the sixth Dye laid into a Robertson fastball and crushed it into the seats in left field, and we were up 2-1.

Of course, we had to make it interesting. (How many laughers have we had this year?) In the ninth, Hermanson gave up a lead-off triple to Ivan Rodriguez, who came up from sliding into third shaking his fist at the Tigers dugout to stir them up. He is a fiery competitor, and he's another example of my theory that the catcher is the difference between championship teams and ordinary ones. With no one out, Ozzie played the infield *back*, and said later that he didn't want to give up a cheap hit to put the winning run on. It was a unique move, and it paid off when Hermanson got Dmitri Young to pop out. *Then* Ozzie moved the infield in, and Hermanson was very, very smart. With the left-handed Monroe up, he kept the ball outside, and Monroe couldn't pull the ball to the right side to score Rodriguez.
Instead, he grounded it to Crede, who glanced at the runner, holding him, then threw Monroe out. Finally, with the infield back again, Shelton grounded to Iguchi, and we had dodged a bullet.

Mr. Slip'N'Slide acknowledged the reason the Sox won again. "The Man upstairs is a Sox fan," he said. "There are games that we shouldn't be winning that we are winning." And I thought, if the Man upstairs is a Sox fan this year, maybe I should start thinking about flying to Vegas and getting a bet down...

The second game I started making plane reservations.

Not at first. In the second, we grabbed an early 2-0 lead after Everett, A.J. and Crede singled for one run, and Detroit's Jason Johnson threw a wild pitch for the second run. The Tigers evened the score in the bottom of the inning when Chris Shelton took a McCarthy pitch the other way to right-center. The Captain blasted a solo shot far over the left field bleachers in the third, and that held up until the seventh, when Shelton tripled and Rondell White flied to center to bring him home.

The Tigers had their chances along the way; in the fourth, Pudge Rodriguez had doubled, and after advancing to third, went on contact when, with the infield in, Shelton grounded right to Uribe, who threw Pudge out at home. In the eighth, against Politte, they loaded the bases with nobody out, but Pudge struck out and Monroe grounded to Uribe, who stepped on second and gunned the fleet Monroe out at first.

But the Sox saved their greatest Houdini moment for the ninth. With Vizcaino pitching, Nook Logan, who has unbelievable speed, dragged a bunt single, then went to third when Brandon Inge singled. After Inge took second unopposed, the Tigers had second and third with two out. Placido Polanco tomahawked a high fastball from Vizcaino toward the hole, and the game was over.

Except for one thing: *the greatest clutch play of the season.* Uribe flashed to his right, and deep. He must have been at least five feet onto the *outfield* grass, in the hole, and unleashed a long throw that bounced once and nestled into the Captain's glove just before Polanco's sliding hand hit the bag. With the game on the line, and the distance of the throw, it had to be the play of the year.

After that, I had no doubt we would win somehow. Of course, since the Sox were 21-8 in one-run games this year, I expected us to win by an eyelash. Sure enough, in the thirteenth, Thomas reached down and practically scooped an outside pitch over the left-field wall. We survived a scare in the bottom half, courtesy of Takatsu, who managed to allow two hits, a sacrifice and an intentional walk to load the bases, but surprisingly, he struck out Inge, and Polanco grounded to Iguchi. We had it in the bag all along.

Game three can be summed up in two words: Freddy Garcia. He was simply dominant. His breaking ball was overpowering, as he threw a complete game and struck out eight. Once we got the lead on a three-run-shot by Crede in the fifth, it was all over. Everett added a two–run HR to left for good measure, and we won 6-1, sweeping the series.

Garcia is 5-0 over his last eight starts. His recent surge is getting lost amid the hoopla surrounding the hot starts of Buehrle and Garland, but I think he's a huge key this year. He's experienced, strong as a bull, and willing to let the other pitchers remain in the spotlight while he quietly does his job. On many other staffs he would be a number one, so I have enormous respect for his positive, team-first attitude. If there's any justice, he'll get his place in the sun sometime.

In a move that will not upset Ben at all, Damaso Marte was placed on the 15-day disabled list with an inflamed left trapezius. That'll put more pressure on the bullpen, so it will be interesting to see what Kenny Williams' response will be. In the meantime, we're 10 ½ games in front. I'm not too worried.

July 3, 2005

I should have worried.
We had to go to Oakland.

When I was growing up, the team I hated losing to more than any other was the Yankees, for obvious reasons. Then in the early seventies, it changed to Oakland, since the great A's team held us off in 1972 to win the division. Somehow, in the intervening years, that never changed. Minnesota has routinely won our division in recent years, but they play good, solid baseball, so I couldn't really hate them. Ozzie even said that he wanted to model the Sox after them. My loathing for Oakland surfaced again with the publication of *Moneyball*, and the elevation to sainthood of Billy Beane and the Bill James school of baseball. I got genuinely pissed off at the cavalier treatment of Kenny Williams in the book, and I'd like nothing better than for us to kick their butts every time we get the chance. The only problem is, somehow they match up well against us, and so I should have worried. And to make matters worse, they had a seven-game win streak.

Game one featured us giving up ten, count 'em, *ten* walks. Of course, you can't blame the whole staff; Contreras gave up seven in barely more than four innings. He just couldn't find the plate. When he left in the middle of the fifth, there were bases loaded, thanks to a bloop double and two more walks. And, oh yeah, he had also thrown not one, not two, but *three* wild pitches already. Kevin Walker (who?) came in, and after getting a pop-out, walked Nick Swisher, forcing in a run. Vizcaino entered, and *he* walked in another run, and we were down 4-2. After the first, we never really mounted a threat, and the walks just killed us. We lost 6-2. After the game, Contreras was quoted as saying, "I can't wait for my next start. The team's playing good and it helps to have games like this because it helps to keep us humble and not become satisfied."

Ummmm, *what?*

The second game was a relief. I wanted us to just get one win out of this series, and I got my wish, thanks to Jon Garland and Joe Crede. Garland won his major-league-leading thirteenth game. It wasn't the dominant performance he had in Oakland April 25, when he threw that four-hit shutout, but it was a gritty job, nonetheless. Just how gritty he's become was revealed in the sixth, when the A's loaded the bases with nobody out and us leading 3-2. Facing the dangerous Eric Chavez, Garland got him to fly to Rowand to score one run, and then got one of the heroes of *Moneyball*, Scott Hatteberg, to foul out to Crede in the huge foul territory at the Coliseum. Kielty grounded to Crede, and we escaped with only giving up one run, tied at 3-3.

Meanwhile, back at the ranch, Crede had already singled in a run when he strode to bat in the seventh. He homered to left, putting us ahead. Crede is beginning to pique my interest as a clutch hitter; I was satisfied for him to be the vacuum cleaner down at third, but lately he's seemed nerveless at bat.

After Politte and Hermanson pitched the last two innings three up three down, Garland was all alone at the top of the majors with thirteen wins. It's the most wins he's ever had in a season, and it's before the All-Star break? Visions of Denny McClain came to mind.

Today, I could feel my own greed manifesting itself. It would have been just beautiful to win two out of three in the devil's lair. We haven't won a series in Oakland since 2000, and everything else has gone our way this year, so why not? And with Buehrle pitching, we had a great chance to pull it off. He was 10-1, with a 2.42 ERA, and Barry Zito was 4-8, with a 4.21 ERA. Looked good to me.

After Thomas hit a massive, massive HR to left in the fourth, and Dye hit another HR in the fifth, we led 2-0. Then, in the sixth, everything collapsed. With runners on first and second, Eric Byrnes hit a perfect double-play ball back to the mound. Buehrle, in as uncharacteristic a move as I've ever seen him make, threw the ball past second base, allowing the lead runner to score. A line drive off his leg and a couple of hits followed, and before you could turn around, it was 4-2 A's, and they never looked back. Buehrle gave up 14 hits, and his record slid to 10-2.

I *hate* that team. I hate playing them, I hate losing to them, and I especially hate the way the Sox play against them. They bring out the worst in the Sox every time we play them. To make matters worse, we get a series against them next week. Ugh.

	W	L	PCT	GB	Home	Away	Div	Streak
Chicago WSox	54	26	.675	---	27-12	27-14	26-5	Lost 1
Minnesota	45	34	.570	8 1/2	26-18	19-16	19-15	Won 3
Cleveland	44	36	.550	10	19-17	25-19	13-19	Won 1
Detroit	37	41	.474	16	19-22	18-19	12-15	Lost 2
Kansas City	26	54	.325	28	15-24	11-30	6-22	Lost 3

July 7, 2005
BEN:

The Tampa Bay series this week was a beautiful reminder that we are a *very* good baseball team. Tampa Bay, though I criticize them all the time, is well-managed by Lou Piniella, and they're likely to be troublemakers sometime down the road. Nonetheless, we swept them to extend our AL Central lead to 11 games.

During the two-hour rain delay before the first game, the Sox stumped for Scotty P. Mercury signed memorabilia for 90 minutes during the rain delay – is that vote buying? – and one of

146

Ozzie's sons held up a sign reading "Vote for Scott." Mark Buehrle, who is one of the classiest fellows on the team, made a stump speech before the July 4 crowd just before the fireworks, pushing Podsednik. It was actually a rather funny situation, since Carl Crawford of the Devil Rays is one of Scotty's competitors in the All-Star race. During the pre-game publicity campaign, Crawford walked out of the dugout, smiling, and held out his hands as if to say "What about me?"

Brendan McCarthy started for us in the first game, and once again, his control wasn't all that impressive. He still looks good at times, but it looks like he's lost his motion because he's getting hit. Hideo Nomo, former Dodger sensation (I remember going to Chavez Ravine when he was pitching – packed house), pitched for Tampa Bay. We got five runs in the first on a single by Scotty, a double by Iguchi, a walk by Thomas, and another single by Konerko. Rowand struck out, but the Silent Assassin hit his 18th HR to right-center on a pitch low and outside. Grand slam, yes!

Dye has been quietly excellent this season, and really has a strong case for All-Star consideration (though he didn't get any). He has more HR (19) than any AL outfielder outside of Manny Ramirez, though his average is a bit low. When Kenny Williams signed Dye this offseason, some believed Dye could never regain his form after struggling somewhat with Oakland. But he's as solid as they come, and is on pace to hit well over 30 HRs (and has an outside shot at 40).

By the end of the fifth, we had a 10-5 lead, thanks to an absolute bomb to center from Juan Uribe. Long man Luis Vizcaino, who came in for the brutal McCarthy in the fourth, was superb. He went two innings, giving up only one hit. Then, our relief disaster. Some guy named Kevin Walker pitched 2/3 of an inning; I haven't heard of him to this point, and I doubt we'll hear much about him after this. He gave up two runs on a Carl Crawford seeing-eye single, a slashed triple to right from Cantu, and a single from Huff. 10-7. Then Ozzie, thinking that the game was still basically over, brought in the man I love to see: Spaghetti Arm Takatsu. He got the final out of the inning, but it wouldn't be a Takatsu appearance without an earned run, which Takatsu surrendered on a long line drive home run to Crawford in the eighth.

Another note: Jermaine Dye and Tad Iguchi put together a beautiful throw to third to catch Joey Gathright, who was trying to stretch a double. That turned out to be big, since the next batter was Crawford, and his bomb would have made the score 10-9. So credit Dye with 6 RBI on the night, a grand slam, and a putout saving a run. Not a bad day's work for the Silent Assassin. Finally, Hermanson shut the door in the ninth, for his 20th save of the season.

After the game, we made some interesting roster moves. McCarthy was sent back down to Triple A, where I hope he can find his control and his edge. Meanwhile, the Sox are bringing up another young pitcher, some guy named Bobby Jenks. What makes this move more interesting than similar moves in the past (Jon Adkins, Jon Rauch) is the fact that Jenks throws 100 mph. We're bringing him up to the majors from Double A, and Ozzie says he won't try to ease him into the majors. He's just going to throw him out there and see what he can do. I think that makes sense, since Jenks is a bit older than some of our other prospects, at 24. He has also had two stress fractures to his pitching elbow in past years from the torque of throwing so hard; last summer, he had surgery to fix the issue. Jenks came over from the Angels organization after they tried to pass him through waivers (go,

Kenny Williams!) – he has reputedly had a drinking problem, but he says that's been solved with his marriage and the birth of his two kids. If he has good control, we're going to have the best bullpen in baseball to go along with the best rotation in baseball.

Game two was more tense than game one. Freddy Garcia was solid, if unspectacular (7 IP, 4 ER), and Mark Hendrickson of Tampa Bay got the better of him for 6 2/3 innings (3 ER). The game seesawed most of the way, and only another Sox comeback (and super pitching from the bullpen – Cotts to Politte to Hermanson) saved this one.

Dye hit another bomb (#19) and a double to lead the way in the early going, but the game was tied 4-4 as we entered the eighth. The Devil Rays have been awful all season in the eighth; they'd been outscored 87-27 in the eighth to this point. They showed why here. Scotty P., silent for most of the game, drove one the other way, hitting the bottom of the left field fence. Tad Iguchi followed with a hard-hit liner to right, which fell in. Because the ball was hit so hard, however, Scotty had to stop at third, setting the table for Big Frank, who has been a power-monster but average-weakling since his return from the DL.

Like clockwork, Thomas extended those massive arms and drove a fat pitch deep into the night. 6-4 Sox. An astonishing 10th HR on the year for Big Frank. The stadium was rocking. And, just like clockwork, Hermanson came in and grabbed his 21st save of the season.

It was a great win. This is the type of game we surely would have lost last season, and it's important to remember that even without Thomas' big bop, we likely would have scored (men on first and third and no outs). Last year, Thomas or Carlos Lee or Ordonez may have hit a home run in the eighth

149

inning – the difference is that this year, Scotty P. and Iguchi are on when someone drives the ball from the yard.

The third game was wonderful for four very special reasons. First, Scotty P. got a nice ovation when he went out to left field as the scoreboard announced he had made the All-Star team. Second, our offense was terrific once again. Third, Jose Contreras looked good. And fourth, Bobby Jenks pitched. My Lord. Somebody wake me up, here: we're leading our division by double digits *and* we just brought up Jenks?

Aubrey Huff put the Rays ahead in the first with yet another bomb. I'm glad this guy is on a rotten team, because add him to the Twins, and I'm thinking our lead looks more like six games instead of 10. In the top of the third, we moved ahead. Ozuna, playing third again, outran the Rays' Casey Fossum in a footrace to the bag after dropping down a bunt to the right side. After Uribe struck out, Mercury smoked a ball through the box and into center field. Another single from Iguchi, and Ozuna scored. Big Hurt walked (he still has the best eye in baseball), and Carl Everett flared one to center, driving in Mercury and Tad. That was all we'd need, though Thomas would add a three-run dinger in the fifth, most notably.

Contreras went six innings, and Ozzie seems to have figured out what Dad and I were crying about in Anaheim – if you get six good innings out of Jose, get him out *now*. More striking than Contreras' performance, however, was the contrast between the eighth and ninth innings for our bullpen.

After a stellar 1 2/3 from Cotts, the Pasta Master, Takatsu, pitched the last 1/3 of the eighth holding a 7-2 lead. As usual, he made things interesting. With two out, Eduardo Perez singled to right, and Takatsu proceeded to walk Damon Hollins before finally inducing a tap-out back to the mound from Nick Green.

Then the ninth. Bobby Jenks. First major league outing. The first pitch was a bit low. It was also 99 mph. *Say what?!* The second pitch was a strike on the outside corner. It was also 99 mph. *Holy &%^$!* Third pitch missed low. 99 mph. He took something off of one. 95 mph. Ball four, 99 mph.

So, speed but no control, huh? Steve Dalkowski, Part II? Not exactly. Johnny Gomes was a bit less fortunate than the previous batter. High cheese, 99. Swing and a miss. Ball, 99. At this point, I began wondering if and when Jenks would ever throw anything off-speed. Not that he needs to, of course. Just for the heck of it. Strike, swinging. 96. Passed ball, 97. High fastball. 97. Say goodbye, Mr. Gomes.

I feel the need. The need for speed.
Their All-Star candidate, Carl Crawford. Ball, 99. Fouled back, 97. Fouled back, 98. Crawford looks like he's swinging in slow motion. So naturally, he barely chops one down to first base on Jenks' first off-speed pitch of the evening, clocking in at 80 mph.

Good night, sweetheart, well, it's time to go . . .
Julio Lugo. Fouled off, 99. Lugo looks tardy up there. Fouled off, 99. Fouled off, 99. Then, the kicker – 85 mph curveball, in the dirt. Lugo can't hold off.

And that's that. 18 pitches, 11 strikes. Every fastball clocking in at 95 or above, and 9 of the 16 at 99 mph. I know Dustin Hermanson is our closer. I know he's been great. But I have *never* seen anybody throw like this. Ever. Big Bad Bobby Jenks. He may look like Bob's big boy, but he throws like Goose Gossage. Whew.

151

July 11, 2005

Going into the All-Star break, we have to feel pretty good about the first half of the season. We're 57-29, and we have a nine-game lead over the second-place Twins. Two of our pitchers are going to the game (Buehrle and Garland) and one of them is starting (Buehrle), thanks to Toronto's Roy Halladay fielding a line drive off his shin, breaking a bone in his leg. Captain Konerko made the team as a backup 1B; Scotty P. made the last slot on the AL team through fan voting, beating out heavyweights Derek Jeter and Hideki Matsui (more on that later). Dustin Hermanson really should be on the team, too.

Ozzie, who is seen by many as the crazy lucky guy who happens to sit on the Sox bench, is runaway favorite for Manager of the Year at this point; Kenny Williams should win any awards for general managers, too. Everyone predicted that the Sox would finish no better than second in the division, and many picked us to finish *behind* Detroit. So much for that bunch of nonsense; barring a Cubs-like collapse, we should win the division and make the playoffs for the first time since 2000. And with our pitching, we can do some serious damage in the playoffs. I also wouldn't be surprised to see Trader Kenny go out and get a big bat near the trading deadline, since he always makes moves after the All-Star break. Current rumor has it that the Sox are checking out another *pitcher*, San Francisco Giants flamethrower Jason Schmidt, which would certainly give us the most formidable rotation of the last twenty years, the way our current guys are pitching.

That's the good news. The bad news is that we can't beat Oakland. I continue to pray that Oakland misses the playoffs, since they've handed us seven losses so far, as opposed to only two wins. The only good news there is that we don't face them

152

again this season. Of course, we do get a lot of New York and Boston, so we'll see how we hold up there.

Oakland swept us. They beat us every which way. They beat us in our kind of ballgame in the first contest – a low-scoring affair, which they took 4-2. They crushed us in game two, 10-1. And then they slowly squeezed us to death in game three, breaking our hearts in the 11th inning.

In the first game, Garland got his fourth loss of the season (he has 13 wins). He only went five innings (throwing an incredible 111 pitches) but he gave up three runs. He got beaten by Kirk Saarloos (who must have found a discount vowel store); Saarloos went six innings and gave up just two runs on seven hits. The only positive highlight for us was All-Star elect Scotty P.'s two stolen bases (bringing his season total to 43).

The second game was an old-fashioned beat-down. Mark "Slip 'N' Slide" Buehrle got hammered. He didn't slip, and he didn't slide. He sort of hit the turf and just stuck there. Through six innings, he had surrendered only two runs (and in the sixth, he made a superb effort on a bunt – he slid to his knees, popped up, and threw out the runner). We were losing anyway, since Barry Zito had held us to a single tally in the sixth. But in the seventh, the wheels came off the bus. Nick Swisher (who sounds as though he should be in an F. Scott Fitzgerald novel) hit a ground ball that ate up Pablo Ozuna at third. A flare from Jason Kendall, and it was first and third. Mark Kotsay made the Sox pay with a tremendous blast to right field.

Buehrle exited at the end of the inning. And Bobby Jenks entered. After his stellar debut against Tampa Bay, he received his initiation into MLB. His first two pitches to Eric Chavez were beauties, with the second clocking at 99 mph; he dropped a change-up in at 84 to run the count to 1-2. Another 86 mph breaking ball. *Throw the cheese! Throw him the high, stinky limburger!* Fastball, 99, and Chavez grounded it to Konerko, who threw to Jenks for the force at first. So far, so good.

That's where the good part ended. Bobby Kielty hit the first 99 mph offering into right-field for a single. Jenks went 1-1 to Eric Byrnes before creating a crater between the mound and home by burning a 55-ft. fastball into the ground, advancing Kielty to second. Byrnes knocked a grounder up the middle; Jenks stabbed at it, but only knocked it to Iguchi, who couldn't throw out Byrnes at first. Can't blame that single on the Big Fella. Byrnes proceeded to steal second on a terrible throw by Chris Widger.

Jenks walked Swisher on five pitches, and it was bases loaded. Up came Scott Hatteberg, Billy Beane's favorite human being. (A funny moment: While Hatteberg warmed up, the camera cut to Freddy Garcia, who was to start game three. Garcia was picking his nose in the dugout. The A's announcer dimwittedly remarked as the camera showed Garcia's mining operation, "There's Freddy, getting ready for tomorrow." So *that's* how Garcia prepares.) Hatteberg showed why by working Jenks for a walk on four pitches, driving in a run.

At that point, Ozzie called on the Linguini Specialist himself, Takatsu. Jenks had to be thinking, "I'm stinking it up out here, but *please*, for the sake of my ERA, *not that guy.*"

Oh yes, it was *that guy.* Hitting Takatsu after seeing Jenks must be like hitting a beach ball after swinging at a speeding golf ball. Mark Ellis grounded a DP ball to Iguchi, but Ellis beat out the throw to first, and Kielty scored. Credit that run to Jenks. Jason Kendall then reached out and poked a low breaking ball (is there any difference between a Takatsu fastball and breaking ball?) into left. Byrnes scored. Credit that run to Jenks.

Way to go there, Shingo. You inherit three runners, and two of them score. Your line at the end of the game reads: 2/3 of an inning, 1 run (which you give up a moment later). Just terrific.

In a 6-1 ballgame, you've got to leave Jenks out there to work out his kinks. At least don't bring in Takatsu to jack Jenks' ERA up to 20.25. On second thought, maybe Ozzie wants to protect Jenks' psyche. We've already got enough loons (read: Marte) in the bullpen.

The third game was simply tragic. It was a battle all the way. The game was slated as a pitcher's duel, with Freddy Garcia going for us and Dan Haren (7-7, 3.96 ERA) going for Oakland, but it didn't end up that way.

We had the lead, 5-4, going into the seventh, thanks to a jack to right field by the subbing Carl Everett in the fifth. Then the unexpected occurred: our situational lefty, Cotts, blew up. His control was off, and he left a ball over the plate for Dan Johnson, who laced it to deep center with two men on for an off-the-wall double. 6-5 A's. Cotts is usually tough on lefties; his tactic is to go slightly outside to them. Here, he seemed unable to keep the ball on the outer half of the plate. The A's got another run before the end of the inning.

We came within one again in the bottom of the seventh when Hambino singled to right to drive in Paul Konerko from third. Then, the ninth. Dustin Hermanson came in to keep it close, and fed Mark Kotsay a fastball down and in. You could almost see Hermanson try to grab the ball after it left his hand and bring it back. No one on the field could bring it back, however, as it landed in the right field bleachers. 8-6. The HR hurt a lot, especially because Hermanson had a 3-2 count with two outs. One more strike . . . nope. If Bobby Jenks had Hermanson's control, we'd have an unstoppable closer. As it stands, when Hermanson misses, it ends up out of the park (that was an 85 mph heater).

Bottom nine. Captain Konerko at the plate. He absolutely drills a ball down the line, and it bounces off the foul pole. Typical Captain. Konerko is so solid, and he's so clutch. That's the first HR A's reliever Huston Street had allowed all year. Fitting that the Captain should christen that ship.

After the bomb, small ball. Carl Everett – today's hero – grounded a ball toward the hole, and ran it out hard enough for an infield single, just beating a beautiful leaping throw by Bobby Crosby. Rowand sacrificed Everett to second, and pinch runner Willie Harris entered the game.

Up came A.J. Unfortunately, down he went. Hambino was called out on an inside strike, and A.J., always demonstrative, flipped his bat as he strode angrily back to the dugout. *And the ump threw him out.* For flipping his bat. That's just ridiculous. It's a tense ballgame, and he doesn't even speak to the ump. He throws away the bat. Normally in these types of situations, I side with the ump, but that's silliness. Ozzie came charging out of the dugout to challenge the call, but to no avail.

Juan Uribe was due up next, but Ozzie pulled him in favor of Timo Perez. Timo is another excellent bench player. He has occasional pop, and he has above-average speed. Perhaps Ozzie's prolonged argument with the ump iced Street, because on the second pitch, Timo lined a gapper into right center, scoring Harris and tying the ballgame.

We lost the ballgame in the eleventh. Of course, that was rather predictable after Ozzie removed Hermanson in favor of

Luis Vizcaino. Vizcaino ranks third on my relievers' doghouse list, after Marte and Takatsu. I'd rather have Jenks in there than Vizcaino – Vizcaino has mediocre stuff and mediocre control. He committed the cardinal sin of walking Eric Chavez, the leadoff man. Dan Johnson nubbed one down the third base line, and it was first and second with no outs. Bobby Kielty laid down a terrific bunt to advance the runners.

Here the limitations of Vizcaino began to show more than usual. Instead of intentionally walking Nick Swisher, a hard-hitting lefty, to load the bases and get to Marco Scutaro, Vizcaino pitched to Swisher because we couldn't risk him walking in a run. Swisher made us pay with a long double to deep right. In came Chavez, but Dan Johnson was dogging it around the bases, and we put together a beautiful relay to nab him at the plate. Perez threw it in to Harris (playing second now) who rifled it to substitute catcher Chris Widger for the out. So it remained 9-8. We still had a shot.

Except that we went down silently in the bottom of the eleventh, and got swept.

I *hate* the A's.

On the upside, publicity for the book is going well. The pain of the A's series was assuaged by a wonderful incident on Fox News on July 8. I've known Ann Coulter for a few years now, ever since the start of my syndicated column, and she's a terrific lady. Friday night, before Sabbath, she was on Fox News' *Hannity and Colmes* to discuss the new vacancy on the Supreme Court. The conversation went like this:

COLMES: Who do you want?
COULTER: Thank you for asking. I want Ben Shapiro.
COLMES: Ben Shapiro.

COULTER: Yes. He just finished his first year at Harvard Law, 21 years old.

COLMES: You mean for a date or for the court?

COULTER: No, for the court. He's my candidate. He's very bright. He's already written one best-selling book.

(CROSSTALK)

COLMES: You want to put a 21-year-old guy on the court?

COULTER: Twenty-one, and he's just finished first year of Harvard Law.

COLMES: So you want someone who's going to be on the court for 50, 60 years? Is that — is that the whole idea?

COULTER: No, I just happen to like Ben Shapiro.

It was a real crackup – just hilarious. And then, today, David Limbaugh was on Fox News, and *he* recommended me for the Supreme Court. The Court is such a disaster at this point (and the concept of judicial supremacy in every area of American life is so repugnant to the basic framework of our government) that we need some judges who realize the difference between adjudicating and legislating.

Anyway, into the All-Star break we go. Good luck, Mark, Jon, Scotty and Paul! (And Kenny, can we *please* get rid of Vizcaino, Marte and Takatsu quietly, while all the focus is on the festivities in Detroit?)

	W	L	PCT	GB	Home	Away	Div	Streak
Chicago WSox	57	29	.663	---	30-15	27-14	26-5	Lost 3
Minnesota	48	38	.558	9	26-18	22-20	21-17	Won 1
Cleveland	47	41	.534	11	21-19	26-22	15-21	Lost 1
Detroit	42	44	.488	15	19-22	23-22	14-17	Won 1
Kansas City	30	57	.345	27 ½	19-27	11-30	8-24	Lost 1

July 12, 2005
DAD:

So Ben and I watched the All-Star Game together, and as we did, I reminisced about famous All-Star games I have seen. The one that will always stand out in my memory is the 1964 game, when the hated National League finally caught the American League and tied the series. For the next twenty years, they went on to win every game but one.

The game itself was a classic. I should have known something would happen when Mantle was replaced in center field in the bottom of the ninth as the NL came to bat. Dick Radatz, the huge flame-throwing reliever of the Red Sox, was on the mound in the ninth with the AL leading 4-3. These weren't the days of Mariano Rivera, who pitches one inning only; Radatz was on the mound for his third inning. Willie Mays, who owned the All-Star game, worked Radatz for a walk, stole second, and tied the score on an Orlando Cepeda bloop single to right when Joe Pepitone threw wildly to the plate as Cepeda went to second on the throw. Ken Boyer popped out, but Johnny Edwards, who batted lefty, was walked intentionally to set up the double play as Hank Aaron strode to the plate. Aaron never got the publicity in those days that he later received; I knew he was a great hitter, but because he played in the NL I didn't know how truly dangerous he was. Radatz somehow struck Aaron out, and I relaxed; two outs and Johnny Callison was up. I figured extra innings we'd get 'em. Then Callison got hold of one and launched it into the right-field bleachers; the NL had scored four runs in the ninth to win. It was awful. Had I known what would ensue the next twenty years, I really would have been upset.

Yet as the years went by, the All-Star game became less and less interesting, aside from occasional flashes like Pete Rose

159

slamming into Ray Fosse at the plate to win the 1970 game in the twelfth inning. So I was glad when baseball decided to revivify the game two years ago by upping the ante; the winning league got the home-field advantage in the World Series. And with the Sox on a tear, this game had real importance to me for the first time in forever.

Because Roy Halladay was hurt, Buehrle got the start. He was typically modest, saying Garland might have deserved it more. In the first, he gave up a lead-off single to Bobby Abreu, and then Carlos Beltran hit a bullet up the middle. I felt bad for Buehrle; he is such a great guy, and he was in trouble already. I didn't reckon with Miguel Tejada, the AL's shortstop. He flashed to his left, snared the ball, and flipped to his teammate Brian Roberts to start a spectacular double play. After that, Buehrle settled down, striking out three over the first two innings: Derrek Lee on a pitch high and tight that tied him up, Piazza on a pitch that dove and sent Piazza fishing, and freezing Jeff Kent with a breaking ball. Tejada hit a monster shot to left to put the AL ahead, and by the time Garland entered in the sixth the AL was up 5-0. Garland was a little shaky, walking two, but it was his first All-Star appearance (Buehrle's second) and he got out of it, leaving me looking forward to seeing Konerko and Podsednik get in some swings. Konerko did, striking out, but Scotty just got in as a defensive replacement. Still, it was the first time since 1994 the Sox have had four players on the team, and it felt great. After the NL had narrowed the lead to 7-5, Rivera shut the door in the ninth, and all I could think was if we can get to the Series, this game might matter a lot.

But, being a lifelong Sox fan, I know that's a big if.

July 17, 2005
BEN:

I'm thinking when, not if, after the series in Cleveland. Cleveland has some good young talent, and a pitching staff with a lot of potential (C.C. Sabathia, Jake Westbrook, etc.). They were roundly picked to finish ahead of us in the AL Central this year. We smoked 'em, pure and simple. Four up, four down. And we've got Detroit next. I love it.

The first game was a shocker: Jose Contreras did not give up a big inning. Seriously. Okay, you can stop laughing now. He went seven powerhouse innings, giving up only three hits. He struck out seven. When his control is decent, Contreras is tough to stop. That forkball falls right off the table, and he has the arm to chuck the fastball in the mid-90s. That made for a long day for the Indians.

We had a long day too, scoring only one run in the first inning off of Kevin Millwood. Tad Iguchi bounced one up the middle, and Millwood stupidly reached up with his bare hand to stab at it – he was lucky he missed it (he probably saved himself some DL time). Iguchi got a monster jump on the 1-1 pitch to Big Frank, and stole second easily. Frank proceeded to yank a low outside breaking ball all the way to the left field wall – in most other ballparks, it would have been gone (which is amazing, since Frank got very little of it). Jacobs Field, however, has that higher left-field wall, and Coco Crisp (who certainly has the best name in baseball, and possibly of all time) scaled it but couldn't keep the ball in his glove. 1-0, Sox.

That's how it stayed. We had some opportunities. The first ended with the bases loaded; in the top of the fifth, Scotty P. singled and stole second easily, but was stranded. The Indians had their opportunities as well – Contreras looked poised to give up his patented Big Inning in the fifth, when Jhonny Peralta smoked a one-out double into the right field corner. Aaron Boone followed with a sure single up the middle, except that Juan Uribe made a diving catch of his sizzling liner. Uribe is looking more and more like a Gold Glove candidate this year, although his glove had better be good since his bat leaves so much to be desired (.243 BA). But the play of the game was made by Aaron Rowand, who saved Scotty P. out there. In the bottom of the sixth, Travis Hafner hit a long fly ball into left field. Scotty didn't see it off the bat. He stood there with his arms out, puzzled, as Rowand raced over to help. Rowand caught the ball 15 ft. *behind* Podsednik to make the put-out.

Very heads up by Rowand – that's the sort of hustle we haven't seen in CF for the Sox in a long, long time. It was a day of good all-around defense on our part, though. Paulie made a beautiful over-the-shoulder grab on a pop-up down the right field line in the seventh. He's really an underrated defensive player to go along with that power bat.

If I was surprised by Contreras' performance, I was shocked by the bullpen situation. Cliff Politte got the first out in the eighth – no surprise there. But then Ozzie brought in The Loon, Damaso Marte, to pitch to Cleveland's lefties. He struck two out in a row. He was bringing the heat, and his control was there. Why can't he pitch like this all the time? In the ninth, he got another strikeout. Maybe the Sox have discovered the solution to the Marte problem. Has Marte had a breakthrough? Has he been reading Freud in his spare time? Has he discovered the lithium hidden in the clubhouse? Or is this simply an aberration?

Once again, Hermanson got the save. He pitched the final two outs and gave up a hit, but somehow induced a soft fly ball to Rowand to end the game. One more note: Scotty P. had three stolen bases, bringing his total on the year to 47. He truly makes the game exciting.

Game two was far less stressful. We got another great start from Freddy Garcia, who won his sixth decision in a row and hasn't lost in his last 11 starts, since May 14. His record is now 9-3. This time, he went seven innings, giving up only one run. Our Big Three – Buehrle, Garland, Garcia – is looking *very* strong.

More surprisingly, the Sox pinned a loss on C.C. Sabathia, Cleveland's big lefthander. Sabathia has killed us since he entered the league, but we put up four runs in the first inning. After inducing a Pablo Ozuna groundout and an Iguchi strikeout, Sabathia walked Big Frank and Paulie. He then struck out Carl Everett, but the pitch got past the catcher, and the bases were loaded. Jermaine Dye worked Sabathia for a walk, and we were up 1-0. Our two-outs-and-men-in-scoring-position machine, Rowand, smacked a sinking liner into center, and it dropped in to score Konerko and Everett. After Chris Widger (playing because he is a righty) lined a single into right, it was 4-0. We never looked back. In the sixth, we got two more runs on a wild pitch and a squeeze play – Ozzieball strikes again!

Final score: 7-1 Sox.

The third game looked like a repeat of the first two in terms of starting pitching. This time it was Mr. Slip 'N' Slide's turn, and he went seven innings, surrendering two runs. He didn't need to be as slippery as usual today; he gave up only three hits and no walks on the day.

We got our first run of the day in the second. After Paulie grounded out sharply to third and Hambino struck out on a good inside breaking ball, Jake Westbrook nailed Jermaine Dye

163

with a fastball on the knee. That was retaliation for Buehrle's first inning fastball to Travis Hafner's head, which was just plain dangerous – Hafner had to come out of the ballgame. The Westbrook retaliation was solid baseball any way you slice it, and the ump came out to warn both sides. After the ump-managers pow-wow, Dye immediately took off for second, catching the Indians sleeping, since no one was covering for them. Joe Crede made the Indians pay with a double past third base. It would be good to see Crede get going – I feel bad for him because his back's been bad this year, but I'd be lying if I said he hasn't been disappointing to this point in his career. He might be the most obvious piece of the puzzle right now that we can upgrade. He's a Gold Glover at third, and he can hit in the clutch, however, so that gives him some inherent value. I hope that the clutch side of him emerges down the stretch.

We got a couple more runs in the top of the third. Westbrook couldn't get the third out for the second straight inning. Rowand singled to right. Everett hit what looked like a blooper to left off the bat, but carried all the way to the wall for a stand-up double. Then the Captain cranked one off the left field wall for another double. 3-0.

Three more in the fifth. Mercury (sporting a strange-looking goatee) hit an infield single, and then his buddy Rowand hit one off the knuckles into center. Everett grounded out to the right side, advancing the runners, and the Indians intentionally walked Konerko. Westbrook is a ground ball pitcher, so it was a good move. Except that Hambino grounded a ball past Belliard at second base, and two runs scored. They gave Hambino an RBI and gave an error to Belliard. Dye grounded into a fielder's choice, but we got another run nonetheless: 6-0, Sox.

The Indians got two back in the bottom half, after Buehrle hit Casey Blake in the knee on an inside fastball. It was accidental, and everyone knew it. Belliard followed by ripping a double down the left-field line; Buehrle left the pitch in the middle of the plate and up in the zone, a real hitter's pitch. Both runners came around to score, Blake on a groundout by Aaron Boone and Belliard on a groundout by a catcher named Bard (his groundout was less lyrical than his name would suggest).

We got one back in the seventh, and went into the ninth with a 7-2 lead. What could go wrong?

Two words. Shingo. Takatsu.

Yes, he's still on the team after the All-Star break. Yes, his arm is still spaghetti. And yes, he almost blew this game for us.

He came on to start the ninth. Pitching to Casey Blake, Takatsu went from an 0-2 count to a walk. Ronnie Belliard fell down 0-2 before walking. It's as though with two strikes, Takatsu begins playing around. You can almost see him muttering to himself out there a la Jack Nicholson: "All work and no play makes Shingo a dull boy." Aaron Boone finally got a bat on the ball from Takatsu, hitting a single into left and scoring Blake. Out came Takatsu. Now what could go wrong?

Two words. Luis. Vizcaino.

Yes, he's still on the team. Yes, he's still having control problems. Yes, he almost blew the game for us.

He walked the first batter he saw, Victor Martinez. Out came Vizcaino. We were still up four runs. Now what could go wrong?

Two words. Damaso. Marte.

So much for my lithium theory. The first batter he faced, Grady Sizemore, flared one to center, scoring two. 7-5, men on

165

first and second, Marte pitching. At this point, pitching coach Don Cooper looked as though he was going to need some lithium himself. Coco Crisp strode to the plate, his lone hit against Marte on his career being a home run. Marte quickly went up 0-2 on Crisp, however, and the end looked near.

Not quite. Marte first went 3-2 on Crisp. Crisp then grounded one to Juan Uribe, who gunned low to first, where the Captain made a beautiful pick. Out. Game over.

Ozzie, for the sake of preserving your health, can you *please* convince Kenny to dump these guys?

Game four was back to normal for us. Jon Garland picked up his league-leading 14th win of the season, going six shutout innings before Cotts and Politte came in to mop up the rest. We got four runs in the first three innings. In the first, Scotty P. lined a double over the outstretched glove of Coco Crisp. He moved to third on a lineout to center by Iguchi, and scored on a tapper down the third-base line by Big Frank. In the second, with a man on first, Hambino absolutely drilled a ball over the center-field wall on a pitch around his ankles – the first HR by either team in the series. We got our last run in the fourth when Tad Iguchi crunched one into the left-field seats. The most telling statistic: we had eight hits in the game. So did the Indians. We got four runs. They got zero. That's the mark of a great ballclub.

That makes four consecutive quality starts from our staff. But that's been the recipe all year – great starting pitching, just enough hitting. Now if only our bullpen could come together …

Despite the stroke-inducing antics of our cadre of *One Flew Over the Cuckoo's Nest* relievers, we're divisional monsters – 30-5 within the division at this point. No wonder we've got that huge lead. That record should only get better with our trip to Detroit.

July 18, 2005
DAD:

It's been a heady time for the Sox and for Ben. For the Sox, sweeping the Indians may have put them in our dust for good. With Ann Coulter and David Limbaugh endorsing Ben for the Supreme Court on national TV, I reminded him to enjoy the moment. Ben and I spoke about the dovetailing of his success and the team's, and we were reminding ourselves to be cautious, quoting one of our favorite films, *Patton*.

At the end of the movie, George C. Scott as Patton (in one of the most acclaimed performances ever) is heard on the voice-over recalling the triumphal return of Roman conquerors, and what happened after the victory parade: "A slave stood behind the conqueror, holding a golden crown, and whispering in his ear a warning: that all glory is fleeting."

Of course, Ben knows all that; he just thinks it's hilarious that Ann and David did that. He also knows that it's true; they know how uncompromising Ben is. That's the real message: that they want someone on the court who will stick to his guns, and someone who will be there for fifty or sixty years.

I suppose his uncompromising stance can be traced in part to me; I'm a stickler for loyalty to principle. It goes for baseball, too. Wherever I've lived, I've been a die-hard Sox fan. I raised my kids in Los Angeles, but there was never any question of which team they would root for.

For a long time, I didn't think that was enough. Of course, we went to Angels' games when they played the Sox, and when we visited our folks in Chicago we went to the Sox games, but I felt there was something lacking.

That feeling was assuaged one day in 1990. Ben was six, and I stopped by a small baseball card store in Burbank to get him some cards. To my astonishment, there was a huge brown metal sign that read Comiskey Park with an arrow pointing the way. It had a big hole at the top where it had been anchored to the concrete post, and had obviously been used over the Dan Ryan Expressway. I excitedly asked the proprietor of the store where he got it.

"When they tore down old Comiskey last year, there was some stuff lying around," he said. "They put up new signs, so they left this on the ground, and I picked it up."

"How much do you want for it?"

"Oh . . . twenty-five dollars?"

"Great!"

I answered so quickly, he was probably angry at himself for not asking for more. When I got home, I proudly showed it to my wife. I wanted to keep it in the house, but since we had a small house, that got nipped in the bud, so it went in the backyard.

That night, it started to rain, hard. I leaped out of bed, threw my robe on, and headed for the door.

"Where are you going?" my wife asked, confused.

"I've gotta get the sign!" I called back.

"Wait, David, wait!" she called, laughing.

"*What*," I said, irritated at her for delaying me, as I paused at the door.

She caught up to me and held my arm. "David, that sign has been over the highway for years . . . *outside*. In the snow, and rain, and sleet." She waited to see my reaction, trying to keep herself from laughing.

"Oh, yeah. That was pretty dumb, I guess . . ."

The success of our marriage is that my wife never has to have the last word.

We got the last word today. Well, actually it was Joe Crede who got the last word. He stole the show. After El Duque gave up a lead-off HR to Inge on the first pitch, Crede robbed Rodriguez in the second with a leaping catch of a liner, twisting his body so he could stab the ball high to his right. In the third, he doubled to right-center and scored on Scotty's sac fly, narrowly beating the throw to the plate.

By the seventh, it was 4-1 Detroit, and our winning streak looked to be over at four. But in the seventh, after Sean Douglass had made it look easy against us, allowing only three hits and two walks, Alan Trammell brought in Chris Spurling, who was 2-0 with a 2.10 ERA. We hammered him. First, Konerko hit a high fly ball that somehow carried just over the left-field wall. Then Dye doubled, A.J. singled, and Crede was up. Spurling hung a breaking ball, and Crede absolutely walloped it. It landed somewhere between the left-field wall and the planet Venus, and I think Venus may have been closer. As soon as Crede hit it, he dropped his bat and clenched his fists. It's the most emotion I've seen out of him all year. Uribe immediately followed with a liner over the same wall, Thomas muscled one out in the eighth, and we won going away, 7-5. It was a terrific comeback, and this time we won by two runs! At this rate, we won't need a bullpen.

Just kidding, of course, but perhaps I'm not alone in my thinking. Shingo Takatsu was designated for assignment, and no more spaghetti in the Cell. Apparently, Ozzie and Kenny have decided that they are going to give Jenks all the time he needs to master the craft. Kenny was quoted as saying, "We've got something special that cannot only help us in the short term, but in the long term as well. When you look out on the open market for those types of guys that possibly could be available toward the end of the month, you very quickly realize they're not available. They're not out there. If we can grow one of our own into the role with the time we have left, we're going to be better off."

At the rate we're going, Jenks will have all the time in the world.

July 24, 2005
DAD:

Maybe not. The Tigers killed us in the second game of the series, broke our hearts in the third game and set us up for the entrance of the defending world champion Red Sox for a four-game set.

The second game of the Tigers series can be summed up simply: Jeremy Bonderman pitched well, Contreras stunk. Bonderman went eight, giving up only three hits, two walks and one run. Contreras did his usual I've-got-a-secret-horrendous-inning-stuffed-up-my-sleeve-guess-which-one-it-is   routine, except that this time there was a surprise: there were two horrendous innings, the second and the sixth. The man simply loses focus. In the second, after Crede couldn't handle a bullet to his left (I can't blame him, it was a rifle shot) Infante hit a three-run HR. In the sixth, Contreras came apart, giving up four doubles in five batters. We lost, 7-1.

Aside from that, Contreras was just *fine*. Will someone please give this guy some No-Doz?

The rubber game of the series was truly disheartening, because we deserved to lose. Freddy Garcia had good stuff, but he hung a pitch to Shelton for a two-run blast in the first, and we were playing catch-up all day long. In the sixth, Freddy wild-pitched Pudge Rodriguez home, and it was 4-2, Tigers. How many wild pitches does he have this year, anyway? Chris Widger cut the lead to 4-3 with a solo shot in the seventh, but in the ninth, the Tigers finally routed Garcia, with an Infante HR and a line shot through the middle that almost took Freddy's head off. Ozzie, who had kept Garcia in out of loyalty, (to try for the win should the Sox come back?) pulled him in favor of Politte, who simply didn't have it, and by the time the dust had cleared from his work and Cotts' the Tigers had smoked us for four runs, and our comeback in the ninth was too high a mountain to climb. Although, to be fair, we got it to 8-6 with two on and had the winning run at the plate with Iguchi, but he tapped back to the pitcher to end the game. Yuck.

BEN: In Boston they're probably taking the White Sox for granted.

DAD: They're entitled; they're the champs and we haven't done anything yet.

The Red Sox series really meant something to everyone. The general consensus in the media seems to be that the White Sox are simply not in the same class as the Yankees and Red Sox, and I was eager for the Sox to prove that was a lot of hooey.

The first game, the atmosphere was electric, like a play-off game. It had to be a learning experience for our Sox. They made three critical errors, and it cost them big-time. There's just no margin for error when you play a team this good. The Red Sox got away with their sometimes sloppy play in the Series last year because they had that monster lineup, but we don't have the hitting to afford such mistakes.

We hit Clement reasonably hard. Everett slammed a two-run HR in the first, the Captain and Knievel (hmmmm, sounds like a pop group) both went deep in the fourth, and we were up 4-1. Mr. Slip'N'Slide slipped in the fifth, when Damon doubled, Renteria hit one deep that glanced of a racing Knievel's glove for a double (a ball that he probably should have caught), and then Ortiz blooped one barely over a leaping Crede, and it was 4-3. The first key play occurred in the seventh, when with Damon and Renteria on first and second, Ortiz lined one to Iguchi's right, and Iguchi booted it toward center. Then he compounded his mistake by throwing badly to home, allowing Damon to score, tie the game, and the other runners to move up. After a walk to load the bases, Politte entered, struck out Varitek, and induced Millar to fly to right. Timo saw there was no way to get Renteria at home, so instead he gunned to third to get Ortiz, but Renteria had scored before the tag on Ortiz, so it was 5-4 Red Sox.

Curt Schilling relieved in the eighth. I like Schilling. A lot. When sports pundits speak of athletes as warriors, I want to throw up, but he's one of the few to whom it applies. Of course, after pitching at great risk last year in the playoffs and Series that's hardly a state secret. It was the most courageous performance I've seen since what I think is the greatest game anyone ever threw: Koufax's seventh game shutout of the Twins on two days' rest in the seventh game of the '65 Series, a game that I watched in awe because the Twins had a line-up that matched today's Red Sox for power.

I have another reason to like Schilling: he's an overtly religious man, and anyone who sincerely gives credit to God for his athletic achievements is okay by me.

Schilling entered, and although I admire him, that doesn't supersede my love for the Sox. With one out, Rowand doubled, and then Crede doubled him home, tying the score 5-5. Another clutch hit by Crede; it's becoming a habit, but he died on second when Uribe grounded out.

I felt confident entering the ninth, we were at home, but I did have misgivings with Vizcaino on the mound. With one out, Manny Ramirez was at the plate, and he lofted a high foul ball that Crede, running toward the stands, should have caught, although it was a tough play. He slightly overran the ball, and waved at it as it came down. It popped out of his glove (two hands, Joe!) for our third error, and on the next pitch Manny drilled a HR to left. Ballgame.

The mistakes killed us, and the Sox knew it. Buehrle said after the game, "We've got to get back to playing our kind of baseball. The past few games we've had a couple errors, haven't been hitting the ball, we haven't been pitching, and we haven't been playing the type of White Sox baseball we did at the beginning of the season." Yup.

The second game we beat them the way they're supposed to beat us: with power. Wakefield had us baffled the first time around; nine up, nine down. Then Rowand tied the score at 1-1 when he homered to left in the fourth, and in the sixth, we sank their battleship with two torpedoes. The first was a three-run shot to right by Hambino, who caught a knuckler just as it dipped low and golfed it into the right field bleachers. Moments later, after Graffanino (the Red Sox just acquired him from the Royals – hope we don't see *him* in the playoffs) had booted a grounder,

Uribe lined a three-run shot to left, and we were up 7-1, ultimately winning 8-4. Garland looked exceptionally strong, winning his fifteenth, and the other great pitching story was Jenks, who struck out the only two batters he faced, Millar and Mirabelli, with fall-off-the-table curveballs. This from a guy who throws 100 mph heat. Whew. If he can always throw like that, Rivera will soon be a memory.

I liked our chances in game three. El Duque was 7-2 and Wade Miller was 2-4, and we were coming off a strong game. But we wasted an excellent performance by El Duque. He made one mistake, a two-run blast to Manny (who else?) in the first, but after that he was masterful, allowing only three hits. We had two chances; one in the third and one in the ninth. In the third, we loaded the bases with one out, but Everett struck out and Konerko (who, I've become convinced, goes to another level in the clutch) uncharacteristically flied out to right. In the eighth, Marte hung a curve to Varitek, who pounced on it and jolted it out to right, giving them an extra run to play with, 3-0. In the ninth Schilling came in and gave up a liner off the wall by the Captain and then a blooper by Hambino to put runners on the corners, but Schilling proved to be our match. Rowand, the tying run, hit a hard grounder up the middle, but Schilling ain't Schilling just for throwing. He has good fielding form, too, which he displayed by snaring the grounder and turning it into a 1-6-3 double play. Two batters later, we were done. It looked as though we could play with the Bosox in this one, but they had the extra edge that comes with having won the whole thing before.

I'm convinced there is nothing more important than experience (at almost fifty, that seems like a useful bromide to sell to my four children), and I've always wondered why teams, when they're hiring managers or players, don't look to see who has won before. Notice how championships seem to follow certain players around, like Pete Rose or Jack Morris? They knew how to win. That's why I'm glad the Sox picked Ozzie to manage; he had won the whole thing with the Marlins as their third-base coach, and he saw how it was done. The Bosox have that extra confidence that comes from being champs, and I hoped that we could learn from them how it's done.

If the last game was any indication, we did. Contreras pitched extremely well, considering that he was facing the Bosox. Ortiz hit a solo HR in the first, and they picked up another run in the second, but there weren't any hugely bad innings from him, which was a surprise. Meanwhile, Konerko doubled home two in the first, helped by Manny playing the field the way only he can, kicking the ball for a while (Manny giveth, and Manny taketh away). In the second, after they had tied it at 2-2, Scotty doubled, and Iguchi, who was the real hero of this game, homered to left. When Varitek homered in the sixth, and the Bosox got two men on, Ozzie went to Cotts, who was magnificent. He ended the inning by getting Damon a fly ball to Scotty, then fanned two of the next three in the seventh, setting the stage for Politte, who after giving up a hit, retired the side.

Leading 5-3 in the seventh, we got a key insurance run. Damon was cheating, playing Scotty shallow, and Mercury made him pay by lashing one deep to left-center. Damon gave it all he had, but he couldn't quite get there, and Scotty had a double, later coming around to score. Marte came on in the ninth; I understood Ozzie wanted to play the percentages, Marte, a lefty, against Damon, Mueller, and Ortiz. So what does Marte do? He walks Damon, gets Mueller, and *walks* Ortiz, bringing the tying run (Manny, who else?) to the plate. On the broadcast, Hawk said disgustedly, ". . . second walk of the inning." The Goateed one entered to face Manny, and I thought, not again. We won a moral victory, though, Manny only singled, making it 6-4, and then Hermanson got Nixon to fly out to Scotty and Olerud to end the game by grounding out to Iguchi, appropriately enough, and we had a split with the big boys.

By golly, I think we *are* in their class. Damon said after the game, "They go out there with little fanfare, and are quietly taking care of business." I like that Very Much.

	W	L	PCT	GB	Home	Away	Div	Streak
Chicago WSox	64	33	.660	---	33-19	31-14	31-7	Won 1
Minnesota	53	45	.541	11 1/2	29-22	24-23	23-20	Lost 1
Cleveland	51	48	.515	14	25-26	26-22	17-27	Won 2
Detroit	49	49	.500	15 1/2	24-26	25-23	21-22	Won 1
Kansas City	36	62	.367	28 1/2	21-28	15-34	12-28	Won 1

August 2, 2005
BEN:

I just got back in town from Oklahoma City, where I was hosting a local talk radio program. It was a lot of fun – I've always wondered what it would be like to host a show, rather than be a guest on one. It's a very different job. You control the callers, the topics, and the guests, which means you have to be over-prepared all of the time. Callers and guests make the situation a lot easier, but this was a three-hour show, and since Oklahoma City is a relatively small market and I was hosting a midday program, the number of calls was low. That meant that I had to monologue for about two hours every day, and since I speak so quickly anyway, I covered a ton of material. The higher-ups at WKY were pretty happy with my performance, especially since this was the first time I had ever hosted. I'm sending the CDs of those shows to some people over at WSB in Atlanta, which is a much larger station (Neal Boortz's flag station, Sean Hannity's former flag station); they have spoken about having me guest-host a night show. The key for me is to keep a sense of humor on the air (I often get very serious when I talk politics) and to *slow down*. That means preparing far less, since I can think on my feet and let the audience think along with me. After hosting, I've got the basic idea now: it's a conversation, not a monologue, despite the fact that you're the only one with the microphone. No matter what happens, it was a fantastic learning experience.

Oklahoma City was an interesting place in and of itself. The Midwest is much friendlier than big coastal cities like LA or NY. The first thing that struck me was the fact that when you walk down the street and you catch someone's eye, you don't immediately look away (as you do in Los Angeles, for fear that the person might have road rage) – instead, you greet them. The first time someone did that, I was taken aback, but it certainly creates a better community atmosphere than the "better look away" mentality so prevalent in the cities.

I also liked Oklahoma City because nobody was afraid of the word "God" there. You could bring Him up in conversation without having to couch it in terms of "I happen to believe that . . ." or "Listen, I know you probably don't agree, but . . ." Having respect for the Bible in common with other citizens does build a nice sense of commonality.

On a far smaller scale, baseball does the same thing. No matter the political or moral perspective of the person you're talking to, you can usually talk baseball. It's become a part of our common heritage. Is it as important as sharing a common morality? Of course not. But having *something* in common is certainly helpful.

If the Sox keep playing like this, everyone should be talking about them. After blowing two out of three to pitiful Kansas City, we went into Baltimore and swept a four-game series. Our lead in the AL Central is now a whopping 15 games, and Dad and I are both thinking World Series. Of course, we'll have to see how we fare against Boston and New York first.

The first game against Kansas City went the way it was supposed to. We took it, 14-6. Freddy Garcia didn't pitch well, giving up five runs in six innings, but he pitched well enough for the win, since we absolutely smoked Zack Greinke. This despite a lineup featuring Timo Perez in the two-hole and Aaron Rowand batting third, due to Frank Thomas' visit to a doctor to discuss his left ankle again. This is the problem with signing big long-term contracts – even if the player looks healthy at the time, he could wear down, as Thomas obviously has.

It didn't matter much to our offense. Rowand singled down the third-base line in the first, and was followed by soft liner to center from the Captain. Hambino crunched a fat fastball off the right-field wall, and Rowand came around to score.
Jermaine Dye lined one into left-center, and both Hambino and Paulie scored. Joe Crede smoked the ball into left field for another single, and Dye came around to score on a botched tag attempt by the Royals' "Ranger" John Buck. Willie Harris flared one to center, and Crede scored. 5-0.

It was 9-3 in the bottom of the sixth when the Royals began to come back. David Dejesus hit a single into right, and Terrence Long followed with a bomb to right. All of a sudden, it looked like this might become a game. Mike Sweeney lacerated the first pitch he hit to deep right field, and Dye took off running after it. At the last moment, he leaped up and grabbed it, saving us a HR and basically ending the Royals' night. After Dye's problems with a spider bite last week (his lymph nodes inflated and he had to be put on IV), players started calling him Spiderman. Apparently, he has indeed mutated into a wall-crawler.

We just kept pouring it on all night long. We ended up with 22 hits, and Pierzynski hit another HR. The only other highlight worth mentioning was the performance of Bobby Jenks, who went two innings and gave up one run in relief.

Before the game, Ozzie said that he thought we wouldn't make any powerhouse trades, despite all the rumors flying about Jason Schmidt and A.J. Burnett. After this game, it didn't look like we'd need much of anything to maintain our winning ways.

Then there was game two. Buehrle started for us, and was fantastic through five innings before suddenly deciding it was time for an impromptu imitation of Jose Contreras. In the sixth, he got racked. He gave up a single to Chip Ambres. Mike Sweeney, who saw Pablo Ozuna playing deep at third, dropped down a beautiful bunt and beat it out. Sweeney is one of the most solid players in baseball year in and year out – how many power hitters know how to drop a bunt like that? (Note: Every time he comes to bat, the title song from *Sweeney Todd* runs through my head. "Swing your bat, high, Sweeney! Hold it to the sky!")

Emil Brown followed with a double down the right-field line, scoring Ambres, and it was 2-1. Matt Stairs (boy, do the Royals have a team full of great names; it's as though they recruit by name alone; then again, maybe they do – look at their record) grounded to short, and Juan Uribe, who is often Gold Glove caliber, made a dumb throw to the plate to try to cut down

Sweeney. He threw wildly, and Sweeney scored easily. 3-1. After Angel Berroa was intentionally walked, Mark Teahen golfed a grounder down the right field line. Everyone scored (including Teahen) when the ball was thrown wildly to the plate. In this game, it looked like the Sox had chosen players solely based on their inability to throw the ball to the plate.

Or to hit. Jose Lima, who was brought to the mound via Moped, threw aside his walker long enough to shut us completely down. He went six innings, giving up five hits and only one run. Final score: 7-1 Royals. What was that about no major trades, Ozzie? How about a bat?

The third game was a heartbreaker. When you play the Royals, you shouldn't have to be in the position of having your heart broken. But then again, we didn't look very much like ourselves in this series.

Jon Garland got the start for us, and he pitched very well yet again, going seven innings and surrendering three runs. He should have gotten his sixteenth win, but instead got a no-decision. Runelvys Hernandez got the start for them, and he, too, pitched well until the fifth and sixth, when he gave up five runs total. Still, this one went to the 13th before we lost it.

It was a shutout ballgame until the fifth, with both sides playing solid baseball. Our defense was spectacular. In the bottom of the second, Uribe made a terrific play up the middle. Matt Stairs grounded one past second base; Uribe raced over, slid to one knee, turned around, popped up, and gunned to first for the putout. In the bottom of the third, Jermaine Dye loped to a sinking liner, slid, and came up with it.

We got our first run in the fifth, when Uribe followed up his great defensive effort with a sac fly to drive in Joe Crede from third. In the sixth, Dye followed up *his* great defensive effort with a three-run bomb over the left field wall, making it 4-0 Sox. We got another run on a Joe Crede rocket to extend our lead to 5-0 before Hernandez got out of the inning.

Then it all came unraveled. In the sixth, Mike Sweeney took a low, outside breaking ball and yanked it out of the park for a two-run blast ("He knew how civilized men behaved, he never forgot and he never forgave"). Then, in the eighth, after Garland's exit, Neal Cotts came in. He's usually solid, and this outing was no exception. The big mistake was made by substitute first baseman Ross Gload (or, as my younger sister likes to call him, Fat Gload – he's actually in pretty good shape), who blew a sure double play ball, leaving runners on first and third for the Royals. Cliff Politte entered, and Mike Sweeney gave him the same treatment he gave Garland, taking him deep and tying up the ballgame. ("For power he deserves a nod. Does Sweeney Todd. The Demon Royal of Fleet Street.") When Sweeney hit it, all twelve of the Royals fans in attendance went berserk.

Damaso Marte pitched well in relief, going 1 1/3 innings and striking out three while walking two. Today must have been his manic day (rather than his depressive day). So did Hermanson, who went 1 1/3 and gave up only a hit and a walk. So did Bobby Jenks, who pitched two innings and struck out only two while shutting out the Royals.

In the twelfth, we had a terrible sequence when Juan Uribe, who was on first, took off for second on a hit and run. Unfortunately, Scotty missed the ball completely, and Ranger Buck threw out Uribe. Then, Scotty got on base and was picked off first. Yuck and double yuck.

Then, in the thirteenth, with Takatsu off the team, in came the newly elevated second man on my relief totem pole of stinkage: Luis Vizcaino. When you look in the dictionary under "mediocre," there is a picture of Luis Vizcaino. He promptly gave up a single to David Dejesus, another single to Chip Ambres, and *another* single to Sweeney. ("Sweeney was smooth. Sweeney was subtle. Sweeney would blink, the Sox would scuttle.") Bases loaded. Rowand made a play on that Sweeney ball that was interesting, by the way – he faked as though he could catch the ball, and it kept Dejesus from scoring. Ozzie pulled in Dye to play up the middle, and Scotty and Rowand to play as shallow as possible. It looked like a softball field out there.

Of course, none of this maneuvering ended up mattering. After striking out Joe McEwing (and with Dye moving back to RF), Vizcaino served up a fat breaking ball to Emil Brown, who shot it into left for a single to win the ballgame.

What an awful series.

	W	L	PCT	GB	Home	Away	Div	Streak
Chicago WSox	65	35	.650	---	33-19	32-16	32-9	Lost 2
Minnesota	54	46	.540	11	29-22	25-24	23-20	Won 1
Cleveland	52	50	.510	14	25-26	27-24	17-27	Lost 1
Detroit	50	51	.495	15 1/2	24-26	26-25	21-22	Lost 1
Kansas City	38	63	.376	27 1/2	23-29	15-34	14-29	Won 2

The Sox announced before the first Baltimore game that Big Frank was likely out for the season. On the one hand, this was a big blow – it meant that we're going to go the rest of the season without a big bat aside from Konerko. On the other hand, this also means that the grind-it-out style of play we utilized before Thomas' return will be the main style of play from now on. With Thomas gone, our lineup is more predictable, less power-oriented. And to be honest, centering the lineup around

Thomas seems problematic to me anyway, since he was such a clubhouse cancer before this season.

For a lot of Sox fans, losing Big Frank for the season means we'll have to try to make it without our key player; that we'll have to suck it up that much more. I called Dad to get his reaction, and he reminded me of an incident in Little League that I'd forgotten . . .

DAD:

"Joey's mom called last night and told me that he can't come to the game tomorrow," I informed Ben, as we drove across through the city to the game.

"That means Phil will have to catch, right, Dad?" he asked.

"Guess so." Phil was our back-up catcher, and did a pretty fair job, but Joey was irreplaceable at bat, so he'd be sorely missed.

"Is Papa coming today?"

"Yup. He's meeting us at the field."

"Cool," Ben said.

Twenty minutes later, we arrived at the field, and as we unloaded the bag of bats and balls from the car, we were met by four kids from the team, who charged up to us yelling at the same time. My father was already there, waiting on the field with the rest of the team, and waved to us as we headed his way, surrounded by the shouting boys.

"Mr. Shapiro! Mr. Shapiro!"

"Whoa! One at a time, guys," I cautioned them, still crossing toward my father.

The shortstop yelled, "Let me tell him!" The other boys quieted down.

"What's the problem," I asked, as we reached the field and my father hugged Ben.

"Phil can't come. He's real sick," the shortstop said. "Who's gonna catch?"

"Anyone volunteer?" I asked, reaching down to take the bats out of the bag.

Silence.

I stood up, with three bats in my hands, and looked around at the team. "Anyone interested?"

More silence.

"Well, someone's got to catch, guys," I said, slightly exasperated.

No one said a word.

"Sure, I'll catch, Dad," Ben said from behind me.

"No one else wants to try?" I asked again.

"Let Ben do it," one of the boys said.

"I don't want you to catch," I said quietly to Ben.

He gave me a knowing glance. "I'll be okay, Dad," he reassured me, reaching down to strap on his shin guards. "The team needs me to do it."

"Make sure you keep your bare hand behind you," I reminded him. "If Johnny Bench could do it, so can you."

"I will, Dad."

My father approached me. "You're going to let him catch?" he said worriedly. "What about his hands?"

"I know, I know," I muttered.

I had been playing piano since I was six, and when I was fourteen, I started playing in clubs around Chicago. When I was a sophomore in high school, the football coach, Hal Samorian, asked me if I'd like to try out for the football team, since I was reasonably big. Excited, I told my parents that night, and to my surprise, my father adamantly refused to let me play on the team. He said he was worried that I would rack up my hands. (He was also worried that I'd tear up a knee, but I didn't learn that until years later.) As a catcher in Little League, I had injured my hands more than once, and my father knew football was a lot rougher. When he refused to let me play football, I was severely disappointed, but later I realized he was probably right.

Now I was letting Ben play catcher, and the problem was that Ben, at eleven, had become a terrific violinist, playing for events around the city. (When he played at one event, Larry King introduced him as someone who wanted to be "the first Orthodox rabbi to sit on the Supreme Court and give a recital at Carnegie Hall . . . meaning the Court will have to close early on Fridays.")

My father continued, "You're really going to let him catch?"

I grimaced. "Do I have a choice?"

That game was the most stomach-churning game I ever watched. Every time a pitch was thrown, I went nuts inside. My father was the most vocal I had ever seen him at a game.

"Great catching, Ben," he'd shout. Or, "Way to block that ball, Ben," as Ben would block a ball in the dirt. As the coach of the team, I had to restrain myself from cheering too much for Ben, but I was never prouder of him. Ben never forgot to keep his right hand behind him when the pitches were thrown, and even threw a runner out at second base. We won, and after the game, Ben exhaustedly ripped off his mask as the team excitedly ran off the field, amazed that we had won without Joey. No one congratulated him on the job he did, but he trudged up to me and my father with his eyes shining.

"I did okay, Papa?" he asked my father.

"You were terrific, Ben," my father chortled, hugging him. "Just terrific!"

"You okay, Dad?" Ben asked, turning to me as I knelt to help him take off his shin guards.

I took off one shin guard without looking up at him. "Piece of cake," I said.

Then I looked up at him and my father. They were both grinning.

BEN:

Dad said that on that day, he learned two lessons: that he had to let go and let my life take whatever course it would, and that sometimes the best thing that can happen for a team is to lose its best player so the team learns self-reliance. I wondered how the Sox would respond in Baltimore after the loss of Big Frank.

The first game in Baltimore was a showcase for El Duque, who is now 8-3. He was in trouble throughout, but his Houdini-esque escapes were a wonder to behold. His finest was in the fourth, when up 4-1 (because of a three-run bomb from the Captain) with two Orioles on base, he hung a 3-2 pitch to an off-the-juice Sammy Sosa, who smashed it down the left field line. It looked like a HR for sure, but curved foul. On the next pitch, Hernandez struck Sosa out. It was so typical. The man looks positively nervous with the bases empty.

Carl Everett added a two-run dinger to extend the final score to 7-2; Politte was great in relief, and shockingly, so were Marte and Vizcaino. Boy, baseball seems easy when you win.

Game two was more difficult. We literally knocked out their starter, Daniel Cabrera, in the first inning, when Joe Crede lined a ball off Cabrera's hand. The O's relief was pretty good,

though. Jose Contreras was starting for us, which automatically meant that victory would be more difficult. This time his "secret inning" was the third, when he surrendered four runs. We were up 2-0 at the time, so that put us in a hole. Their leadoff man, Jay Gibbons, chopped one toward short, and Crede cut over to take it. He threw wildly to first, and Gibbons was on. Sal Fasano, the O's backup catcher, hit a chopper up the middle.
David Newhan worked Contreras for a walk. Bases loaded for Brian Roberts, the season's biggest surprise. He doubled down the left field line, tying up the game. Ozzie came out to the mound, trying to get Contreras to pull himself together. That's somewhat like telling Kirstie Alley to stop acting like an idiot. Contreras heeded Ozzie's advice by throwing a wild pitch, scoring Newhan. Eric Byrnes then hit an RBI double down the left field line. 4-2.

We tied it in the top of the fifth. Bruce Chen, who makes spot starts for the O's, came in. Joe Crede reached down on a low breaking ball, and drove the ball into the left field stands. Crede might be starting to hit, which would be good for him, since there are a few available 3Bs on the market. Uribe then doubled down the right field line and scored on a hard single to right-center by Tad Iguchi, who has been rather silent of late.

The O's struck back in the sixth against Contreras, who pulled a second "secret inning" out of his hat. He started the inning by walking Miguel Tejada. Don Cooper came out to talk to Contreras, who was not too receptive to the message: on the next pitch, Rafael Palmiero lofted a ball into the right field stands. A pan of the dugout showed Don Cooper, who looked like he was ready to go out there and punch Contreras in the gut.

A brief digression. Palmiero has a beautiful swing. He impressed me earlier this year when he appeared before Congress and, glaring into the camera, stated that he had never taken steroids. Today, Palmiero was suspended by the MLB for testing positive for steroids. This is just repulsive. Steroids in baseball are a sin – I've written before calling for all records set by steroid freaks to be wiped from the books (including the McGwire and Bonds HR records, which should be given back to Roger Maris). For Palmiero to sit before Congress and the American people and lie about his steroid use is beyond disgusting. The league shouldn't suspend Palmiero, they should ban him for life.

Anyway, back to the game. All remained silent until the eighth, when the Sox took the game back in dramatic fashion. Chris Ray, a young gun for the O's, came into the game. Ray came in with an 0.92 ERA. He left with a 2.61 ERA. He issued a walk to Tad Iguchi to lead off the inning. Everett popped up to Tejada, but Captain laced one into the gap in left-center, putting men on first and third with one out. Hambino, who had doubled and singled earlier, came to the plate. Ray threw a low breaking ball over the meat of the plate, and Hambino went down and *got it*. He *murdered* it. And all of a sudden, it was 7-6. We got another run in the eighth, and one in the ninth. Jenks and Marte to Hermanson, and it was all over, 9-6.

Game three was a laugher. That was nice, after all the drama of the previous game. Freddy Garcia did his usual workmanlike job, going seven innings and giving up three runs. And we tore apart Rodrigo Lopez, one of the up-and-coming starters for the O's. The game was over after two innings. It was 5-0 after the first, thanks to two RBI from Dye, two from Crede, who *is* warming up, and an RBI from Uribe. It was 8-1 after the second (score RBI for Konerko, Rowand, and Dye).

That was the game. Except that beanball wars broke out. Aside from hitting Rowand in the first, in the top of the third,

Todd Williams nailed Tad Iguchi with a purpose fastball to the ribs. Or maybe it got away from the O's, since the O's pitching couldn't hit the broad side of a barn.

We poured it on some more in the sweep game, which we took 6-3. The big story of the game wasn't our solid play, though – it was the ejection of Mark Buehrle in the sixth. His ejection broke his 49-game six-inning-per-game streak. It was amazing.

But first some back-story. Daniel Cabrera started for the O's and immediately gave up a run in the first when he walked Timo Perez, wild-pitched him to second, allowed Pablo Ozuna to move Perez to third on a slow roller down the third-base line, and surrendered a sizzling liner to center to Carl Everett, scoring Perez.

Our story truly begins in the top of the sixth. Everett singled to left to lead it off. Paulie struck out, but Cabrera chucked one up and in to Hambino, nailing him on the shoulder. Dye singled to right to score Everett, and the Sox had the lead.

Now, that beanball to Hambino looked like it got away from Cabrera – who throws a purpose pitch in a tie ballgame with one out and a man on? Still, as a pitcher, you can't tolerate that sort of stuff. So after Buehrle got the first two outs and Sammy Sosa singled to right, Buehrle threw a fastball behind B.J. Surhoff. The ump immediately tossed him.

Good for Buehrle. After the game, he told the press, "We had a guy hit yesterday and then A.J. gets hit," Buehrle said. "Their catcher sets up away and the pitcher comes up and in and hits [Pierzynski]. Obviously, you guys were out there and you've seen the game. People who know baseball know what happened." Of the streak, he stated, "It was fun while it lasted and unfortunate the way it ended. But we won the game, and I'll just start up another one." Ozzie was (as usual) more blunt about the streak: "We don't care about the streak. . . . If Buehrle don't make the Hall of Fame because of that, then blame it on me, the team or the umpire. We are not here to break records. Our record is to win games and everyone in that room knows that."

This is the type of incident that can define a team. It takes real unity to make that kind of pitch. And the Sox went out and took it to the O's from there on, scoring one in the seventh and three in the eighth, one on a bomb by Hambino, which he thoroughly enjoyed. Ozzie remarked on the mettle of the team, saying that they won this one "for Buehrle."

It's been a busy week. Our big trade deadline move was picking up Geoff Blum (who?) from San Diego. He's a bench player who can sub at first or third. Not exactly Griffey or Schmidt. Meanwhile, Torii Hunter of Minnesota is out for the season after hurting himself severely while leaping for a fly ball. You never like to see that, but as a Sox partisan, it does make things easier for us in the Central. Of course, I wasn't too worried about the Twins anyway, the way we're playing (or Cleveland either, which just passed the Twins for second in the division). We're barely visible on the horizon to Minnesota and Cleveland, and we're pulling away even further.

It's really starting to hit me: could this be for real?

August 7, 2005
DAD:

Now I know how it feels to be a Yankee fan. One week into August, we've played .500 baseball in the last six games, and our lead has shrunk from fifteen games to thirteen. Yawn. Instead of the anxiety that comes from worrying about every game, slowly I'm taking the long view: just play decent baseball and the division is a lock.

With that in mind, each game becomes slightly less important and I start to examine how individuals are doing; looking for potential weaknesses in the team, wondering as the trade deadline approaches whether the Sox should make a deal. One strong rumor being floated around is a deal for Ken Griffey Jr.

Now, call me irresponsible, call me unreliable, call me anything you darn want to, but *don't* call me and tell me you're a Sox fan and you don't salivate at the very idea of adding Griffey to the lineup. I don't care that he's thirty-five; even if he were fifty per cent of what he once was he would still be a tremendous force in the lineup. According to reports, the Sox would have to pay him through 2008. If we can shelter Frank Thomas through his numerous injuries, we can shelter Griffey. Griffey would have to agree to the trade, and strangely, he has mentioned four teams to which he would be willing to go, and the Sox aren't one of them, presumably because the Sox train in Tucson, and he makes his home in Orlando. This sounds fishy to me. For one month out of the year he'd pass up a chance to play for a World Series ring? If it's true, it just goes to show that there are people out there who still don't believe we're that good. If it's true, the heck with *him*.

So what *do* we need? Our bullpen has been solid lately, we generally play good defense, we have the horses on our staff. The only thing missing is a big bat to help Konerko and Dye, since Everett runs hot and cold.

The last six games, the lack of another bat is beginning to tell. Against Toronto and Seattle, we had one game where we scored five runs, one with four runs, three with three runs and one with two. We're just not hitting. I'm not horribly worried, because in the end, it always comes back to pitching, but it would increase everyone's comfort level if another bat could be obtained.

The first game of the series against Toronto was no contest. Garland had his first truly bad outing in a while, giving up thirteen hits and seven runs. The only bright spot was Bobby Jenks, who threw two innings of perfect relief, throwing twelve out of sixteen pitches for strikes. The beanball wars that started in Baltimore continued; Josh Towers of the Jays hit Hambino (the second time in two games he's been hit, and knowing A.J., someone will pay). When Justin Speier relieved him, he immediately hit Dye. Jon Adkins, whom we just called up, hit Russ Adams in retaliation in the ninth, which had to have been called from the dugout, since Adkins was a newcomer. The question was, who made the call? Ozzie had been ejected in the fourth, only the second time this year he's been thrown out, for arguing balls and strikes. Don Cooper? Joey Cora? Or was it Ozzie from back in the clubhouse? Doesn't matter. The message is getting pretty clear to the league: you hit our guys, we're coming after you. It's not only a winning attitude, it's a vital part of the team's closeness. They really are looking out for each other.

The second game El Duque did a Contreras, giving up four runs in the first. The Jays loaded the bases on two walks and a hit batsman, and then Zaun doubled them all home, later scoring on a base hit. After that El Duque was terrific, shutting them out for the next six innings, but the damage was done. And our offense showed exactly why we need another bat, missing numerous chances to drive in runs. Everett hit a moon shot to right in the first for one run, and Konerko hit a two-run shot later,

192

but in a game we lost 4-3, here's a short list of missed opportunities:

1. 2nd inning: runner on second, two out, Scotty fouls out.
2. 3rd inning: runner on third, one out, Konerko taps back to pitcher, A.J. fouls out.
3. 4th inning: runner on second one out, Rowand grounds to short, Uribe pop fly to center.
4. 7th inning: runners at second and third, two out, Konerko grounds out to short.
5. 8th inning, runners on first and second, one out, Crede fouls out, Blum strikes out.

This game should have been won, and there really wasn't anything in which to take comfort.

The third game against the Jays seemed like a replay of the second with the teams switching uniforms. This time we got four runs in the first, with Konerko singling in a run and Rowand following with a three-run blast to center. With a four-run lead, I was waiting to see which inning would Contreras come apart, hoping against hope that he would stay together long enough so our bullpen could hold the fort.

Sure enough, in the fourth he gave up a single and a walk. Alex Rios bounced softly toward shortstop, and Crede charged, looked back at second, and threw wildly to first, allowing one run to score and two more to follow when Adams tripled to center. In the eighth, Marte allowed a leadoff single, and then hung a curve to Adams, who leaped on it and drove it to right-center for a double. Ozzie went to Vizcaino (where is Jenks?). After Adams was bunted to third, Evel made one of the best plays all year, which ultimately saved the game. Vernon Wells blooped on toward very short center. Knievel raced in, and I mean *raced*, and caught it at his ankles in full stride, then rifled a throw to Widger to hold the runner at third. It was an amaaaaazing catch and wonderful throw. Hillenbrand then fouled to Widger, and we dodged a bullet, going into the bottom of the inning tied 4-4.

Ozzie was recently asked who the MVP of the team was this year, and he answered Iguchi. It makes sense; he's been our most consistent hitter all year, and although I might have nominated Scotty, who jump-starts our offense, he's been cold lately, going 2 for his last 27. On one swing in the second Jays game, he looked as though he was favoring one leg a little, almost swinging flat-footed.

Back to Iguchi. Leading off in the bottom of the eighth, he hit Justin Speier's first pitch over the right-field wall. It happened so fast, it was almost anti-climactic. There wasn't even time for us to start a rally. Hawk said that Iguchi had tremendously quick hands, and you could see it on that pitch.
More than that, you could see Iguchi outguess the pitcher. The first pitch was a slider that caught the outside corner for a strike. Speier tried the same pitch right away, but Tad saw it coming, and mauled it.

Fool me once, shame on you. Fool me twice . . . except Tad didn't get fooled. Just beautiful hitting. Hermanson followed by striking out the side in the ninth (has he been watching Jenks?) and we had salvaged a game out of the series.

BEN: Getting shut down by the Jays' staff isn't good new, Dad.

DAD: I think our bats are termite-infested.

The series with Seattle featured great pitching and practically no offense at all. Freddy Garcia pitched game one and lost, which is no surprise since he is 9-1 on the road and 2-4 with a 5.01 ERA at the Cell. We picked up two solo HRs, by Knievel and A.J., but that was it. Back to missed opportunities. Scotty and Iguchi left Blum and Uribe on in the seventh, among other opportunities, and in the last two innings, the last six hitters went down so fast you'd think they had a train to catch, swinging at every first pitch. Meanwhile Freddy Garcia had a mediocre outing, giving up four runs, including a HR and double by Richie Sexson that looked as though they had been fired from a bazooka, and although we finally got a glimpse of Jenks (that's all Seattle got of him, too, he pitched two perfect innings and had three K's), it wasn't enough and we lost 4-2.

Two items of note: Scotty had a double down the right field line in the third, and it's very clear to me something's wrong: he's shortstepping in a way that looks like the adductor strain he's had is giving him trouble. The second note is that one of the Sox got hit *again*. This time it was Iguchi, and he got hit in the head. Enough is enough already. When is the league going to wake up and take notice?

We won the second and third games in just the way we've been winning all year: Ozzie ball. In the second game, Buehrle did one of the best slip'n'slides he's done all year. It came in the first inning. With runners on second and third and one out, in stepped Sexson. First Mr. Slip'N'Slide slipped, getting behind 3-0, and then he threw inside for a strike, farther inside, another strike, then sawed Sexson off for a foul ball. Finally, he totally froze Sexson, who by now was looking inside, with a perfect pitch at the knees on the outside corner. A fly ball and he got out of the inning unscathed.

He was rewarded in the bottom half of the first, when Scotty lined one at Beltre's feet at third which Beltre bobbled.

Mercury advanced to second on Iguchi's grounder to second, stole third, then scored on Rowand's sac fly to center. Ozzie Ball took a respite when Konerko then powered a HR to left, but that was all Buehrle needed. From then on, he was on his game, with pinpoint control. He even made the defensive play of the game when he knocked down a vicious line drive by Sexson with one out and a man on third in the sixth. The ball was hit so hard it knocked Buehrle's glove off, but he calmly ran, got the ball, held the runner with a glance, and threw Sexson out. This game was all Buehrle (with relief help from Politte and Hermanson.)

The third game was a replay of game two. Konerko hit a two-run shot that curled inside the foul pole. Garland looked like Buehrle, not only in total pitching command, but also defensively, as he made a dandy catch of a liner with two on that saved a run. He's a great fielding pitcher anyway, so it didn't come as a big surprise, but it was clutch.

The play of the game was made by – drum roll – Evel Knievel. He did it again, with two on and two out in the eighth off of a deep drive to the wall by Sexson. In the replay, it was clear why Rowand *is* Evel Knievel: he never even looked at the wall, running full-tilt and throwing his glove up at the last instant to snare the ball well above his head. It was a great way to end the series, taking the last two with our typical get- three-runs-and-hold-the-dike gameplan. We've got the Yankees, Bosox, and Twins coming up, and even though our thirteen-game lead seems secure, it's still nice to have pitching and defense in place when we need them

We still need hitting, though. . . .

	W	L	PCT	GB	Home	Away	Div	Streak
Chicago WSox	72	38	.655	---	36-22	36-16	32-9	Won 2
Cleveland	60	52	.536	13	27-27	33-25	20-27	Won 3

Minnesota	57	54	.514	15 1/2	32-26	25-28	23-20	Lost 1
Detroit	52	58	.473	20	26-30	26-28	21-25	Lost 3
Kansas City	38	73	.342	34 1/2	23-32	15-41	14-29	Lost 10

August 14, 2005
BEN:

Well, we can stick with 'em. But will sticking with 'em be enough come playoff time? We went into New York and took two of three; we went to Boston and lost the first two (before being rained out with a lead in the third game). Every game was close. So much for the "Sox will fold against good teams" contingent.

The first game in New York featured El Duque going up against New York's consistently underrated ace, Mike Mussina. The Yankees started off the year *very* cold, but they've heated up of late, and they were 59-50 going into the first game with us. It is wonderful that we've got two ex-Yanks on our staff, and they went out and got Jared Wright and Randy Johnson, only to fall behind the Red Sox in the AL East. But you can never count out the Yankees, and I'm sure we'll be seeing them down the road, whether they're the AL East champs or the Wild Card winners.

El Duque couldn't put it together in the first inning. Derek Jeter led off with a rocket to left-center field, and Rowand took off after at. He was running straight back toward the wall at full speed, and at the last second, he threw up his glove, dove, and caught the ball backhanded. It was, as the announcers said, an "unbelievable" play. Rowand has to be a serious candidate for a Gold Glove, especially now that Torii Hunter is out for the season. He proved why *again* on the next play. Robinson Cano, the Yankees' talented rookie 2B, hit a deep drive toward right-center. Rowand made a Willie Mays-type grab over his shoulder.

Unfortunately, El Duque couldn't take advantage of Rowand's spectacular defensive effort. He walked steroid freak Gary Sheffield, and then left a fastball over the plate for A-Rod. Boom. A-Rod has a pretty swing and a quick bat, and he sent that one flying into the left field stands for a fast 2-0 lead. The Yanks got another in the second to make it 3-0 after Posada singled home Tony Womack.

Mussina was on fire all night. He struck out seven, including Dye looking, Crede swinging, and Podsednik looking twice in the first few innings. We mounted our comeback against him in the fifth, when Dye led off with a single through the left side. Rowand followed with a hard-hit double into the left field gap – perhaps only Rowand could have caught that. Dye came around to score easily. Crede tapped one to second base to advance Rowand to third. Uribe brought him home with a deep sac fly to left. 3-2.

In the top of the fifth, El Duque got some more defensive help, this time from Jermaine Dye in right. Sheffield was on first when A-Rod hit another ball deep toward the right field wall. Dye leaped and grabbed it, preventing at least a double off the wall. Dye turned around and flung the ball toward first to try to double off Sheffield, who was running on the play. We didn't get him, mostly because A-Rod (who showed his seamy side last year during the playoffs with his girlie slap at Bronson Arroyo's glove) was too busy walking as slowly as possible back to the dugout after flying out to pay attention to the ball coming his way. It bounced off his shin. He made literally no effort to get out of the way. Luckily, we got out of the inning anyway. A- Rod acting like a spoiled brat after flying out? There's a shocker.

Our relief joined the game in the seventh, when Cotts entered and rocked the Yanks to sleep. Scotty P. helped out with a leaping catch down the left field line, reaching into the seats a la Moises Alou circa 2003 but sans Steve Bartman. Cotts got out of the inning without further incident.

Unfortunately, Tom Gordon rocked us to sleep in the eighth. Jenks pitched a perfect inning in the eighth, which was a good sign – Ozzie isn't afraid of using him in close ballgames anymore. He popped up Sheffield and A-Rod before striking out Matsui. That's serious stuff, especially for a rookie.

It didn't matter. We went down quietly to Mariano Rivera. Then again, who doesn't? Seven pitches, two groundouts, one strikeout. Every pitch was a strike. The guy is only the best closer in baseball history.

Game two went the way game one should have. Jose Contreras, for some strange reason, didn't pull a "secret inning" – he was simply spectacular. He went seven shutout innings, striking out six, and though the Yanks' Shawn Chacon was good (seven innings, one run), he wasn't good enough.

We got our first run in the top of the fourth when Tad Iguchi went deep to right. I'm not sure I've seen a player who goes to right better than Iguchi – it seems like he's a much better hitter when he tries to go with the pitch.

In the bottom of the seventh, Rowand saved us from an extra-base hit by Posada, running down a liner into the right-center gap. He covers *so* much ground out there, it makes it tough for the Yanks to get extra bases.

We got an insurance run in the top of the ninth when the Captain went yard to left off of Alan Embree, who had to be wishing he was back in Boston at this point. It's a good thing we did, because in the bottom half, Cliff Politte gave up a bomb to

A-Rod, who killed our pitching in this series. After the Yanks got another runner, Damaso Marte came in to pitch. *Ozzie, what are you thinking?!* Marte immediately surrendered a single up the middle to Tino Martinez, advancing the runner to third. A batter too late, Ozzie brought in Dustin Hermanson, who pitched inside to Posada. Posada turned on it and mashed the ball down the first-base line – right at Paulie. Game over.

It was a really nice win. We played great baseball all the way through. Contreras was tremendous. Rowand was amazing. Scotty P. made another great play in left. And a fan fell out of the upper deck and into the netting behind the plate. The game was delayed while the moron tried to climb his way out of it. Both teams stood on the top step of the dugout to watch this idiot. Funniest moment: as he was inching his way up the net, the crowd began cheering loudly. When he reached the top, a couple of security guards grabbed him and hoisted him into the field deck – by his belt. Ultimate wedgie. Ouch.

Game three, we gave the Yankees the ultimate wedgie. Freddie Garcia went eight sterling innings, giving up only a run. The Yanks' starter, Aaron Small, was just as good, going seven and giving up only a run. It took until the tenth, but we finally pulled it out in their ballpark, against – *no way!* – Mariano Rivera.

The Yankees took the lead in the bottom of the first, when Gary Sheffield singled home Derek Jeter. Small, who had us swinging at air all night (seven strikeouts) kept that slim lead until the top of the third, when we touched him for a run. With Pablo Ozuna on base, Carl Everett (batting lefty) went the other way with a ball down and away, bouncing it off the left-field wall. Ozuna came around to score.

In the bottom of the third, Chris Widger came up with a big play. Jeter was on first, and he took off for second. The pitch was a high outside fastball to the lefty Cano, and Widger rifled it to second for the Uribe tag. Pierzynski is a wonderful catcher – he calls the pitches well, and he blocks the plate nicely. He doesn't have a great arm, though, and Widger does. Sheffield drilled one to center and Rowand made a nice running grab *again*. He's a Yankee killer out there – I can't imagine that any other CF covers that kind of ground.

In the bottom of the sixth, Rowand did it again. He caught a right-center gapper from Matsui dead on the run for the last out of the inning. The Yankees' announcers couldn't believe it.

We got the benefit of a kind call in the top of the eighth. With two outs, Gary Sheffield grounded to Uribe at short, who couldn't dig the ball out of his glove. He threw high to Konerko, who came down on first base a bit late. But Sheffield got called out. You could almost see Konerko whistling his way back to the dugout.

We got nothing in the top of the ninth. Rivera was pitching, so no surprise there. Cotts put the Yankees away in the bottom of the ninth, and we got to see Mariano Rivera again in the tenth. Widger went down on strikes. Then Juan Uribe drove a ball to right-center and deep. Bernie Williams isn't Aaron Rowand, and it showed here: Uribe made it all the way to third. Scotty P. grounded it to the right side, and Cano threw to the plate. Uribe slid in right under the tag. Sox win again. Two out of three from the Yanks. In the Bronx.

DAD: The Sox are for real.

201

BEN: Now if they'd only start showing us at the top of the show on *SportsCenter*.

Even though we lost two straight in Boston before being rained out in the third game, we re-enforced the fact that we're a *good team* by playing the BoSox tough in Fenway. In the first game, we really should have been blown out. Slip N' Slide Buehrle didn't exactly slip or slide, and got racked for six runs and 12 hits in seven innings. David Wells wasn't much better, and surprisingly, we were still in the ballgame, 6-5, when Buehrle came out.

We got ahead 4-0 in the first two innings. In the first, Mercury singled and moved to third on a sinking liner by the Captain. A good left fielder would have caught it, but thankfully, Manny Ramirez is out there for the Red Sox, and it dropped in (E7, there). Both Pods and Konerko came around to score on a triple to center by Rowand, who golfed a ball around his ankles over the head of rock star Johnny Damon. Damon, by the way, is worshipped in Boston. He's such a goofball, and he's really a clubhouse leader. He's a free agent after this year, too, but I'm sure the BoSox will bring him back simply for the public's sake, despite his age.

In the second, we loaded the bases after A.J. grounded one through the left side, Scotty P. hit an infield single on a bouncer down the third base line, and Iguchi got nicked by an inside fastball. Hambino and Podsednik scored on a soft liner into right off the bat of Carl Everett, who continues to be a veritable RBI machine.

The BoSox got two back in the bottom of the third after a Bill Mueller single, an Edgar Renteria wall-ball, and a David Ortiz smash into the right-field corner. They made it 4-3 in the fourth, when Gabe Kapler singled home Bill Mueller. In the top of the fifth, Carl Everett (batting righty) drove a ball over the Monster in left to give us a 5-3 lead.

That's where our highlight reel ended. Varitek ate up a Buehrle fastball and sent it screaming out of the park for a two-run HR in the bottom of the fifth. In the bottom of the seventh, Buehrle threw a good outside fastball. Unfortunately, the batter was David Ortiz, who goes the other way as well as Tad Iguchi does. The ball ended up in the first row of Monster seats.

Then, the Battle of the Rotten Relievers. Bobby Jenks got beaten, pure and simple. With two men on base, he challenged Ortiz with a fastball low and over the plate. Bye bye, baby, time to hit the road to dreamland. That ball was hit so hard it looked like it might burrow its way *through* the center field bleachers.

Fortunately for us, the BoSox closer is still Schilling. Schill, who will one day be mayor of Boston for his heroics in the 2004 playoffs, is still not fully recovered from that ankle injury. He came into the game with a 5.55 ERA and a .297 opponent batting average. Not good stats. Schilling got two quick outs, but couldn't get the third. First, Tad Iguchi hit a high-flying Fenway pop-up/home run into the left-center seats. Then Carl Everett (who killed his former team) singled to left. Konerko followed by cranking a bomb over the Monster yet again to bring us within a run, 9-8. Unfortunately, that's the way it ended. Schilling went up 0-2 on Aaron Rowand, and then got the benefit of a kind call from the home plate ump on an outside curveball that froze Rowand.

Game one: close but no cigar.

Game two was a similar story – the BoSox built an insurmountable lead off of Jon Garland, who looks weary out there (five runs in just over five innings). Tim Wakefield, the knuckleballer who baffles us on a consistent basis, held us down. We did our best to make up the ground in the late innings, but couldn't get it done. The big story of this game was once again David Ortiz. We put the shift on for him – we had three infielders on the right side, and he still went 3 for 4 on the night. MVP? At this point, it would be hard to question that call.

The bottom line on the NY-Boston swing: we can hang with these guys. If we can beat them is another story. Our pitching staff will have to write that story, since both Buehrle and Garland looked terrible in Beantown. Then again, we're leading the division by a wide margin, so maybe Ozzie can get the staff some rest. Looks like they need it.

	W	L	PCT	GB	Home	Away	Div	Streak
Chicago WSox	74	41	.643	---	36-22	38-19	32-9	Lost 2
Cleveland	63	55	.534	12 1/2	27-30	36-25	23-27	Lost 3
Minnesota	60	57	.513	15	32-26	28-31	23-20	Won 1
Detroit	55	61	.474	19 1/2	26-30	29-31	23-25	Won 2
Kansas City	38	78	.328	36 1/2	23-37	15-41	14-34	Lost 15

August 18, 2005
DAD:

It's an off-day today, and the Sox badly need one. It seems as though all the good luck we've been swimming in has dried up. That's ironic, since the last Boston game had a 4 ½ hour rain delay that turned into a rainout, and we were ahead at the time. That should have been the tip-off that something was rotten in the state of Ozzie. Worse than that, as I had conjectured, Scotty *is* hurt, and on the disabled list resting his strained left adductor. The Sox's downturn has coincided with my own; walking has gotten to be extremely difficult. The Sox's season had served as a balm for me while I've been going through this, an escape from the pain, and their recent doldrums have depressed me almost as much as it must depress them.

The three games against the Twins were a disaster. There was no excuse for it; both Jacque Jones and Torii Hunter were out, but we still managed to get thoroughly outplayed by a team fifteen games out. At this point, all the Twins are talking about is trying to make the wild card, and with the Indians on a roll in front of them, they should have been thinking next season.

No way. They killed us, especially with their defense. The first game, Contreras reverted to form; he was absolutely magnificent the last outing against the Yankees, but I suppose that was an aberration. As usual, he had his one catastrophic inning. This time it was the fourth. He gave up four runs after issuing two walks, but of course every *other* inning he was lights out. Shannon Stewart robbed Konerko of a two-run HR (just to show that they always have at least one Willie Mays out there.) Whoops, I meant two. Lew Ford gunned Crede out at home when he tried to score from second on a base hit. The Minnesota pitchers were excellent, with Kyle Lohse giving up two runs in 5 1/3 and their bullpen shutting us out the rest of the way.

The next day we played the longest game, time-wise, in the history of the Cell. It went 16 innings, and lasted over five hours. We should have won it. Even though they got twenty hits to our twelve, we were ahead 4-3 in the ninth when Dusty gave up a game-tying HR by Cuddyer. In the eleventh, Cuddyer added his bid to join the Twins' Gold Glove contingent. With men on first and second and one out, Uribe popped up, but then Crede rocketed one to Cuddyer's right. He picked it cleanly and fired to first to end the inning. In the sixteenth, after Cotts (one inning), Vizcaino (two), and Jenks (three inning, with four K's) had held them scoreless, the Twins laid into Jon Adkins, scoring five times. Joe Nathan struck out the side, and we lost 9-4. It was particularly disappointing because we had come back from being down 3-1. Freddy Garcia pitched decently, giving up two doubles in the first and a two-run HR by Morneau in the sixth., and after we rallied back to take the lead, I had hopes. But they got it done, we didn't.

The big reason I had hopes for that second game was that I had slim or none for the third. One reason: Johan Santana. You don't have to be a baseball aficionado to know that he's got to be the best pitcher in baseball (with the possible exception of Roger Clemens.) He did exactly what I expected, holding us to one run, while Buehrle was struggling to hold them. I felt bad for Buehrle; pitching against Santana is like holding your thumb in the dike while the water on the other side is being swollen with torrential rain. Mr. Slip'N'Slide did quite well, though, except when he faced Matt Lecroy, who solo-homered twice. The Twins added three more runs in the fifth after a rather strange balk call against Buehrle, but all they really needed was two runs total. Santana's simply that good.

With the Yankees coming to town, the Sox really need some good news. I hope they can keep it together until Scotty gets back in a couple of weeks; I think they miss him more than they even realize. I've been telling Ben you never know exactly where that good news will come from.

In my case, maybe it was that Detroit series last month. I noticed that Magglio Ordonez was hitting well again. When I did some research, it turned out that he had been surgically repaired for something called athletic pubalgia, by a Dr. William Meyers, in Philadelphia. Intrigued, over the last two weeks I have explored further and found that Dr. Meyers operates on the most famous athletes around, and that the symptoms of athletic pubalgia seem similar to mine. With Ben due to leave for Cambridge in a couple of weeks, we're taking the family to San Diego for a couple of days and I've set up a time to talk with Dr. Meyers by phone while we're there. I want to know what he thinks; with all the tests on me coming up negative, no one here will even think of opening me up to take a look. The odd thing is, one of the parts of the surgery Dr. Meyers does is called an adductor release. I don't know what that is, but hey, perhaps I truly am in sync with the Sox. Perhaps Meyers will fix me up (including the adductors) and I'll be able to run like Scotty when he and I both heal. Boy, the fantasies middle-aged men have.

Maybe my luck and the Sox's is about to change.

August 22, 2005
DAD:

"Pa! Pa! The Yankees are comin'! The Yankees are comin'!"

Sheriff John McGarrity stared, dumbfounded, at his nine-year-old son Billy. "I thought they weren't comin' here this year, son. I never thought they'd come here with the sharpshooters we have. Deputy Mark, Deputy Jon, Deputy Fred, Deputy Jose, and old Deputy Orlando should'a scared 'em off."

"Well, they're comin' Pa," Billy said, with a curious glint in his eye.

The Sheriff thought quickly about making a heroic stand, but he'd seen too much blood spilled before. It ain't worth it, he thought. "Hurry, son, tell your mother to pack up the valuables and head for the hills. I'll warn the town and meet you there as soon as I'm able."

"Ya think Tape-Measure Mickey'll be with 'em, Pa?" Billy asked. Tape-Measure Mickey was famous for his range, for he could put a bullet in a thimble from over five hundred feet away. "D'ya think he will, Pa?"

"Tape-Measure Mickey's long gone, Billy. But they've got some pretty good gunslingers to replace him," his father answered.

"Can't I just hide and watch when they come ridin' in, Pa? I never saw 'em before," Billy begged.

"Are you out of your mind, son? They'll shoot you just as soon as they'd shoot me. Age don't make a darn bit of difference to them. They're the coldest, meanest, baddest, evilest, nastiest –"

"I get the picture, Pa," Billy said, rolling his eyes behind his father's back.

"Well, you just hurry along, son."

"Sure, Pa." But once Billy was out of his father's sight, he wedged himself behind a building to wait and see for himself.

That's the way it felt to be a Sox fan in the early sixties. You hated the Yankees, knew they would win, but still watched, fascinated, as they usually beat us to a pulp. Although . . . there was one glorious day in 1972 – that was a little different . . .

"Do we *have* listen to the White Sox game? We heard the first one already," my sister asked. The White Sox were at home playing a doubleheader against the Yankees, and they had listened to the first game, in toto, as our family was on a Sunday drive.

"C'mon, Dad, just the end of it? We've probably missed the whole second game," I pleaded.

"I think let's see how they're doing," my father said as he drove, turning the radio back on.

They weren't doing well. Down 4-1 going into the bottom of the ninth, the Sox needed a great rally to win, which would have made it three out of four from the Yankees, which we badly needed as we were chasing Oakland. (A fate we would face all year; we finished 5 games back, and had I known how truly great that Oakland team was I would have realized what an accomplishment that was.)

To make matters worse, our star player, Dick Allen, who would win the MVP that year, was being given the second game off by Chuck Tanner, who let his volatile star have the run of the place all year. Tanner said no matter what happened, Allen would rest.

We managed to get two men on with one out against Mike Kekich, and then the scenario I feared played out. The Yanks sent in Sparky Lyle, arguably the best reliever in the league, that era's Rivera. I was excited, but our next hitter was Rich Morales, who normally couldn't hit one past the outfield.

"Do we have to listen, Dad?" Suzie asked. As a Cubs fan, she wasn't entirely unhappy that the Sox were about to lose.

"You know, Nate, the girls have been awfully patient," my mother suggested.

"Yeah, Morales can't hit anyway," I said disgustedly.

"You never know, Butch," my father began, but then the announcer said excitedly, "Allen is walking up the steps of the dugout! Allen is going to hit!"

"No way," I said disbelievingly. *"No way!"*

Way.

Gunslinger Lyle delivered, and Sheriff Allen plucked that bullet (actually it was Lyle's famed slider) and shot it, cannon-like, toward the center field bleachers. It landed some 450 feet away. Game *OVER*. I have never heard such noise over the radio. After that blast, Sheriff Allen could have run for governor.

Of course, that's one memory among scores of other, more painful memories of the Yankees, but thanks to my dad, I heard it.

The last three games against the Yankees, two truisms have emerged:
1. Without the power of the Captain and the speed of Mercury, we're a good baseball team, but not good enough to go very far in the playoffs. Konerko and Podsednik are essential parts to our success.
2. Once we get them back to jump-start our offense, we have the defense and pitching to beat anyone.

The first game, truism #1 became abundantly clear. Konerko is out with a back injury, and Scotty's still out, and as a result, we never mounted any offense of note against Mussina. He was typically brilliant, outdueling Garland. For the first six innings, he can be as devastating as any pitcher of the last ten years. There are cases when he collapses after that (see Bosox-Yankees playoffs last year) but I'm convinced he's so focused for the first six innings that sometimes he just runs out of gas. Of course, when Rivera's behind you, it becomes an eight-inning game, so if the Yankees have decent relief for innings seven and eight, they're really tough. Their late-inning man is Tom Gordon, who is reasonably tough, but there was no excuse for the way we swung against him. With a 3-1 lead in the eighth, and Iguchi on first with a base-hit, Everett struck out on a 55-foot curveball, A.J struck out on a pitch at his eyes, and Dye got sawed off for a pop-up. We just looked pitiful all night.

The second game was worse – more of truism #1. Shawn Cacon threw eight shutout innings, gave us leadoff runners as often as he could, and we still couldn't do anything. Meanwhile, El Duque threw away a double-play comebacker into center field, and A-Rod doubled home two. We wound up losing 5-0, our seventh straight loss. The last six losses we scored a total of twelve runs. I don't think it's any coincidence that Mercury was out of the lineup for those six losses.

The only solace in those two losses is that there were some great defensive plays, notably by Crede and Uribe. Crede made some plays reminiscent of Brooks Robinson, charging slow rollers barehanded and firing to first so smoothly I could have sworn he must have been healthy. Ben and I are trying to think of a nickname for Uribe; his arm is so strong that it looks like he's firing missiles at short range.

The third game we finally stopped the losing streak, and in the most unlikely manner possible. Unlikely because we hadn't been hitting a lick, and:

a) we had to face Randy Johnson
b) we had to face Randy Johnson, and
c) ad infinitum . . .

But then truism #2 emerged in the person of the Captain, who returned from his two-game absence to help shrink the Big Unit. And it all happened in the same inning –the fourth. With one out, Iguchi did what he does so well, going the other way to right field for a HR. Moments later, Rowand did the same thing, and suddenly we were up, 2-1. Konerko walked stiffly to the plate, DHing, and I was worried that he might have returned too early. He must have known that the Sox dearly missed his bat.

211

It had to have killed his back, but he reached out and golfed the low, outside pitch with everything he could muster, and it soared far over the left-field wall. Three successive HRs, and we were up 3-1.

But that wasn't all. Dye and Uribe immediately followed the HRs with singles, bringing Chris Widger to the plate. Against Randy Johnson? I'd say he was over-matched. Johnson fired a fastball away, helmet-high, and somehow Widger not only reached out to get it, but *pulled* it, all the way over the left-field wall, and we were ahead 6-1. We won, 6-2, and Contreras was smart, scattering eleven hits a la Buehrle. A most unlikely victory in every respect, but perhaps that was the only way the streak could be snapped.

We have one monstrous problem from here on in: *we only get one day off for the rest of the season.* That rain-out at Boston cost us, because it was rescheduled for the one other day off we should have had, but now there is essentially no rest, and no break. Our once insurmountable fifteen-game lead has shrunk to eight and a half over the Indians, who have won five of their last six and are gaining on us. It's sink-or-swim time.

	W	L	PCT	GB	Home	Away	Div	Streak
Chicago WSox	75	46	.620	---	37-27	38-19	32-12	Won 1
Cleveland	68	56	.548	8 1/2	32-31	36-25	23-27	Won 4
Minnesota	66	58	.532	10 1/2	35-27	31-31	26-20	Won 1
Detroit	60	62	.492	15 1/2	31-31	29-31	23-25	Won 4
Kansas City	40	82	.328	35 1/2	23-37	17-45	14-34	Won 2

Left: The authors, twelve years after the White Sox won the 2005 World Series.

Below: David Shapiro and his sister, Suzie, with Dodgers' all-time great Sandy Koufax, in 1966

Picture of 1965 White Sox Team baseball: In 1965, David won a contest from the White Sox -- and won this signed team baseball. The team would go 95-67, and finish 7 games behind the Minnesota Twins.

David and Cindy Shapiro, 2014

Nathan Shapiro, David Shapiro, and Ben Shapiro, 1989

David Shapiro and Ben Shapiro, 1997

214

Nathan Shapiro and Ben Shapiro, 1986

*The year the Little League White Sox won the World Series,
coached by David. Ben batted second
and played second base (1995).*

Little League - Summer, 1966

Nathan Shapiro (center) coaches David Shapiro (bottom left) in Little League, 1966

Ben in his Little League uniform
-- a Sox fan then, now, and always.

Part IV
Sink

August 25, 2005
BEN:

We're nearing crunch time. And I'm heading back to Cambridge next week. Every year around this time, when I go back to school, I begin thinking how lucky I am to have such a great family. A lot of my friends aren't particularly close to their parents or siblings, but all of the kids in my family are close not only to Dad and Mom, but to each other. Maybe it's because all four kids shared a room until I was 11 – we lived in a two-bedroom, one bathroom house for over a decade. We didn't have central air until we moved, so I vividly remember sitting in front of our unit air conditioner during the summer, trying to get cool. Bedtime was always particularly fun; we used to say goodnight a la *The Waltons*.

We'd probably be as close if we had grown up in a bigger house, just because Dad and Mom are so involved with us. But growing up in close proximity does make for common purpose. It also makes for fighting over the bathroom. Still, it's wonderful to know that if I need anything, I have five people who would be right there. Or six hours away by plane, at least.

Meanwhile, the Sox continue to jell. We went 2-1 against Minnesota, and we really should have gone 3-0, except that we faced an unhittable Johan Santana, who beat Freddy Garcia and his one-hitter in the first game of the road trip. That first game was definitely the toughest of the Minnesota series. It really, really hurt. I'm sure it hurt Freddy Garcia more than me. His location was excellent all night, and he had his good fastball working. The Twins got the bat on the ball and hit it hard a couple of times (a long fly to center that Rowand dragged in, a long liner to the left field wall Everett caught on the warning track). The fifth was interesting for Garcia as Ozuna misplayed a

Cuddyer grounder down the line. Cuddyer ended up on second and advanced to third on a groundout, and with two outs, Nick Punto hammered a ball toward the right field wall. It looked like the Twins' first hit – and their first run. Silent Assassin went flying back, slammed into the wall, and came down with the ball to preserve the no-hitter.

Santana was brilliant throughout, as usual. His changeup had us flailing, and when we did get the bat on the ball, we were hitting high pop-ups. He also has fantastic outfielders. We had the game won in the top of the fourth when, with Everett on base, Konerko crushed one to the top of the left field wall; Shannon Stewart leaped up and grabbed it. So much for that idea.

The Twins' run came in the top of the eighth. Garcia threw a curveball that dropped down into the low strike zone, and Jacque Jones, with his big loopy lefty swing, swatted the ball out of the park. End of no-no, Sox lose.

Garcia took the loss in stride, saying "It's hard to lose like that, but a loss is a loss. We are here to win games. You can give up five runs and win the game." That's a good perspective. I can't say I'd be as gentlemanly about it. The good news about the game is that Freddy is getting into good form. He's been pitching well lately, and this was the best game I've seen pitched by the Sox to this point.

Unfortunately, Cleveland beat Tampa Bay, which put them seven games back. Where did that big lead go?

Luckily, we got that game back the next day, when Cleveland lost and we took the second game from the Twins. Buehrle (who takes his facial hair from Wolverine, apparently) went eight sterling innings, surrendering six hits and one run, and we won the game 6-4. Our offense came alive, as Carl Everett smoked a ball into the upper deck in right for a two-run first inning shot. Everett got a couple more RBI in the fifth, singling home Timo Perez and Iguchi. Pierzynski scored that same inning after doubling and being driven home by Dye. Maybe we don't need another bat. Then again, Joe Mays isn't exactly Santana.

Game three was revenge for game one. This time, we pulled out a slim win on the strength of our starting pitching and bullpen. Jon Garland looked better than he has in a while, going 7 2/3 shutout innings; unfortunately for him, Carlos Silva of the Twins went seven innings and gave up only a run, and our bullpen allowed the Twins to tie the game in the bottom of the ninth.

After Garland's outstanding performance, Ozzie went to the pen. It was a close game, a real nailbiter. Did he go to Cotts? Did he go to Politte? Did he go to Hermanson? Did he go to Jenks? Nah. He went to my favorite guy, Damaso "Charles Manson" Marte. The first batter in the ninth, Nick Punto, smoked a liner up the middle, and Marte found it in his glove. Phew. Naturally, Marte wasn't going to take his piece of good fortune and run with it. He issued a walk to Joe Mauer. *Now* Ozzie called for Hermanson. Hermanson got LeCroy to pop up to Uribe. Two down. Starting to breathe easier.

Then, disaster. Michael Ryan and his .193 average strode to the plate. He scalded a ball down the first base line – it looked *foul*. Except that Konerko reached out and poked it, and the ump called it fair. The ball bounced merrily down the line as Luis Rodriguez, running for Mauer, chugged around the bases. Geoff Blum, playing second, ran out to get the ball, and fired it in to the Captain. We had a play at the plate developing, except that the Captain (who had been lying on the field in anticipation of a foul call) *dropped the ball*. Rodriguez scored. Tie game. A no decision for Garland. Yuck.

In the top of the tenth, we made up for it. Blum (whom I think I shall call "The Producer" after Leo Bloom of Mel Brooks fame) doubled off the base of the center-field wall. Then misfortune struck again. Joe Crede, who has been getting a lot of time off to heal that bad back, tried to bunt at a pitch that nailed him in the finger. It was called a strike, but Crede had to leave the game. This could be a serious problem – time to go out and trade for Joe Randa?

His replacement, Pablo Ozuna, laid down a bunt that bounced right back to pitcher Jesse Crain, who fired to third, beating The Producer by two steps. Except that Blum had the presence of mind to pull up short on the slide, avoiding the swipe tag, and only *then* stick his foot in there. "To come up with that slide and do it consciously, that's the whole game right there as far as once we got out of the ninth inning," Konerko said afterward. Fantastic call by Lance Diaz, the third base ump.
Timo Perez followed with a single to left. Ballgame. (Timo had an excellent game, by the way – he threw out a Twins runner at home in the second, aside from getting the game-winning hit.)

One other note: Bobby Jenks picked up his first career save in the bottom of the tenth. It was pretty smooth sailing, although Twins shortstop Bartlett kept fouling off pitch after pitch before striking out on a curveball in the dirt. Great call by Hambino, who recognized that Bartlett was swinging at everything. Jenks also struck out Lew Ford looking to end the game – on three straight breaking balls. The prospect of the next pitch being a 101-mph sizzler will do that to hitters. Bobby Jenks, future closer?

August 28, 2005
BEN:

Still treading water. Not because we're playing badly, but because Cleveland refuses to lose. Our lead is still eight games despite the fact that we took two out of three in Seattle. Once again, our wins were close and our loss was big. That seems to be the pattern. When we win, we squeak it out. When we lose, Ozzie sends home the starters early.

The first game was a squeaker. Which is to say, we won. Amazingly, the arm of El Duque lasted eight innings, and he gave up only three runs. For him, that's like pitching 12 or 13 innings straight. Felix Hernandez, the Mariners' rookie sensation, was just as good, holding us to three runs over seven innings.

Hernandez's big problem was Brian Anderson. Anderson has been a top prospect for a while now, and he can't break into the outfield. But with our bench depleted due to the loss of Crede, he got the start in center. In the third, he took Hernandez deep to left, which was a first for both of them – the first career HR for Anderson, the first HR surrendered by Hernandez. Four innings later, Anderson did it again, this time a two-run jack to left center. Later in the game (10th inning), Anderson would hit a double off the wall, just missing *another* HR. Will Anderson break Hank Aaron's HR record? Statistically, he's on pace to hit about 160 HR per season (he went 0-4 the next night), so we should know in about five years.

Anderson was very gracious about his performance after the game. "Obviously it feels good any time you hit a home run," Anderson said. "Then you realize when you get back to the dugout that [Hernandez is] only 19. He'll give up his fair share of homers and he'll have his fair share of strikeouts. ... That guy's got a humongous future ahead of him. [Giving up two homers] is probably not going to happen too many times with how electric his stuff is."

We were up 3-2 in the eighth when Willie Bloomquist (who?) hit an RBI double to tie it. The tie lasted all the way until the 12th. Our relief was just terrific – Politte went two scoreless innings, and Vizcaino added one to get the win. Ozzie, thankfully, didn't use Marte.

We finally touched the Mariners in the twelfth. With two outs and Uribe on second, Tad Iguchi drove a high fastball deep to left center. As the announcer put it, "Goodbye, baseball." Hermanson came in for his 32nd save of the season, and that was that.

It was a good win, particularly because we got some bad news before the game – Crede has a fingertip fracture. That might not keep him out long, but it can't be good for his swing, which has been a problem for him all season, despite some decent power numbers. I don't think "Producer" Blum is going to cut it, and Ozuna is only a decent replacement. Kenny, are you listening?

Game two: another squeaker, another win. Jose Contreras provided the stellar start this time out, going seven innings and giving up three runs. He has had a monster month, going 2-1 with a 1.69 ERA. Ozzie is seriously considering giving the big right-hander a rotation slot for the playoffs: "The way he's thrown the last four outings, it's not easy for me [to leave him out of the playoff rotation]." I'm starting to believe, but until I see some more proof, I'd rather have the battle tested Duque out there than the vacillating Contreras.

He was good enough on this night, though. Once again, no secret inning for Contreras. We grabbed a quick lead in the top of the second when the Silent Assassin hit a can o' corn that just kept flying, all the way over the left field fence for a two-run dinger. We got another run in the fourth when Dye once again got it done, doubling into right-center and coming home on a Uribe single to left. Dye had a huge game, doubling again and singling (and stealing two straight bases – yes, that Dye – though he was picked off third during a rundown) before the night was out. We got our fourth run of the night on a bomb from Carl Everett; he was batting righty. I note that only because Everett has an awful, hole-filled swing righty. When he does get the bat on the ball, though, it goes.

Contreras weakened in the seventh, giving up two quick runs on a pair of singles, a hit batsman (the count was 0-2 – blech) and another single. In the eighth, after Contreras gave up a single, Ozzie removed him in favor of Cotts. Cotts promptly gave up a walk to Ichiro (no sin there), and then got a couple outs. In came Big Bobby Jenks, who threw a low outside fastball that Bigger Richie Sexson lined for a hit the other way, down the right field line.

This was the play of the game. One Mariner scored easily. Dye ran over to grab the ball and fire it in to Iguchi; Iguchi rifled it to Hambino as Ichiro rounded third. The throw was off line, but Pierzynski made a terrific swipe tag to nail Ichiro, who slid wide of the plate. That's how it ended: 4-3, despite the best efforts of Damaso "the Ripper" Marte to give it up in the ninth. Jenks should buy Dye and Iguchi dinner after that one.

Game three: not a squeaker. You guessed it – we got creamed. Freddy Garcia, who was so fantastic in Minnesota, got racked by his former team. He went 4 1/3 and gave up an astounding 11 hits and 8 runs. Not much to write about here, since 97-year-old Jamie Moyer, whose age is higher than his velocity, shut us down, holding us to two runs in seven innings. It was a blowout, plain and simple.

There was one piece of good news, however: Jon Adkins, another prospect, relieved Garcia and gave up only one run in 3 2/3 innings. Not bad.

The final verdict is more about Cleveland than the Sox, though. We have maintained an eight-game lead, but the way Cleveland is playing makes me nervous. Then again, maybe I shouldn't be nervous – I'm a Sox fan, and it's a genetic thing.

In other news, I head off to Atlanta tomorrow to guest host on WSB. It's a tremendous opportunity, since they're the flag station for Neal Boortz and the former flag station for Sean Hannity. I'll be interested to hear everyone's advice over there, since they obviously know how to turn out winners.

	W	L	PCT	GB	Home	Away	Div	Streak
Chicago WSox	79	48	.622	---	37-27	42-21	34-13	Lost 1
Cleveland	73	58	.557	8	32-31	41-27	23-27	Won 1
Minnesota	68	62	.523	12 1/2	36-29	32-33	27-22	Lost 1
Detroit	62	66	.484	17 1/2	32-33	30-33	23-25	Lost 1
Kansas City	42	86	.328	37 1/2	25-38	17-48	14-34	Lost 3

August 31, 2005
DAD:

August is over. Good riddance. Our lead shrank from fifteen to seven, Scotty P. was out for fifteen days on the DL, and just as he got back, Joe Crede has to replace him on the DL for another fifteen days. It would be nice to have our lineup intact.

It seems when things go wrong in team sports, it almost doesn't matter how they go wrong. It's almost as if Defeat is beckoning with a long, outstretched, bony finger, summoning the team to the Land of Suffering, where any Bad Thing can happen at Any Moment. We've got one toe over the border now, with these small injuries cropping up, and I hope that we don't enter the land and get sunk in the morass there.

This last series in Texas felt as though Defeat finally had issued its summons. Scotty came back, and sure enough, our offense surged as though we got a new battery.

The first three games we scored five, six, and eight runs. But when Defeat summons you, there's no escape. Instead of losing because of a paucity of hitting, as per usual, our staff went dead. With the hitting we got, we should have won the first three games, or at least the first two, since Buehrle and Garland were hurling those. (The early-season Secret Weapon, Brandon McCarthy, who just came back up from the minors, had the last.)

We won one, and neither Buehrle nor Garland was responsible. In the first game, Buehrle got buffeted, opening with three straight hits and a sac fly, and the Rangers jumped ahead 2-0. Our fielding was atrocious: Iguchi had *three* errors and Uribe had one. The Rangers kept pecking away at Buehrle, scoring seven runs in seven innings, and although we got the tying run to the plate with two on in the ninth, Everett grounded out. Our three through seven hitters had nary an RBI between them.

I worry about the team's exhaustion level. Buehrle had thrown 189 innings by gametime, the most in the league, and he has to be tired. I don't mean physically, although I'm sure there is some of that, but mentally. Garland, who lost the second game and now has one victory in his last six starts, seems to be feeling it, too. And for the normally reliable Iguchi to bobble ball after ball the way he did indicates tiredness, too. I keep hearing in my

227

head General George Patton's famous dictum, often falsely attributed to Vince Lombardi, "Fatigue makes cowards of us all."

Of course, no one remembers the entire quote from Patton, which read, "Fatigue makes cowards of us all. *Men in condition do not tire.*" I think he may have been hyperbolic, though. *Everyone* tires, at some point. And I wonder if the staff, which has carried the team all year, has hit that point now.

I felt that even more strongly when I watched Garland in the second game. He kept leaving pitches belt-high. Something paradoxical was at work; if he *was* tired, shouldn't his sinker be sinking better? Ozzie said after the game, "Garland couldn't command, no strikes or no velocity. It was one of those days where he didn't have anything with him. I was kind of excited because we got some offense, and we come here with Buehrle and Garland. But we don't get it done."

The Sox grabbed the lead early when Everett and A.J drove in a run apiece, but the Rangers tied it 2-2 after Mark Teixeira hit a fly ball that barely made the right-field corner bleachers. We went ahead again in the second when Blum, subbing for Crede at third, singled home a run. But Blum gave it right back, bobbling a slow bouncer in the bottom of the inning, and that led to three unearned runs. We came back to tie it at 5-5 when Rowand delivered a two-run double in the third, but then Teixeira hit another two-run shot, this one to left, and they led 7-5. After Rowand brought home another run with a single in the fourth, out went Joaquin Benoit, and in came C.J. Wilson, who had an 0-6 record and a 8.45 ERA. I thought we were sitting pretty.

Wrong. He threw five innings, giving up two hits and only one run. That was enough because Blum made another error to bequeath the Rangers another run. In the immortal words of Brandon De Wilde in *Shane*, "Come back, Joe! Come back!"

It was a good thing that this was the first game of a double-header, because the Indians won again, cutting our lead to 6 ½ games, which would have left me completely morose the rest of the day. Instead, the Sox lucked out. Brandon McCarthy pitched in the nightcap, and shut them out. This came after the Rangers had scored eleven runs in two games. McCarthy was magnificent, pitching eight innings, and giving up only two hits and one walk. It was probably the most impressive game anyone has thrown all year, considering who's in the Rangers lineup.

He had help from the Silent Assassin, who simply went nuts with the bat. He homered twice, both of them to right field, and drove in six runs. He was aided by Mercury, who got three hits, and Rowand and Everett, who each got clutch RBI singles. But this was a night for the Silent Assassin and the rejuvenated Secret Weapon. Up by seven games again.

We had a chance for a split in the series today, and after we scored in the sixth to take a 2-1 lead, it looked okay. El Duque was throwing well, despite his record of 0-3 this month, and the bullpen was rested. But then, in the bottom of the sixth, El Duque fell apart, giving up five runs. It started when he barely hit David Dellucci. Michael Young homered, and later Alfonso Soriano homered, and we never recovered, losing 6-2. I had to wonder if El Duque simply unraveled in the heat; it was ninety-two degrees on the filed, and he *is* as old as Methuselah.

In any case, the Indians lost to Detroit, 4-3, so we're still up by seven, but we've lost eight games of our lead this month, as we've gone 12-16, and we need a shot of *something*. Seventeen of our next twenty-four games are at home, so that should help. More importantly, we get Detroit at home tomorrow, and we've gone 8-3 against them so far, so maybe they'll be the balm for our wounds. The trading deadline is on Wednesday, and I wonder if we'll pull a fast one.

September 4, 2005

We did, but it was on the Tigers. We creamed them. Four games, four wins, three straight blowouts followed by a tense win today. Our hitting, with the exception of today's game, was ferocious, not to be outdone by our pitching, which was overwhelming. Contreras, Garcia, Buehrle, and Garland all looked as sharp as if it were May.

Game one: the biggest blowout: 12-3. Pass me the highlights envelope, please.

1. We went 6-for-14 with runners in scoring position
2. We got eighteen hits. Every single starter got at least one hit.
3. Contreras threw seven innings, giving up just three runs on four hits. Even better than that, it was the third straight game he hasn't walked a batter. I think he's gaining focus, especially since in his last four starts, he's 4-1. Ozzie said after the game, "We know he's got one of the best arms, maybe the best arm, in my rotation, and he's showing right now what kind of pitcher he is."
4. A.J got his first HR in his last seventy-seven at-bats.
5. Dye hit a towering, and I mean *towering*, HR to left. He's 6'5", and if he were any bigger, that ball would have gone into orbit.
6. Cleveland was idle; we're up by 7 ½.

Game two: a very comfortable win, 9-1. The envelope?

1. Freddy Garcia being rewarded for that devastating 1-0 one-hit loss to Minnesota in August. He was overpowering, throwing seven innings, giving up two hits and one run, and got rewarded for his labors with:
2. Nine runs, including three HRs, the unlikeliest coming off the bat of . . .
3. *Willie Harris? Hello?* The speedster's first HR of the year, over the right-field fence. I always figured that when Willie hit a HR it would have been a Little League HR: where the hitter hits a ball to the outfield that gets misplayed long enough for him to round the bases. But, no, this was legit . . . I think. . . .
4. Everett and Uribe's twin three-run-shots.

A word here about Everett. He has truly harnessed his temper this year, and I doubt there is anyone in the dugout who wanted to win more than he does. I had misgivings about bringing him back, but I was wrong, and Kenny Williams was right. He's had numerous clutch hits, and I'm reaaaaaallllly glad I was wrong.

Game three: a more normal 6-2 victory, punctuated by Iguchi returning to the lineup and barely missing hitting for the cycle. In the eighth, after hitting a single, double, and triple, he struck out swinging. And he was going for it, too, which was funny, because he doesn't usually look like Dave Kingman up there. Mr. Slip'N'Slide, who had allowed fifteen runs in his last four starts while going 1-3, quelled my concerns about his tiredness. It was vintage Buehrle, scattering nine hits over seven innings to give up only one run. Dye hit another HR, and with Cleveland losing, our lead grew to 8 ½ again.

Today was game four. The Indians and Twins were seesawing back and forth the first six innings of their game, while we were hanging on for dear life. We grabbed a lead in the first, when Scotty singled, took second on a wild pitch by Bonderman, then scored when Iguchi lined one off Bonderman's glove that changed direction and eluded the second baseman.

The crucial moments came in the fourth. The Tigers had runners on first and third with two out, still trailing 1-0. Monroe absolutely ripped a vicious shot down the third base line. Our luck was with us. Ozzie had given Uribe the day off, necessitating Blum to play shortstop (not third, thank you) and Pablo Ozuna to play third. Ozuna dove to his right, snared the ball, leaped to his feet and gunned the ball to Konerko. Monroe was out by at least five steps. If Ozuna doesn't make that play, both runners score, since they were running on the play. As if scripted, in the bottom of the inning, Konerko drilled a solo shot over the left-field wall to make it 2-0. We made the plays, they didn't.

It was mostly due to Garland, who shut out the Tigers for the second time this year. And Garland was quick to acknowledge Ozzie after the game for leaving him in when he got in trouble in the eighth inning. "He's (Ozzie) shown the confidence in us and let us go the distance pretty much all year if it's our game," he said. "That's good to see out of a manager. Without that short leash, he's always giving you a chance to win a ballgame."

Meanwhile, the Twins beat Cleveland 7-5, and our lead is back up to 9 ½.

BEN: Can we just play Detroit the rest of the year?
DAD: I'll call Bud Selig right away.

	W	L	PCT	GB	Home	Away	Div	Streak
Chicago WSox	84	51	.622	---	41-27	43-24	38-13	Won 4

Cleveland	75	61	.551	9 1/2		33-32	42-29	25-30	Lost 2
Minnesota	72	64	.529	12 1/2		38-30	34-34	31-24	Won 2
Detroit	63	71	.470	20 1/2		32-33	31-38	24-30	Lost 4
Kansas City	44	91	.326	40		27-43	17-48	15-36	Won 1

September 6, 2005
BEN:

Remember that game that got rained out against Boston a while back? Well, yesterday we made it up in Boston. It was glorious. Fenway is the most beautiful park in the majors (sorry, Cubs fans), and it was a bright sunny day. Perfect for baseball. Rumor had it before the game that Ozzie was thinking about forfeiting the game simply to give the guys a day off. Good thing we didn't, since we thoroughly dominated the defending champs. "Can we play with them?" Better question: can they play with us?

Brendan McCarthy, who has been renewed since his late season call-up (there's been some talk that he restored his correct arm angle), was fantastic against the BoSox, going seven shutout innings and striking out seven. His fastball, which clocks in the low 90s, comes out of his hand the same as his changeup, which rolls up to the plate at 77 or so. He had the Red Sox fooled all night. This is against a lineup including Manny Ramirez (1-4) and David Ortiz (0-3). This is the McCarthy we saw in spring training. He's baaack.

On the other side of the ball, there was Curt Schilling. He still doesn't look good; earlier in the year, we racked him when he was still their closer. We touched him up for 9 hits and four runs in 6 1/3 innings. In the top of the fourth, the Captain doubled down the left field line, and he came around to score on a Timo Perez single to left. Timo has certainly been a valuable commodity this year – our bench is tremendous. I love Ozuna's ability, and The Producer has been excellent thus far (except for some plays at third).

Speaking of Producer Blum, he scored in the top of the fifth when he singled to left on a ball down in the zone, then was doubled in by Juan Uribe, who went high off the Green Monster. Uribe scored too, after Mercury bunted him to third; Iguchi squeezed him home. The squeeze was executed to perfection – they had no chance at Uribe at the plate. 3-0. In the top of the sixth, Konerko made it 4-0 with a solo rocket over the Monster. We got our fifth and final run against Chad Harville (who came in with a 27.00 ERA), when Uribe, who had a tremendous day, ripped a rising line-drive HR into the left field seats.

Our relief was good – Politte and Marte were both excellent (shockingly enough). Then Bobby Jenks made a ballgame of it. He struck out Manny Ramirez on a 92-mph *off speed pitch*, then got Trot Nixon to chop a grounder to Tad Iguchi. Except Iguchi dropped it. Oops. Jenks froze Jason Varitek on a change. Then Kevin Millar, who has been awful this year, crushed an off-speed pitch off the Monster. Tony Graffanino (why didn't he stay with the Royals?!) cranked another off-speed pitch over the Monster, and it was 5-3. Fortunately, that's the way it ended – Gabe Kapler grounded a ball to Konerko for the final out.

A note on Jenks: he was throwing too much off-speed junk out there. Every hit came on an off-speed pitch. No one is going to catch up to the fastball, Big Guy – bring the heat.

I'm back in Cambridge now, and classes have started. I'm taking a lot of constitutional history and law, which is fascinating stuff – I developed a love for it in college, and I've read a good deal of material on it, which means I have a nice background. That, in turn, means that I can spend more time

234

watching the Sox and less time reading the opinions of Justice O'Connor. Ah, the joy of the pennant race. How I love it. And I actually get to watch two pennant races – Yankees vs. BoSox is going to go down to the wire again. Right now, the BoSox are up four games. It shouldn't affect my White Sox, but it's baseball drama, that's for sure. It was fascinating living in Boston during the Red Sox's championship year – it was though all the years of futility were washed away. Now it's the Yankees who are reeling.

I just hope that it's the Twins, Indians, Red Sox, Angels *and* Yankees who are reeling after this season.

September 8, 2005
BEN:

A few weeks ago, I was worried. Now, I'm not. We took two out of three from the Royals, and we're up 8.5 games with 23 games to go. Whom do we face in the first round?

One thing's for sure: it ain't Kansas City. The first game was a close one, and as usual, we pulled it out. We built a huge lead in the first two innings off of Jose Lima, who doddered onto the hill before the ump told him he couldn't keep his cane out there. Scotty scored the first run – he singled, Iguchi hit a double, and Konerko hit a sac fly to left to bring home Mercury. Rowand doubled into the right field gap, bringing home Iguchi. 2-0. In the bottom of the second, Uribe continued his hot hitting with a long fly that *just* made it over the left field fence for a dinger. Ozuna tripled into the right field gap, and Mercury walked. Ozuna scored easily when Iguchi lofted a fly into deep right. 4-0. After a walk to Carl Everett, Konerko went the other way with a pitch down and outside, and grounded it through to drive in Scotty. 5-0.

With El Duque on the mound, the game looked to be over. Hernandez wove a gem through five. In the sixth, he gave up a run on a triple and a balk. Then, in the seventh, he fell apart. Mark Teahen smashed a double down the right field line. Ranger Joe Buck followed with a Herculean clout to left field. 5-3. Our bullpen didn't exactly shut the door. Neal Cotts didn't have it, as he plunked Aaron Guiel and surrendered a single to Terrence Long. Ozzie brought in Vizcaino to get the last out.

We got one back when the Captain blasted a sky-high home run to left. That was barely enough. Ozzie called for the psychotic lefty Marte, who promptly hung a breaking ball to Matt Stairs, which Stairs laced into left for a single. He then left a fastball over the plate, which Emil Brown slashed into the left field bleachers. 6-5. Note to Kenny Williams: can we *please* dump this guy? Or at least check him into Bellevue?

Mercifully, Cliff Politte and Hermanson came in to shut it down. That's Hermanson's 33rd save of the season. What a year for the unsung hero. Hermanson is hurting, and he's open about it, telling the press, "I don't have my best stuff . . . I haven't had it for a while since this has been going. But I don't feel terrible out there." He's playing through it. I hope he heals; the good news is that if he doesn't, Jenks is ready out in the bullpen.

Game two, Contreras was the story. What a turnaround he's had. He thoroughly dominated the hapless Royals, going 7 2/3 shutout innings and giving up only six hits. His secret inning problem seems to be gone. He's locating, and he's concentrating. The way he's pitched, I think we'll probably go into the playoffs with a rotation sans El Duque. Then the question becomes whether El Duque should even be on the playoff roster with McCarthy pitching the way he is. I like El

Duque's experience, but it's tough to say that he should beat out McCarthy for the roster spot.

We got our only run of the night off of Mike Wood. Fittingly, it came off the bat of the Captain, a true bomb to left center, number 36 on the year. Boy, the Dodgers must be crying their eyes out now – they traded him long ago to the Reds for an elderly late inning reliever named Jeff Shaw. The Reds have to be crying as well – they got Mike Cameron in return for Konerko.

Defensive play of the night: Jermaine Dye and Willie Harris. Mike Sweeney ("he shaved the faces of gentlemen who never thereafter were heard of again") was on first in the top of the fifth when Emil Brown smoked a liner past Harris at second base. Sweeney froze, thinking the ball would be caught. The Silent Assassin, playing shallow, came up firing, and rifled the ball to Harris at second base on one hop to force out Sweeney. Heads-up play by both parties.

We lost game three after our bats went into a coma. Freddy Garcia pitched well, going seven innings and giving up only three runs, but we only scored two for the game. We were no-hit for 4 2/3 innings by J.P "Thurston" Howell "III." The only bright spot was a play we see far too rarely in baseball: a steal of home by Pablo Ozuna in the fifth. We actually grabbed the lead in the fifth after Scotty P. singled home Chris Widger. Ozuna, who was on first, ended up on third. When Mr. Howell went to first to try to hold on Podsednik, Ozuna took off for home and slid in under Ranger Joe's tag. 2-0. Of course, Garcia gave up three runs the following inning, so it didn't matter much. Final score: 4-2 Royals.

The second win against KC made it a seven game win streak. Our lead was back up to 9.5 over the second-place

Indians. Game three was a tough loss, but we're still in good shape. One problem I foresee, however: we didn't hit well against a rotten pitching staff. For the three-game series, our total output was 9 runs. That's unspectacular at best. Against a good pitching staff (read: A's or Angels) that could spell trouble.

The good news: Ozzie is getting wise to the status of his bullpen. Jenks is being prepared to take over at closer. "Right now, hopefully nothing bad happens to Hermie where he can't go," says Jenks. "But if they call on me in that type of situation, I believe I can do it. Absolutely. I have enough confidence, and trust myself to get the job done." Hermanson, who is nothing but class, says that Jenks is ready to take over for him at closer, too.

Meanwhile – it's about time – Ozzie is getting ticked at Damaso "I'm Crazier Than The Menendez Brothers Combined" Marte (40 hits and 30 walks in 42 innings). "I don't like it when Marte goes out there and doesn't want to attack people. . . . He doesn't want to pitch the way he should pitch. It can be a lot of things. Mental, guts. I think physically he's pretty fine. But like I told him, 'We need you. We need you to step up and do a good job because I count on you.'" Don't count on him too much, Ozzie.

In other news, Evel Knievel has been nominated for the Clemente Award for his public service. He's a solid community guy, and he really deserves the nomination. Of course, we have a team full of solid community guys. It's good to be a Sox fan. Even if you're a Yankees fan, you're fond of fellows like whiny A-Rod and steroid freaks Sheffield and Giambi. The Hawk is right – we're a team of good guys.

Dad's heading into Philadelphia for surgery next week, and we're all praying that it helps. We're excited that someone is actually going to take a look at what's going on inside – so many doctors are afraid to do that. If we're lucky, they'll find something clear-cut they can operate on. We'll find out soon enough.

The Sox get the Angels next, and that's a potential playoff match-up. Please, somebody, wake up the bats!

	W	L	PCT	GB	Home	Away	Div	Streak
Chicago WSox	87	52	.626	---	43-28	44-24	40-14	Lost 1
Cleveland	79	61	.564	8 1/2	34-32	45-29	29-30	Won 4
Minnesota	73	66	.525	14	39-32	34-34	31-24	Won 1
Detroit	63	75	.457	23 1/2	32-36	31-39	24-34	Lost 8
Kansas City	45	93	.326	41 1/2	27-43	18-50	16-38	Won 1

September 12, 2005
DAD:

I can't believe this. *We had a fifteen-game lead.* Now it's down to five and a half. Five and a half! I'm on the plane for Philadelphia to have Dr. Meyers cut me open, and I'm so furious about the Sox that I'm not even thinking about whether the surgery will work or not. Of course, we have the Angels to blame for that. They came in to the Cell and swept us.
Meanwhile, the Indians swept the Twins. This is the only day the Sox have off for the rest of the season, and I hope they're as furious as I am. It's no shame to lose to the Angels, but to be swept at home is a revoltin' development.

Being a White Sox fan makes me feel like Daffy Duck. He would have to make a decision, and above him on one side would be a small Daffy dressed as the devil, urging him to do evil things, while the Daffy angel on the other side counseled virtue. Except my angel and devil aren't about how to behave; they're about pessimism and optimism. Instead of an angel and devil, they're more like Winnie the Pooh (read: optimist) and

239

Eeyore (read pessimist). To make matters worse, they aren't above quoting every movie I've ever seen as they argue in my mind. They've been having a field day arguing lately as they fight about the Sox's collapse.

Eeyore: They're melting! They're melting!

Pooh: That's not funny. Who ever told you that you were funny?

Eeyore: A.A. Milne isn't around right now, okay? I'll bet when he's not looking you spit some of that honey out.

Pooh: No, I don't. I *like* honey.

Eeyore: Sure you do. (calling out) They're melting!

Pooh: (accusingly) You haven't even seen *The Wizard of Oz*.

Eeyore: Yes, I have. I watched it the other day. You know who reminded me of the Sox?

Pooh: (guardedly) Who?

Eeyore: The Wicked Witch of the East.

Pooh: But she's not even in the movie. We don't even see her. I mean, the only time she's in it is when Dorothy's house ---

Eeyore: Exactly.

Pooh: That's not funny.

Eeyore: "You've got to ask yourself one question: 'Do I feel lucky?'"

Pooh: *You're* quoting Clint Eastwood? Here: Robin Williams. "Carpe diem. Seize the day, boys."

Eeyore: Jack Nicholson: "You can't handle the truth!"

Pooh: Peter Finch: "I'm as mad as hell, and I'm not going to take this anymore!"

Eeyore: (pause) That doesn't sound like you at all.

Pooh: My honey jar is empty.

Eeyore: Oh. May I sum up?

Pooh: (giving up as he starts to waddle away.) Fine. I have to go look for more honey.

Eeyore: Then this is appropriate for you and your Sox. "Hasta la vista, baby!"

I think, at the moment, Eeyore is winning.

The first game against the Angels was incredibly painful to watch. Buehrle was hit all over the lot, giving up ten hits and five runs in six innings. Yet it was tied 5-5, because we scored four runs in the fourth after Dye tripled Konerko and Rowand home, scored on a Hambino groundout, and Uribe followed with a two-run blast. At that point we led 4-3, and I was actually laughing, because when Dye tripled, Rowand was running so fast he caught up with Konerko as they rounded third base. He almost ran up the Captain's back. They caught us in the sixth, when Robb (if Rob is short for Robert, what is Robb short for? Robber baron?) Quinlan hit a two-run shot to right. In the seventh, Carl Everett robbed Cabrera of a HR with a leaping catch at the left-field wall, and the way our relief corps pitched, we should have been okay. Bobby Jenks, in particular, was outstanding, striking out five in three innings. In the eleventh, Rowand was on second with one out, and Uribe singled to left, but Juan Rivera fired a strike to the plate on the fly and they nipped Rowand by an eyelash.

Then came the twelfth, and justice was ill-served. Vlad Guerrero launched a bomb (at least it looked like one when it left the bat) and just stood at the plate, admiring his work. I *hate* that. The Captain doesn't do it, Dye doesn't do it, and players who have class don't do it.

Not Guerrero. He is a great, great player, but what he did stunk. When he realized the ball wouldn't clear the wall, he made a mad dash and barely beat the throw to second. Bengie Molina popped a bunt down the third-base line, and Blum raced down to throw him out at first. Guerrero, who had already done one stupid thing, wasn't finished. He ignored the third base coach's sign, and ran for home. Iguchi, covering first, immediately realized what was happening and fired to the plate.

There was one problem. Ross Gload, playing first, had gone into foul territory after running in from first on the bunt, and now, thinking the play was over, walked back *across* the first-base line, blocking Iguchi's way. The best Iguchi could do was fire the ball low and up the line at third, leaving A.J. out of position to tag Guerrero. Guerrero scored, as Justice proved blind, and after the game everyone was complimenting him on his "aggressive play." Bull. He was trying to make up for his earlier stupidity, and got lucky. We went down in the bottom of the inning, and that was that.

The second game was hyped as a battle between Cy Young candidates: Jon Garland (17-8) and Bartolo Colon (18-7). Colon was listed as questionable before the game with an ailing back. He showed up, though. The first two innings it looked as though Garland had the edge; Colon gave up two runs, including three consecutive walks in the second, while the Angels went six up, six down. The Sox could've broken the game open in the second, when Rowand was up with bases loaded and two outs. Iguchi had just sweated through a 3-2 count, fouling off a couple before he held up on a pitch just outside to force in a run.

Rowand wasn't so patient, swinging at the first pitch and flying out. He said later, "There are two ways to look at it. He walks three guys, so take until I get a strike. OK. That's one way.

Another way is, he wasn't wild during those walks and he didn't get a couple of calls, and they were upset about the calls he didn't get. I know what pitch he's going to give me. He tried to set up middle away and throw a strike, and that's exactly what I was thinking. It didn't work out."

Nope, and it came back to haunt us later. Finley homered to give them a 3-2 lead in the fourth, and then Anderson crushed a three-run home run to right on a 2-2 pitch from Garland an inning later. As an indication of how far Garland has fallen, neither Finley nor Anderson had hit a HR in a month. Not only that, but the Angels' 10-5 victory was only the second time in their last 29 games that they reached double figures.

Anderson commented after the game, "It was about making mistakes out over the plate by them." That just about summed it up.

By the third game yesterday, with our lead over the Indians down to 6 ½, and our losing streak at three, I didn't have a good feeling. John Lackey was throwing for them with El Duque for us, and I didn't like our chances, even playing at home.

Eeyore: I knew it all along.

Pooh: You're a fair-weather fan.

Eeyore: I am not. Fair-weather fans ride high when their team wins. I *always* think they'll find a way to lose.

Pooh: If we didn't have to be in books together, I'd dump you.

Lackey, who pitched so brilliantly in the seventh game of the 2002 Series, then had two mediocre seasons, is back in form, and yesterday he showed how far back he's come. He threw seven shutout innings while he was staked to a 5-0 lead. The Angels killed El Duque, homering three times in the first. They would have had a fourth, but Evel robbed Guerrero with a leaping catch over the wall in center. The stated plan for the Sox was for El Duque to throw five innings or so, and for McCarthy to follow.

It didn't work out that way. El Duque was gone in the third, and McCarthy threw almost six innings of good relief, but Lackey was too tough. The Indians won again, but with our lead down to 5 ½, the Sox still acted confident. Scotty said, "You have ups and downs throughout a 162-game schedule. We had a rough homestand here, but we play good on the road. So, we will bounce back." Konerko was also unruffled. "There are always momentum shifts, and right now, the Indians seem to have the momentum and we are down. There's no doubt it stinks when you aren't playing well, but it doesn't mean it has to be like that on Tuesday. We feel like if we put together a good game of hitting and pitching, we are going to win."

Eeyore: Can you say "Whistling in the dark?"
Pooh: Shut up.
Me: I'll give you a movie star quote of my own.
Pooh/Eeyore: What's that?
Me: All things considered, I'd rather be in Philadelphia.

	W	L	PCT	GB	Home	Away	Div	Streak
Chicago WSox	87	55	.613	---	43-31	44-24	40-14	Lost 4
Cleveland	82	61	.573	5 1/2	37-32	45-29	32-30	Won 7
Minnesota	73	69	.514	14	39-32	34-37	31-27	Lost 3
Detroit	65	76	.461	21 1/2	34-37	31-39	26-35	Won 2
Kansas City	46	95	.326	40 1/2	27-43	19-52	17-40	Lost 2

September 15, 2005
BEN:

The good news: Dad is out of the hospital and back home. Dr. Meyers found that Dad's rectus abdominus muscles on both sides had essentially torn loose from the pelvic floor. This necessitated making incisions roughly 3-4 inches on either side of his pelvis, pulling down the rectus abdominus muscles and pulling up the pelvic floor, then sewing them together. Because the pelvic floor is attached to the adductor muscles, Dr. Meyers had to also cut between the adductor muscles and the pelvic floor to release the muscles and then reattach them. It's a helluva surgery – in layman's language, it makes typical hernia surgery look like child's play. Still, Mom and the girls and I are all glad that Meyers found *something*.

The bad news: the collapse continues. All of a sudden, our lead is down to 4.5 games with 17 games to go. Cleveland refuses to lose. And we lost two of three to *Kansas City*. The wonderful thing about a big lead is that it takes a long time to lose. The bad thing is that if you lose it, you challenge the 1969 Cubs for the "Chokers of the Century" award.

We took the first game from the Royals rather easily, 6-4, to break a four-game losing streak. Jose Contreras, who has been our best pitcher in the second half of the season (he's 8-2), went 5 2/3, giving up four runs, three of them earned. Unfortunately, his secret inning problem reared its ugly head once more; he pitched well through five, and then couldn't get it done in the sixth.

It was 5-1 in the sixth when Contreras opened the door for the Royals. Joe Crede fielded a bad-hop grounder from Ambres off his shoulder. Long hit a broken-bat flare to right to put two men on. Then it was Mike Sweeney ("Sweeney pondered and Sweeney planned, like a perfect machine he planned") doubling to right on a low, outside pitch, scoring Ambres. Contreras threw wildly to the plate, and it was 5-3. Politte relieved, and Angel Berroa hit a high chopper over the mound. There was no play, and the score was 5-4. Uh-oh. Not again.

We got an insurance run in the eighth on a Crede double and a Scotty P. single to give us some breathing room. Then it was time for Big Bobby Jenks. He was simply dominant. He went two innings, shutting the Royals down.

Game two was a high-scoring heartbreaker. It was painful because Dustin Hermanson blew a two-run lead in the ninth. We were leading 9-7 going into the bottom half. Our offense had been stellar, with everyone in the lineup getting a hit, and Uribe, Iguchi, and Crede homering. Our pitching had been less than satisfactory, with Garcia surrendering seven runs in just over five innings before giving way to Cotts, Vizcaino and Politte. But it all came apart in the ninth. Hermanson struck out Sweeney, and I thought we were getting back on track. But Stairs singled up the middle, and Emil Brown followed with another single up the middle. Teahen rifled a single to right, and it was 9-8. Angel Berroa singled to right, and it was tied up. But – oh, no – Dye misplayed the single, and all of a sudden here came Teahen around third with the winning run. No play at the plate. From 9-7 to 10-9. We lose. Yuck, yuck, and yuck. Where are you, Ozzie? How many singles does a guy need to give up before you yank him?

We needed that game badly. Cleveland won, of course, so our lead shrank from six games to five going into the series finale. I thought we had a good shot at this game going in, with Buehrle (15-7, 3.13) on the hill and Greinke (4-16, 6.06 ERA) going for the Royals. After all, Buehrle is steady as the rock of Gibraltar, if kooky as Goldie Hawn circa 1968.

The game was all tied up at two going into the seventh. That's when Buehrle lost it. Chip Ambres led off with a double to left. After Buehrle got an out, Emil Brown smoked a liner to left, scoring Ambres and giving the Royals the lead. It was still a close game. So who did Ozzie go to? Politte? Cotts? Try again – it was Vizcaino time. He immediately gave up a single to Berroa, and then hung a breaking ball to Ranger Joe, who rocketed it down the left field line, scoring two more. All of a sudden, it was 5-2 KC. Vizcaino intentionally walked Teahen, then struck out some guy named Justin Huber, bringing .192 Andres Blanco to the plate. Blanco chopped one between the mound and first base, and Vizcaino badly misplayed it, loading the bases. Naturally, Vizcaino walked Aaron Guiel to force in a run and make it 6-2.

The game was over from there. We scored three in the eighth to make it 6-5 (walks to Harris and Everett, a single by Rowand, a double by Iguchi driving in all three of them). It wasn't enough. Final score: 7-5 Royals.

Remember that famous Gary Larson cartoon of a man looking at his car's sideview mirror and seeing a gigantic eye staring right into it? The caption at the bottom of the mirror reads "objects closer than they appear." Cleveland is closer than they appear. We can feel them breathing down our neck. In fact, we face them right after a series in Minnesota, and Minnesota always plays us tough. They way we're playing, I can definitely see us going into the Cleveland series with a 1.5 game lead. Somebody hit the panic button.

Ozzie is rightfully ticked (although he deserves a share of blame here for picking the wrong relievers at the wrong time). "We've played good all year long catching the ball, making the plays and making the big pitch," said the inimitable Oz. "Right now, it's not there. There's no doubt about it, we flat out stink."

In other news, Damaso Marte's nuttiness is wearing thin. Ozzie sent him home from the ballpark a couple of days ago after Marte showed up late to practice. Marte supposedly said he went to see a doctor to check out his arm. It was a lie. "It seems like he is OK (physically)," said Ozzie. "I don't want this kid just to make an excuse like he was hurt just because he was giving it up. A lot of guys in this game give up home runs, base hits.........I don't want him to use it as an excuse to fake injury. I'm not saying he was. I just worry about it. Because he was not performing the way he thinks he can perform. To me, I'd rather have a guy hurt physically than be hurt mentally. . . . Mentally, we need guys to show up every day. I don't know if Marte is ready to do that for the team. If the decision I made on Sunday hurt his feelings, I care less. That's my team. That's my rules. If you don't like it, get out of here." Oz went further than that, stating "I'm going to talk to Kenny (Williams) and see if he (Marte) is ready to help this team. If Marte is not ready to help this team, he can have a nice trip to the Dominican Republic and enjoy himself. He has to come and show me he's ready to play."

Good. It's about time. But why did Marte have to wait to implode until we're in the middle of a team implosion? Just what we need. Distractions going into Minnesota. This could be a *really* depressing week.

	W	L	PCT	GB	Home	Away	Div	Streak
Chicago WSox	88	57	.607	---	43-31	45-26	41-16	Lost 2
Cleveland	84	62	.575	4 1/2	39-33	45-29	32-30	Won 2
Minnesota	75	70	.517	13	39-32	36-38	33-28	Lost 1
Detroit	67	78	.462	21	35-39	32-39	27-37	Won 2
Kansas City	48	96	.333	39 1/2	29-44	19-52	19-41	Won 2

September 18, 2005

DAD:

I can't cough or laugh without wincing, so for the first time in my life I'm watching the Sox without any apparent emotion. Inside, of course, my stomach is doing its version of *The Poseidon Adventure.* But I'm back home from Philadelphia, and the Sox are back home, awaiting Cleveland, both of us hanging on for dear life.

With a 4 ½ game lead going into the Twins series, and the Indians coming to the Cell immediately after that, we needed to win two out of three so our lead would be at least 3 ½ and a Cleveland sweep wouldn't put us into second place. Did Yankees fans ever think this pessimistically? Hmmmm, perhaps I'm thinking that way because I'm back home recovering and on narcotics for the post-surgical pain. Or perhaps it's because Marte rejoined the team. He made a 15-minute apology to the team, and Ozzie commented, "To come up and do what he did, I think it convinced his teammates he was sorry. It was up to them if he was coming or not. They made the decision to do it, and I respect that decision. He's going to be with us for the rest of the season." Nooooooo . . . .

But I need to say thank you to Minnesota. We scored five runs in three games and somehow managed to win two out of three, even with the Great Santana hurling the middle game. Of course, he shut us out, again, and in the four games he's pitched against us this year he has given up 2, 1, 0, and 0 runs in that order. Buehrle lost to him the first two times, then Garcia, and the middle game of this series El Duque. I would guess that pitching against him must feel like you're the sacrificial virgin being led to the funeral pyre.

With his victory a foregone conclusion, and Cleveland on fire as they swept Kansas City, it was imperative that the Sox win the other two games. We got the two games, but not without help from the Twins. If we hang on and win the division, I'll have to send a thank-you note to all my relatives in the Twin Cities.

And just why, you may ask, should we thank them?

Because not once in the three-game series did the Twins execute a sacrifice bunt.

We won both the first and last games 2-1, and they couldn't or wouldn't bunt. It cost them. In the first game, they had the leadoff man on base five of the first six innings, and they never bunted him over. They had a rookie, Scott Baker, throwing, and he was terrific, allowing only two hits in seven innings. Meanwhile, Jon Garland pitched heroically in a crucial game, scattering six hits over eight innings, and only allowing a run on Jacque Jones' fourth inning solo HR. We got our run in the top half of that inning, when two-out hits by Crede, Scotty, and Iguchi brought a run home.

After Marte(!) had gotten two batters in the ninth and Jenks had finished that inning, the game went into the tenth. Dye and A.J. had seeing-eye singles under the shortstop and second baseman's gloves, respectively, and then Uribe popped a bunt to the first-base side of the pitcher's mound. Jesse Crain, their reliever, ran in and kicked it into foul territory. He probably booted it because the Twins had forgotten what a bunt was.

Bases loaded, no one out. Crede then lined one off of Crain's leg for a run, putting us up 2-1, but we couldn't score again. Big Bobby Jenks blew them away in their half, and we escaped with a win.

Game two: Santana. 13 strikeouts, two hits in eight innings. Is there anyone else remotely this good? He left in the ninth, after loading the bases on two hits and a walk, but they were leading 5-0, and Joe Nathan struck out the side to end it. The only story for the Sox was that El Duque got roughed up again, and McCarthy came in and pitched well, which complicates matters for the playoffs. Which one do you keep on the roster?

That's assuming that we make the playoffs.

Game three my stomach went from *The Poseidon Adventure* to *Earthquake*. Our lead was down to 3 ½ and this game was more than crucial, it was pivotal.

Contreras pitched the game of his life. He gave up one run and five hits over eight innings. He was matched by Kyle Lohse and Jesse Crain, who combined for one run and seven hits over seven innings.

Contreras had help from the Twins. In the third, Nick Punto tripled. When Jason Bartlett hit a hard grounder to Iguchi, Punto waited for a moment, then tried to score after Iguchi fired to first. Konerko threw him out by five feet. In the fourth, with the game 1-1, Lew Ford tried to bunt with runners on first and second. He bunted it just in front of the plate, and because he dallied, watching it, Hambino pounced on it and fired to Crede for a force at third, who then fired to Konerko for a double play.

But by the eighth it was still 1-1 (Rowand had sharply singled in a run in the fourth) and I was swallowing every antacid in the house. With two out, Konerko got his biggest hit of the season, and it was a tough one. Fighting off a high inside pitch, he fisted it into right for a Texas leaguer. Hambino then lined one over the shortstop, leaving it up to Dye. He hit a hard grounder to Punto's right at second base. Punto, like a matador, attempted to wave it down instead of blocking it with his body, and the ball skipped under his glove as Konerko scored. The man from Bellevue, Marte, got two quick outs in the ninth, Big Bobby

251

Jenks blew away the last batter with a 99 mph fastball, we had taken two out of three, and our lead remained 3 ½ games.

Tomorrow the Indians are here. We have 14 games left to play.

If we sweep them it's over. (Pooh)

If we win two out of three, our lead goes up to 4 ½ and we'll have some momentum. (Ben)

If we win one out of three, we'll be only 2 ½ in front, but still be in first place. (Me)

I am ignoring Eeyore.

Part V
Shut Up, Eeyore

September 19, 2005
DAD:

I love movies. Growing up, my mom and I would stay up on school nights watching the late show on WGN, and I saw more old movies than any kid I knew. I passed that love of old movies down to my own kids, and they've seen every great movie between the 1930's and the 1970's.

This Sox season has felt like a movie: a little surreal, since they've been in first place the whole season. I don't remember that ever happening before. And with my own illness, their season has taken on even more importance for me than it normally would have. Their success has been a welcome distraction from the pain, and the thought that they could fall short is even more painful than it ever was. It seems like a kid's perspective, but I've never fully understood the use of sports as a healthy distraction until now. I want them to win so badly that I have to remind myself that it's only a game.

So I wonder, now that their season has followed the standard exposition and development of a good story line, what will the outcome be? We've had the wonderful, joy-filled beginning, when everything went the hero's way. We followed that with the plunge into the dramatic abyss, with the hero holding on to the cliff by his fingernails. Now, will he fall? Or will he find a miraculous way to save himself?

Today, the hero, who was holding on with both hands, lost the grip of one of them. The game was a reverse microcosm of our season. Freddy Garcia got knocked about, giving up four runs in six-plus innings. Travis Hafner, who kills us, doubled in a run in the first, homered in the fifth, and along with Aaron Boone's HR in the second, the Indians jumped out to a 4-0 lead going into the bottom of the fifth. It looked as though it wasn't our night, because in the third both Crede and Iguchi hammered Millwood's pitches to left, but they were both caught. I thought about calling Ben, but I was too depressed to talk about it.

I called him after the fifth. Rowand led off by lofting a ball to deep right field. Casey Blake should have had it, but it glanced off his glove and Rowand took second base. Uribe fanned, but then Crede, who is growing a goatee (Ben thinks he looks just like Luke Skywalker) fouled off a couple of 3-2 curves before grounding a low fastball past Millwood into center field, making it 4-1. Mercury pounced on a Millwood hanging curve for a base hit to right, sending Crede to third, and Iguchi followed with a base hit to left, scoring Crede and sending Mercury flying to third and Iguchi taking second on the throw. 4-2, and the tying runs in scoring position. But Everett, who hadn't an extra base hit since September 7, popped out to short. Two down, and the Captain stepped in. I figured, he's the best we've got.

He is, and he proved it by lacing a curve to left-center for a two-run double.

> **DAD:** Did you see that? Did you see that!
> **BEN:** He's awesome. Just awesome.
> **DAD:** If we don't re-sign him at the end of the season, I will personally go to his house and beg him.

Seventh inning, still 4-4, Everett up. He launched one to right so hard, so little doubt, that the Cleveland announcer said simply, "Home run."

My response was somewhat different.

DAD: You can put it on the board, you friggin' Indians,
Yes!

BEN: (laughing) Pull the phone out of your mouth, Dad.

5-4, Sox, and life looked good. Then the eighth, and disaster.

Marte gave up a one-out walk to Hafner and a double to Martinez, and after he struck out Broussard, he was pulled so that Bobby Jenks could face Boone, mano a mano. Jenks threw a 2-2 fastball down and away, and Boone, to his credit, turned on it and ripped it to left for two runs to give them the lead.

DAD: $#@!$#@!

BEN: Grrrrrrr. . . .

We had two more chances. In the eighth, Ozuna, leading off, doubled, but was stranded at third when Uribe popped out. In the bottom half of the ninth, after Hafner had doubled another runner home in the top of the inning, making it 7-5, Scotty singled with one out but Iguchi fanned. Bob Wickman, their great reliever, was careful with Everett up, walking him on four pitches. Runners on first and second and the winning run at the plate; the right guy, again: the Captain.

The outfielders were plastered against the walls; no ball was getting by them to score the run from first. The crowd, on its feet, was as anxious as I was. The Captain fought the count to 2-2, then lined a shot just foul down the third–base line. The next pitch, Wickman threw a fastball, and Konerko just missed it, popping the ball to short center, and immediately sinking to his knees in frustration. The ball game was over, and our lead was 2 ½. Not only that, but the Yankees won, and our lead over them for a simple playoff spot is now four games.

The Sox still sounded confident in post-game interviews.

Everett: "I always say that as long as there's no games back behind your name, you are still on top. There's no sense of holding your head down."

Buehrle: "You can't say tomorrow is it. If we lose tomorrow, it ain't the end of the season. If we play like we did today, things will turn out good for us."

Konerko: "Just because we lost all that ground it doesn't mean that two weeks from now we have to be on the losing end. I believe we are going to do it, and if we do, I believe we will be dangerous after that's done."

DAD: How can they talk like that? Are they asleep?

BEN: I don't get it either.

DAD: If they lose tomorrow, it's over. OVER!

BEN: Do you want to call me tomorrow, or me call you?

DAD: I can't even think about it now. I'll try to be more coherent tomorrow.

BEN: Keep taking deep breaths, Dad.

DAD: I will as soon as I get this plastic bag off of my head.

September 20, 2005
BEN:

Wow, wow, wow, wow, and wow. Can Dad and I start breathing again? The Sox just took the second game of the

258

Cleveland series, which they needed desperately. A loss would have left us up 1.5 games and in position to finish the series only a half game up on the red-hot Tribe. Dad and I were calling each other between innings to give our appraisals. Before the game, the conversation went something like this:

> **DAD:** I think we're going to take this one. We should have had that game last night; this is really the crucial one. We lose this, we lose the division.
>
> **BEN:** I think we probably lose the division even *if* we win this ballgame. I think we need to take the next two to pull it out. Look at Cleveland's schedule the rest of the way: Kansas City, Tampa Bay, and us. Meanwhile, we get Minnesota and Detroit. Realistically speaking, we could go into the final series with Cleveland *down* four games.
>
> **DAD:** I don't think Cleveland will go undefeated the rest of the way. Even if we don't take the division, we'll win the Wild Card. But it's *sick* that we have to think about winning the stupid Wild Card after leading this division by 15 games.

Then, the game. I was feeling nervous, to say the least. We had Buehrle on the hill, and they had youngster Jake Westbrook. This, I thought, was not the time for a Slip N' Slide performance. In the first, Coco Crisp hit a single up the middle, and Jhonny Peralta followed with a flare to right. In came a charging Silent Assassin, who dove at the last minute and came up with the ball. Hafner grounded out to end the half. Westbrook put us down easily in order in our half.

In the top of the second, Buehrle walked Jose Hernandez, then left a fastball over the plate, which Aaron Boone put in the left field bleachers. 2-0. In our half, we went down in order once again, this time with the Captain, Hambino, and the Silent Assassin all striking out swinging.

BEN: Ugh.
DAD: They're making Westbrook look like Cy Young.
BEN: And Buehrle look like Westbrook.

Cleveland went down 1-2-3 in the third. Then we struck back. With a man on, Joe Crede turned on an outside fastball and drove it deep into the Chicago night. With fireworks bursting, he rounded the bases to make it 2-2.

DAD: Crede? Joe Crede?
BEN: Look at his hair. He was obviously using an Old Jedi Mind Trick.
DAD: He *does* look like Mark Hamill with that haircut.

Cleveland immediately took back the lead in the fourth on a solo bomb by Travis Hafner. In the bottom of the inning, the Captain got us started with a hard-hit double down the line. Hambino did his job, grounding out to the right side to advance Konerko, and then Dye walked. Rowand popped up to the shortstop, leaving Juan Uribe in the unenviable position of having to get a hit with two outs. Except that Uribe got it done, rifling the ball into right and scoring Konerko. Crede almost followed up with a single, but Coco Crisp got a good jump on the ball and made a sliding catch.

BEN: We should have had more there. It's still 3-3. Rowand has to hit the ball to the outfield there.

DAD: Ozzie needs to forget this six-inning garbage and get Buehrle out of there. He's getting hit all over the lot.

In the fifth, Buehrle slipped n' slid his way out of a double/walk situation; Westbrook pitched his way out of a single/error situation. We should have had a run here. If Konerko were faster, he would have beaten out what would have been an error by the second baseman. Then Hambino couldn't chug out a slow roller, and he got thrown out to end the inning.

DAD: Asking Konerko and A.J. to beat out infield grounders is like asking Rosie O'Donnell to outrun Michael Johnson.

All was smooth for Buehrle in the sixth, and though we got singles from Dye and Uribe in the bottom half, we couldn't score.

BEN: This game is starting to look like *Lost*, we've stranded so many men.

Buehrle left in the seventh after Casey Blake hit a line shot that kept carrying, carrying, carrying all the way into the stands in center. Cotts came in, gave up two more singles, and then Travis Hafner drove one home with a double into the right field corner. After a walk to load the bases, Cliff Politte came on to relieve. Ronnie Belliard leaped on a high fastball and smashed a grounder down the third base line. Crede stabbed it, stepped on third for the force, and gunned to first for the double play.

In the bottom half, with the Sox down 5-3, Carl Everett led off with a double, and Konerko walked. Hambino crushed a ball down the right field line for a double, with Everett scoring. Despite Everett's wild hand motions egging Konerko to go for home, he stopped on third. After an intentional walk to Dye, Rowand lofted a sac fly to Casey Blake in right. Blake threw home, but Ronnie Belliard cut off the throw and fired to third in an attempt to nail Hambino. His throw was low and wild, and the ball got away from Aaron Boone. Hambino never stopped motoring, coming all the way home to give us the lead, 6-5.

BEN: Is Cleveland trying to give this game away?
DAD: I'll take it.

The top of the eighth was as exciting as any half-inning I've ever seen. After Politte got two quick outs, he gave up a bloop to right. Another bloop to center, with Rowand breaking the wrong way, and there were men on first and third. Coco Crisp grounded a ball into the hole, a sure single. But Uribe backhanded the ball, jumped, and from mid-air flung the ball to first, nabbing Crisp by a step.

DAD: Yessssssssssssss!!!!! That's Gold Glove stuff! That is perhaps the most clutch play I've ever seen from the Sox. Ever.

We went down easily in the bottom of the eighth. Then, the top of the ninth. Ozzie brought in Big Bobby Jenks, not Hermanson, who has been ailing. Jenks walked the first batter, Peralta, on four pitches. Uh-oh. Don Cooper came out to chat, and then Jenks struck out Hafner on a killer inside fastball.

262

Victor Martinez took a low fastball and hit it hard to center. It should have been a routine fly ball, except that Rowand broke in on it. Realizing his error, he began sprinting toward the center-field wall. He awkwardly turned and jumped, but the ball dropped *just* over his glove for a double. With men on second and third and one out, Belliard grounded one slowly to Iguchi, who threw him out. The tying run scored.

&^%$!

With the count 0-2 on Ben Broussard, A.J. blocked a breaking ball in the dirt to save a run. Finally, Jenks struck Broussard out on an outside curveball.

> **BEN:** Rowand. Can't believe it was Rowand.
> **DAD:** That's a tough ball to read off the bat. Still, I don't understand why the heck Ozzie didn't intentionally walk Belliard to give us a chance at a force. What was he thinking?
> **BEN:** (muttering) Rowand. Rowand. Rowand.

In the bottom half, we had our chance. With one out, Konerko singled to left, and we sent in Willie Harris to pinch-run. A.J. singled to center; Dye moved the runners up with a short nubber to third. Rowand took one for the team, loading the bases and bringing up Uribe with two out and a chance to be a hero. He declined, popping out to right.

> **DAD:** I can't stand this . . .

Top of the tenth. Hermanson came on in relief, and immediately gave up a single. Casey Blake tried to put down a bunt, but couldn't execute and struck out. Grady Sizemore hit a slow grounder toward short, and Crede tried to cut it off to flip to second, but he missed it. Luckily, Uribe was playing in proper position, and grabbed it for the force at second. Coco Crisp came up with Sizemore on first, but overeager, swung at the first pitch and flied to center.

DAD: I'm thinking bad thoughts.
BEN: Like what?
DAD: You're not old enough for me to tell you.

Bottom of the tenth.
Second pitch.
Fat fastball to Joe Crede.
Ballgame.
The ball was absolutely crushed, off the meat of the bat. A no-doubter. Good night. Don't forget to turn out the lights.

BEN: Never underestimate the power of the Force!
DAD: Joe Crede. I'm sending money to charity in his name.
BEN: So's Aaron Rowand. (Jabba the Hut voice) Ho, ho, ho, ha, ha, ha. He was using an Old Jedi Mind Trick!

Until tomorrow night, sign off Dad and me, singing the theme from *Star Wars.*

September 21, 2005
DAD:
Where's that plastic bag again?
This was awful. I mean, AWFUL. We had a chance to bury the Indians, and instead they buried us. Scott Elarton, who

was 3-0 with a 1.22 ERA this month, pitched even better than that, throwing seven-plus innings of shutout ball, and inducing pop-up after pop-up after pop-up. Our hitters looked like they were overeager, running after the pitches just like Jessica Simpson runs after publicity at a photo-op.

She might have hit better.

We couldn't do anything. Meanwhile, Travis Hafner homered twice, and his second HR, in the ninth off of Jeff Bajenaru, left the bat somewhat faster than the speed of light. Garland pitched well, holding them to two runs, but after Hafner hit his three-run shot in the eighth to make it 5-0, the game was over.

If we somehow right this sinking ship, I have a strong feeling it will be because of the fire of one man: Hambino. After the game, he was genuinely angry. "It would have been nice one time in this series to jump on them early. We never did that. It always seemed like we were behind. It's a lot of pressure to keep throwing on our pitchers, to keep holding them and keep holding them, when we can't score early. We didn't play very well, and that's what was disappointing. I didn't feel the energy tonight, and you can't have that right now. We have to play better than we did tonight. That wasn't a good effort at all."

Good. I'm glad *someone's* angry. Now we have to go on the road and face the Twins for four games, and I'm sure they can't wait to knock us out of the race, since they're done. The Indians get Kansas City for four games, and with our lead at 2 ½, the road just got much, much tougher. Great.

DAD: There's nothing to say, is there.
BEN: I'm worn out.

265

DAD: At least they didn't get swept. A.J. was furious after the game.

BEN: And now he gets to go back to where he started, and they'll be looking to nail him.

DAD: I think Cleveland is gonna roll over Kansas City. I'm just hoping Piniella will fire up Tampa Bay so they can take a game from the Indians.

BEN: We're going to need some help.

DAD: I wonder if Papa can put in a good word…

```
                 W     L    PCT    GB    Home  Away   Div    Streak
Chicago WSox    91    60   .603   ---   44-33 47-27  44-19  Lost 1
Cleveland       89    63   .586  2 1/2  42-33 47-30  37-31  Won 1
Minnesota       77    74   .510  14     40-34 37-40  34-30  Won 1
Detroit         67    85   .441  24 1/2 35-39 32-46  27-41  Lost 7
Kansas City     52    99   .344  39     33-44 19-55  23-44  Won 4
```

September 22, 2005
BEN:

I'm starting to feel like Charlton Heston at the end of *Planet of the Apes*. "We really finally did it. . . . You maniacs! You blew it up! Ah, damn you!" Or maybe Jim Carrey in *Liar, Liar*: "I'm kickin' my ass. D'you mind?!" But mostly, like Roy Scheider in *Jaws*: "We're gonna need a bigger boat."

Because now it's too close for comfort. After losing two out of three to the Indians, we went into the Minnesota series up 2.5 games. One game later, it's down to 1.5. We needed this game, and we didn't get it. As painful as it is to relive the game, here we go:

Brendan McCarthy started the game for us and threw a gem, going eight innings of four hit, one-run ball. He matched Minnesota's ace Santana pitch for pitch. His fastball was really darting, and he was getting help from the defense. In the first, Juan Uribe made a terrific play up the middle, catching a slow grounder on the run and throwing to first for the third out. In the second, we got a 5-4-3 double play after McCarthy gave up a leadoff walk. Top four, McCarthy struck out two straight Twins, one on a nasty changeup that dropped off the table and the other on a deceptive fastball that leaped out of his hand. In the fifth, Rowand made a great catch running back toward the center field, flipping his glove up at the last minute to snare a hard-hit liner. In the sixth, McCarthy worked out of a two-on, one-out jam by inducing a grounder to Crede, who stepped on third and fired smoothly to first for a DP.

In the bottom half, Crede played hero once more on a breaking ball he powered out of the park to left. He really had to go down to get it; it wasn't a bad pitch by any means (Santana hardly ever throws a bad pitch), but he got good wood on it, and full extension. "There is no try, only do!" I yelled. "You are a Jedi, like your father before you!"

Unfortunately, McCarthy immediately gave the run back on an inside fastball to Jacque Jones, who turned on it (the same way he turned on an inside pitch from Garcia earlier this year to break up that no-no) and drove it out of the park to right. Jones is so arrogant I wanted to punch the computer. He started with his "pimp roll" (as Tom Wolfe calls it) and flipped the bat snootily toward the dugout. If it weren't a close game, I would have been tempted to have a Sox pitcher drill him next time around.

We got a leadoff walk in the bottom of the seventh, but Rowand turned over his hands and hit into an easy double play. We returned the favor in top of the eighth, when McCarthy gave up a leadoff single, but then induced a 1-4-3 double play.

In the bottom of the eighth, we blew a big opportunity. With two outs, Widger hit a seeing-eye single through the left side of the infield, and Jedi Crede followed with a bouncer up the middle. With men on first and third, Ozuna popped out to end the inning. *Where is Scotty P???*

We got away with one in the ninth. Ozzie brought in Marte. I almost flung my cup of water at the wall. It's a 1-1 ballgame, the Indians are playing the Royals, which means they'll win, and you're bringing in the Unabomber? Of course, Marte walked the leadoff man, bringing a chorus of boos raining down upon his head. Politte came in, and after a stolen base and walk, he induced a flyout to Rowand for the first out. We got another out, and then Cotts came in with men on first and third. Jacque Jones hit a chopper over Cotts head, a recipe for a sure infield single. But through the middle of the infield stormed a charging Uribe, who gloved it and fired an absolute laser to first to nail a sliding Jones. Take that, Jones!

Our big opportunity came in the bottom of the ninth. Juan Rincon relieved Santana, which was a relief, and Tad Iguchi greeted him with a single up the middle. Rincon recovered to strike out Everett, but Captain Konerko lined one through to left. Rowand walked on a 3-2 count, and it was bases loaded, one out. Up came Jermaine Dye. I thought we had this one. If there's one player who has executed well practically the whole year, it's the Silent Assassin.

And he failed.

After going down 0-2, he popped up to the right side. Uribe followed suit, and the inning was over.

Unbe-freaking-lievable.

We got a huge 3-6-1 double play in the top of the tenth to bail Cotts out of a leadoff single. The Twins gave us a break in the bottom of the tenth. Scotty P., pinch hitting, hit a grounder up the middle that their shortstop bobbled, and our leadoff man was on. Crede, who was executing well all night, sacrificed down the first base line, and we had Scotty in scoring position for Hambino, pinch hitting for Ozuna. Jesse Crain intentionally walked him to get to Iguchi. Iguchi didn't come through; he pulled the ball down the third base line. DP, 5-3.

In-freaking-conceivable.

Bobby Jenks came in to pitch the top of the eleventh. Lew Ford took a low pitch and dumped it into short center, and Rowand broke back instead of forward. He tried to recover but couldn't get there, and Ford ended up on second. That's the second straight series that Rowand's defense has hurt us. He has speed, but his reads need work. Now was an inconvenient time for him to work on them.

Jenks got a little nubber back to the mound for the first out, and then settled down to face Joe Mauer. They intentionally walked Mauer and moved on to Matthew LeCroy. LeCroy turned over on a high fastball and grounded through the left side, scoring Ford and giving the Twins the lead. This time, I threw the cup.

While I went to get a towel to clean up the mess, Jacque Jones hit a rocket into the right field gap on a 95-mph fastball down the pipe, scoring two more. I threw the towel.

We went down silently in the eleventh, and that was that.

The Indians beat the Royals 11-6, and that was that.

We're 1.5 up, and that is that.

In the words of Peter Finch in *Network*, "I'm going to blow my brains out, right on this program, a week from today. So, tune in next Tuesday, that should give the public relations people a week to promote the show."

That is, unless the Sox can turn this around.

I'm not optimistic.

September 24, 2005
DAD:

Note: **During the course of the Sabbath, we are forbidden to use the phone, or electricity, so for 25 hours we don't really know what's going on outside in the world. Needless to say, Ben and I were both going crazy between Friday at sunset and Saturday an hour after sundown, since we were both in the dark about the results of the Friday night game. Then, it was finally Saturday night.**
Los Angeles, 7:15 p.m.

DAD: Hello?
BEN: Hey!
DAD: Did I have a good Shabbos? (Sabbath)
BEN: You had a very good Shabbos.
DAD: I take it we won last night.
BEN: First, I've got to tell you, Kenny and Ozzie have lost it. Kenny lectured the hitters before the Thursday game, telling them that they have to stop swinging for the fences, and Ozzie yelled at them *after* the game, and slammed the door to his office.
DAD: I'm glad. It must have helped.
BEN: I'm not sure it helped the hitters, Dad. We still only got three runs because Dye hit a bullet for a three-run HR in the first. That was good because of his failure the other night. The real story was Contreras. He was so clutch you wouldn't have believed it. He threw a

complete game, struck out nine, gave up one run, and we won 3-1.

DAD: Contreras made it hold up for the entire game?

BEN: He was almost unhittable, Dad. His forkball looked like it was dropping off a table, and his fastball was incredibly live. We were ahead 3-1 in the ninth, when Punto singled off Contreras to lead-off. He took off on a pitch to Mauer, and Mauer hit a ball toward the hole that Uribe left when he took off to cover second. Uribe somehow stopped on a dime, reversed course, and grabbed the ball for a quick flip to Iguchi at second that forced Punto by a heartbeat. Then Lecroy hit a grounder off of Contreras, and Iguchi raced in, picked it up and threw – and got Lecroy by another heartbeat.

DAD: Leaving Mauer at second with two out and the tying run at the plate. Who was up? Jones?

BEN: Yup. And Contreras struck him out on a forkball that plummeted two feet to end the game.

DAD: Wow! Cleveland?

BEN: Won on a gift from the Royals, and they're winning big tonight. Have you got the computer on yet? We're winning big tonight, too. Crede singled a run in the second –

DAD: The guy is a great clutch hitter –

BEN: And in the third, we went crazy. Scotty doubled. Iguchi laid down a perfect bunt down the third-base line and Mays fell down, so first and third, and Hambino doubled Scotty home.

DAD: Ozzie moving him to the three slot was a good idea.

BEN: Konerko reached out and poked a single to right, scoring Tad –

DAD: A.J didn't score?

BEN: We're not talking Mercury, here, Dad.

DAD: Good point. . . .

BEN: But it didn't matter – the Silent Assassin launched a bazooka to right for three runs.

DAD: No way!

BEN: Way. Mays left the game, and the crowd started singing –

DAD/BEN: Nan-na-na-na, na-na-na-na, hey, hey, hey, goodbye!

DAD: My computer's on now. Got the game going. Are you staying up for the end? Call you after?

BEN: Oh, yeah.

8:15 p.m

DAD: Garcia was awesome. If the Indians would lose just once . . .

BEN: Don't count on it. I've never seen a team so hot down the stretch.

DAD: You weren't around in 1978. Everyone talks of the Bosox collapse, but no one talks about the fact that the Yankees went 41-13 in their last 54 games. It was unbelievable. They were a veteran team, too. The Indians are good, but they're young, so maybe they'll screw up somewhere. We can't expect the Royals or Tampa Bay to beat them. Buehrle better win tomorrow, because after the Indians sweep the Royals, we've got to hope we can keep beating Detroit.

BEN: You feeling okay?

DAD: I think this recovery might take a little while, but I'll be okay eventually.

BEN: Love you, Dad.

DAD: Love you, too. I'll call you tomorrow when the game starts.

September 25, 2005
BEN:

Finally, some breathing room. Okay, it's only 2.5 games, but it's breathing room nonetheless. Before the Sox game started today (during an hour-long rain delay), Dad called to tell me the Indians had blown their 4-3 lead to Kansas City. I had stopped watching the Cleveland/Kansas City game when Cleveland took the lead late in the ballgame – that nasty ache in the pit of my stomach forced me to turn away – but I quickly switched back to it.

The end of the game was shocking . . . and convinced me that God was still on the side of the South Siders. The Tribe had jumped out to a 3-0 lead in the first on a three-run bomb to right by Victor Martinez. In the sixth, the Royals tied it up on a single, an error, another single, and a home run by Emil Brown. Ok, I thought, we have a shot here. Go, Kansas City! In the bottom of the seventh, my faith was justified. Teahen drilled one off the right field wall for a double, and after a bunt and a wild pitch, the score was 4-3 KC. Hold on, baby, just hold on.

KC missed a big opportunity in the eighth, but then again, they're a really bad team. It was bases loaded, no outs, and they didn't get a single run out of it. First Jhonny Peralta made a beautiful play on a grounder, throwing home across his body for the force at the plate. Then a groundout and a popout. No wonder this team is about 1,976 games back of the Sox.

Top nine. Mike McDougal, the Royals closer, pitching. Belliard led off with a bouncer up the middle that went for a single. I groaned as the stomach pain set in. Another infield single for Ben Broussard. Winning run on base. Now I went to look for the Tums. Aaron Boone got down a bunt, and both runners moved into scoring position. Casey Blake chopped one up to second, scoring the tying run. 4-4.

That's when I turned off the game. Five minutes later, Dad called to tell me that it was still 4-4 in the bottom of the ninth, but that the Royals were threatening. I grabbed the antacid and turned on the game. Angel Berroa had led off with a single. Huber, playing first base for the absent Sweeney, bunted Berroa to second. Paul Phillips, who is my new best friend, hit a long fly into center. Still, it should have been easy work for Grady Sizemore. But Sizemore looked confused out there; he couldn't see the ball because it got lost in the sun. The ball plummeted from the sky and plunked him right in the arm, bouncing merrily away. Berroa took off and didn't stop running until he crossed the plate.

It was beautiful. Beautiful. Beautiful.

Ozzie Guillen owes Grady Sizemore a thank-you card.

We owe the Royals a bottle of wine.

And 30,000 grateful fans at the Cell gave a standing ovation as the final was posted on the scoreboard.

Of course, there was still the little matter of the game against Minnesota. Minnesota is always tough, and we had Buehrle going. Would he be the dominating Buehrle, with his mixture of off-speed corner cutting stuff, or the six-inning workman who surrenders four runs?

He was brilliant. He went all the way: nine innings, one run, four hits, six strikeouts. The Twins got *nothing*.

Meanwhile, we got four runs in the first three innings. In the second, Silent Assassin singled, then stole second. With two down, Joe Crede (*again!!*) reached out and poked a soft liner into center that dropped just before the center fielder could reach it. The throw to the plate got away, and as Dye scored, Crede moved to second. "A Jedi's strength flows from the Force!" I informed the screen. Uribe popped up to end the inning, but we had the lead.

We extended it in the third. Rowand tripled on an outside changeup that he pushed into the right field gap, bringing home Tad Iguchi to make it 2-0; Konerko followed with a dinger to left. 4-0. The Twins got one in the fifth, but that was it.

And we're 2.5 up on the Tribe. Dad called to celebrate.

DAD: If we split with Detroit and they sweep Tampa Bay, they still come into the Cell behind us by a game.
BEN: I love Joe Crede. LOVE HIM. Did I say trade him? Silly me.
DAD: I think we're going to take three of four from Detroit.
BEN: I still get the feeling it won't be that easy. (Yoda voice) Detroit . . . is strong with the dark side of the Force. A domain of evil it is. In we must go.
DAD: It'll be okay. To quote *The Court Jester*, let's get in, get on with it, get it over with and get out. Get it?
BEN: Got it.
DAD: Good.

September 26, 2005
DAD:
No, no, NO!

No.

No way we lose to the Tigers today.

We finally don't see a Cleveland win on the scoreboard and we lose?

All right, all right, Cleveland was idle today, but still . . . we could've pushed our lead to three games.

What went wrong?

For our pitching staff, three pitches: two that Jon Garland threw to Brandon Inge, which he hit for HRs in the fourth (two-run) and sixth (solo), and one that Cliff Politte threw to Curtis Granderson, who hit a walk-off HR to lead off the ninth. Despite a two-run shot in the first by the Captain that put us up 2-0, and a solo shot by our resident Jedi in the fifth that put us up 3-2, our offense blew some opportunities.

Hambino had a tough day. In the third, after singles by Scotty and Tad, A.J. hit into a double play. In the eighth, with runners on second and third and one out, and the score tied 3-3, he struck out. Konerko walked, to load the bases, but Dye struck out to end the inning.

But the play that made me yell at the screen came in the ninth. Everett, for the second time in the game, was hit by a pitch, putting the go-ahead run on with nobody out. Rowand, who hasn't been hitting much of late, needed to bunt him over.

On the first pitch, a fastball belt-high, Rowand stabbed at the ball. The bat was slanted down toward the barrel, and as a result he popped it right to the first baseman. I think if he had crouched a bit more he might have gotten the bat level, but he didn't. "You've gotta get the bunt down!" I yelled. Nobody expects Rowand to hit like Willie Mays, but even great power hitters like Mays and Mantle would have gotten the bunt down.

Sure enough, that killed the inning, as Crede and Uribe grounded out.

In a close game like this one, failure to execute is the kiss of death. Moments later, Granderson kissed the ball out of the park. Crap. A huge opportunity to gain on the Indians, and it's gone. The lead is down to two, and now we face the Tigers for three more while Cleveland gets Tampa Bay. CRAP.

DAD: I just found my first baseball manual: a pamphlet Papa bought for me at the Merchandise Mart in Chicago in the early 60's called *How to Improve Your Baseball.*
BEN: I assume there's some correlation between this piece of information and the disaster we just saw?
DAD: "The forearm of the forward arm should be approximately *parallel* with the ground and the angle between the forearm and upper arm should be approximately a right angle."
BEN: When bunting?
DAD: When bunting.
BEN: "The fingers of the right and left hands should be barely touching at the back of the neck and the thumbs should meet at the front of the throat."
DAD: When choking?
BEN: When choking.
DAD: One bunt. One blasted bunt. If we can't beat the Tigers after we've thrashed them all year, what the heck is going to save us now?

September 27, 2005
BEN:

Five words never before uttered in order: thank God for Tampa Bay. The Devil Rays are saving our rears. Remember how I said that Tampa Bay gets no fans? How they're not very good? All is forgiven. Lou Piniella, you join Paul Phillips in my pantheon of new friends.

We lost our second straight game against the Tigers. Brendan McCarthy started and pitched well again – six innings, three runs – but was outdone by Detroit's Nate Robertson, who went six and gave up only one tally. We deserved to lose this game. Revoltingly, we left twelve men on base. We scored only two runs despite getting nine hits and eight walks.

We were already at a disadvantage when the game started. Jedi Joe Crede was out of action after flying home to care for his wife, who was suffering from pregnancy complications. That meant that our hottest and most clutch hitter (.404 over his last 16 games, six HRs, 13 RBI) was out, and that light-hitting but speedy Pablo Ozuna was in.

Detroit took a 1-0 lead in the bottom of the third when Omar Infante lashed a long fly ball over the fence in left. We got three walks in the top of the fourth but couldn't score a single run; Rowand grounded into a double play (he's making that a habit) to kill one walk, and Everett grounded out to third with two men on to end the inning. In the top of the fifth we got on the board. Ozuna hit a single to left, stole second, moved over on a ground ball, and then scored on a single to right by Juan Uribe to tie the game at one. We should have gotten a couple more runs, but Rowand turned over his hands again and grounded out to short (Rowand's LOB: 6). "You're killing me, Aaron!" I shouted.

Detroit responded in the bottom of the fifth with a solo HR to left from Craig Monroe to take the lead again. They

278

extended it in the bottom of the sixth on a blooper to center from Magglio Ordonez (ah, the cruelest cut of all), scoring Carlos Guillen from third. We blew a big chance in the top of the eighth. With the bases loaded, Ozzie pinch-hit for Chris Widger. He brought in our big mid-season acquisition, Geoff "The Producer" Blum. Blum promptly hit a comebacker to the pitcher, who threw home for the force; Ivan Rodriguez threw to first for the double play. Great pickup there, Kenny – Ken Griffey Jr.? Nah. Geoff Blum, that's who we need!

We had another shot in the top of the ninth. With men on first and third and two outs, the Captain singled through the left side, bringing home Uribe, but Dye looped a ball weakly to the center fielder to end the game. We lose. Again. To the Tigers. Where did I put that cyanide?

I grabbed the nearest object (a Corporations textbook) and prepared to fire it against the wall. But before I did, I switched over to the Cleveland/Tampa Bay game. Slowly, gently, a smile crept over my face. Tampa Bay was winning 5-0 in the sixth.

Just as slowly, the smile receded. In the bottom of the sixth, the Indians got on the board with an RBI single from Aaron Boone. Figuring that I was likely doubling the Tampa Bay fan base, I went and got my Sox hat and re-shaped it into a rally cap. "You can do it, Devil Rays!" It worked, because the Rays got through the heart of the order. Just two more innings, and the Sox would maintain their two game lead.

Then I remembered. It was the eighth. The Devil Rays have been awful all year long in the eighth. Oh, crap.

Crap was right. Joe Borowski, Tampa Bay's so-called set-up man, gave up a single to Belliard. Ben Broussard, pinch hitting, sliced a liner down the right field line, doubling home

279

Belliard and bringing Cleveland within three, 5-2. Casey Blake powered one to left. "Stay in the park, stay in the park!" I yelled. It did, but not by much, and Blake ended up on second, with Broussard scoring. 5-3.

Luckily, Tampa Bay got out of the inning with the score still 5-3. But the Tribe wasn't done. Speedy Coco Crisp (part of your complete breakfast) smoked a double down the right field line to lead things off in the ninth. After walking Peralta, Rays closer Danys Baez faced the dreaded and red-hot Travis Hafner, representing the winning run. Somehow, Baez induced Hafner to ground into a force at second.

Okay . . . first and third, one out . . .

Victor Martinez followed with a basehit to right-center, scoring Crisp and making it 5-4. Men on first and third, one out.

At that point, I chucked my Corporations book, which made a satisfyingly loud BANG! as it hurtled into the wall.

But Baez somehow got Belliard to ground one up the middle, on the right side of second base. Jorge Cantu bent down, scooped it, carefully tossed to Jose Lugo, and Lugo fired to first to end the ballgame.

After the game, Dad and I spoke.

BEN: Lou Piniella deserves the Congressional Medal of Honor.
DAD: We can't count on this kind of luck the rest of the way. When does Crede get back?
BEN: They're saying he should be back ASAP.
DAD: Good. Ozzie must be sweating bullets.
BEN: Um, Dad? Quick question for you. Any idea how to patch up a hole in the wall?
DAD: No, why?

BEN: Just asking.

September 28, 2005
DAD:

Mercury on second after a single and stolen base, Iguchi up, first inning, nobody out.

Strikeout.

Hambino?

Fly out, left field.

Captain?

Bouncer to third, 5-3. No runs. Blown opportunity. Aaargh.

Dye on third, Everett on second, Uribe up, second inning, two out, still 0-0.

Long fly ball . . . back . . . back . . . back . . . over the left-field wall!

Caught by Monroe on a fantastic leaping catch.

Aaaaaaaaarrrrrgggggggghhhhh.

Carlos Pena at bat, Contreras pitching (7-0 in last seven starts, four starts giving up either 0 or 1 run) second inning.

Long fly ball . . . back . . . back . . . back . . . over the left-field wall.

No fantastic catch by Podsednik. 1-0 Tigers.

Aaaaaaaaaaaaaaaaaaaaaaaaarrrrrrrrrrrrrrrrrrrrggggggggggggg gghhhhhhhhhhhhhhhh.

Mercury on second, Captain on first, Silent Assassin up, third inning, two out.

My fingernails are in dire jeopardy.

3-2 pitch . . .

It's inside, but J.D muscles it somehow to left field . . . Monroe racing in . . . he dives . . .

It falls in. Mercury is across the plate before Monroe picks up the ball. The Silent Assassin has struck again! 1-1.

Okay . . . Jose?

Jose. He is dominant. They can't dent him -- he's striking out half the Tiger team. His forkball is downright *malignant.*

He also gets help in the fourth. Polanco doubles to lead off but brain-cramps when he takes off on a grounder to Uribe, who throws him out at third.

Fifth inning, and Cleveland and Tampa Bay are scoreless in their fifth inning. Captain on second, Silent Assassin on first, one out.

Everett up, 13 for his last 82.

1-2 pitch.

Get ready for aaaaaaaaaargh.

What?

WHAT????

He laces one, LACES one to right-center. Captain will score, Assassin will score, Everett chugs around . . . for a triple?

SAY WHAT?

Eeyore is yelling "aaarrgh!!!" 'cause Pooh is dancing on his throat.

Good.

Sixth inning, Uribe on third after a Scotty hit and run base-hit, nobody out, and Iguchi double-plays Uribe home. No RBI, Tad, but I'll take it. 4-1.

Goooooood . . .

Eighth inning, now 4-2. Uribe up.

Long fly ball . . . back . . . back . . . back . . . over the center-field wall.

Caught by Granderson on a fantastic leaping – no – off his glove – Homer!

Better . . .

Bottom of eighth, bases loaded with Tigers, Monroe at bat. Uhhhh-ohhhhhhh . . .

Easy 6-4-3 DP.

Betterrrrrrrrr . . .

Ninth inning. Two on for us, Rowand up.

Long fly ball . . . back . . . back . . . waaaaayyyyyyy back . . . over the left-field wall.

No one catches this one. 8-2 Sox.

Almost Best.

Almost best? What do you mean, *almost*?

Because the best is this:

Tampa Bay 1, Cleveland 0.

Believe it. It *happened.*

Seth McClung (6-11) for Tampa Bay, outdueled Cliff Lee (18-4), giving up only four hits, and the Tribe lost 1-0.

We have a three-game lead, and assuming we win tomorrow, and the Tribe does, too, the worst we can do is lose three at the Jake and finish the season tied, guaranteeing us a playoff spot. *That's* what's best.

DAD: I can breathe again. I can't remember the last time I took a deep breath and thought about the Sox at the same time.

BEN: It's Garcia tomorrow, Dad. Play it safe, will you?

DAD: I know, I know, I'll bring the oxygen tank.

September 29, 2005
BEN:

We won the division. We won the freaking division.

Of course, we crept up on it. Nobody had this bizarre system figured out before the game. I only realized we had it clinched when Hawk Harrelson began celebrating.

Here's the deal. We're three up on Cleveland going into our series with them this weekend. Normally, this would mean that there's a shot Cleveland could tie us for the division crown. But we have a very complicated scenario here. Both the Red Sox and the Indians are 93-66. The Yankees are a game up on the Red Sox in the AL East. That means that the Wild Card candidate from the AL East can finish no better than 94-68. If the Indians sweep us and finish with the same record as the White Sox, they finish with a 96-66 record. They would then win the Wild Card due to tiebreaker (the Sox win the season series against the Tribe, 11-8).

On this, our division winning day, we played the kind of baseball that got us here. Brilliant pitching, great bullpen, terrific defense, and just enough hitting. Freddy Garcia got the start, and went seven innings, giving up only two runs. His stuff was moving beautifully, and he shut out the Tigers until the seventh.

Meanwhile, our offense got going in the first. The Silent Assassin, batting in the three-hole (obviously Ozzie doesn't want to use Rowand there anymore), hammered a pitch off the top of the left field wall. Konerko walked, and Carl Everett, the forgotten man of late, whipped a low fastball to deep center field. It looked like their center fielder, Granderson, had a bead on it, but he couldn't pull it in, and both runners came around to score. 2-0 Sox.

We got another run in the top of the second. Hambino yanked an outside fastball to the right field corner, and ended up on second. Uribe bunted Hambino to third, and Scotty P. hit a long fly to left to score him. 3-0.

Uribe made the defensive play of the game in the bottom of the fifth. Omar Infante grounded sharply in the hole. Uribe got there, and from at least seven feet onto the outfield grass, pegged the ball to first for the out. The man has a cannon for an arm. He also has a barrel for a chest. He also has occasional pop. He also has a goatee. Dad and I have been trying to come up with a nickname for Uribe all season. I'm thinking Long Juan Silver. Yarrrrr! He's a pirrrrrate! I'll have to get Dad's take on it.

Top six, the Captain of our vessel got his 40th HR of the year, taking Jason Grilli deep to left. 4-0. Fitting that the Captain should get our last run in the clinching game.

Good thing he did, because Garcia almost gave the game back to the Tigers. In the bottom of the seventh, he gave up two consecutive singles. The next batter hit a surefire single toward right, but Willie Harris, subbing for Tad, made a tremendous play to his left, tossing to second for the force. Unfortunately, Garcia threw a wild pitch a few seconds later to bring home a run. In the bottom of the eighth, Garcia surrendered an immediate single and came out in favor of Cliff Politte. Politte got a pop-out, then Magglio Ordonez popped a low fastball to deep center field, over the outstretched arm of Rowand for a double. 4-2.

In came our lefty ace, Neal Cotts, who got a quick strikeout. That made way for Big Bobby Jenks, closing this one out in stylish fashion. He ended the eighth by inducing a groundout on a heavy yellow hammer (read: curveball). In the ninth, he started off roughly, giving up a single to right by Inge. The next batter, Vance Wilson, hit a chopper to Crede, who bobbled it. Two on, no out. I was beginning to grit my teeth.

But Jenks is Jenks, not Marte. He struck out Dmitri Young swinging on a nasty curveball. He struck out Granderson looking on another *nasty* outside curve.

One out away from glory.

It happened as fast as a Jenks fastball. Placido Polanco (I am starting a new chapter of Sox Fans for Polanco) fisted a liner toward Konerko.

The Captain leaped.

The ball slapped into his glove.

The Sox are AL Central Champs.

And the most beautiful thing is that it doesn't matter whether Cleveland won or lost. (They won, 6-0.)

Let's get ready for the playoffs.

DAD: I didn't even know we won the division.

BEN: Neither did I. But we did it!

DAD: I hope we can beat the snot out of Cleveland this weekend anyway, get some momentum going.

BEN: I think we will. I'm still afraid of the Yanks and Angels, though.

DAD: Ben, let's just breathe a bit and enjoy the moment.

We've got a week to breathe. Then, neither of us will breathe until the beginning of November – at least I hope so!

October 1, 2005
BEN:

Good night, Travis. Good night, C.C. Good night, Tribe.

286

The Indians are virtually out of the playoffs.

For the last month, all we've heard has been "Sox are choking" talk. In the last week of the season, it was the Indians, not the Sox, who lost it.

It's good to be AL Central champs.

We just took the first two games from the Indians, basically knocking them out of the Wild Card hunt. They had to win two out of three against us to assure themselves of a Wild Card shot.

They didn't get it done.

It's not as though Ozzie didn't give them a chance. After clinching the AL Central in Detroit, Ozzie decided to rest a bunch of our starters, and in Friday's contest, he suited up seven subs. The whining could have been heard all the way from Beantown to the Bronx.

Our subs made the issue moot by winning the first game in thirteen innings. It was a heck of a game, and it's a good thing that we've already won the division, because otherwise I would have had my heart in my throat watching the tape.

The game was billed as a pitchers' duel, and it ended up that way – pitchers combined for an astounding 31 strikeouts for the game. Kevin Millwood, coming into the ballgame with a stellar 2.92 ERA, started for Cleveland. Mark Buehrle (16-8) pitched for us, and he was on his game – 5 2/3 innings, 3 hits, 0 runs, 6 strikeouts.

Millwood had his stuff going. His curve was really biting, and his fastball was riding in on the hitters. He is also a very good defensive pitcher, and he proved it by barehanding a hard grounder up the middle on one bounce, then tossing to first to get Willie Harris in the second inning.

We scored our first run in the top of the fifth. Chris Widger (subbing for Hambino) singled up the middle. Geoff "The Producer" Blum (subbing for Uribe at shortstop) smashed a grounder off Millwood's leg, and it bounced into right, sending Widger to third. Willie Harris (subbing for Tad Iguchi) popped a soft liner into right, and we were up 1-0.

That lead stood up until the ninth, when Ozzie strangely continued to utilize our resident nut, Damaso "Escaped Patient #8907" Marte, who had entered the game in the eighth. Naturally, Marte imploded, giving up a single and a double, and leaving Dustin Hermanson with a second and third, no outs situation. The next batter, Belliard, grounded to short, but the game was tied 1-1.

Hermanson intentionally walked Ben Broussard, and induced a double play ball from Aaron Boone to keep the game tied. All was calm until the eleventh, when Neal Cotts worked his way out of a bases-loaded, one-out situation. That storm receded until the thirteenth.

Francisco Cabrera, a great young Cleveland reliever, was pitching. Willie Harris led off with a triple over the head of right-fielder Casey Blake. It was a beautiful piece of hitting, and the ball almost ended up in the right field seats. Scotty P. tried to bunt him home with a suicide squeeze, but Harris inexplicably took off late from third, and was cut down at the plate. That's Joey Cora's fault – he has to let Harris know when to take off. Podsednik advanced to second on the throw home, so we still had a man in scoring position with one out.

After Ozzie pinch-hit Konerko for Brian Anderson (another sub), the Indians intentionally walked him, putting two on with one out. Pablo Ozuna (yet another sub) was brought in to run for Konerko. Ross Gload, the left-handed bench player who has never really had a chance to break in with the Sox, stepped to the plate.

And he smoked it.

The ball carried all the way to the center field wall as Scotty and Ozuna scampered home to give us a 3-1 lead.

That was the game. Jenks came in and struck out the first two batters on nasty inside curveballs, then gave up a solo shot to Belliard. That was it for the Indians.

And after today's game, the Indians are holding on by their fingernails. This one was another thriller; we took it in the seventh with a four-run burst.

Jon Garland started for us, and got his 18th win of the season, shattering his former career high of 12. Ozzie started four subs, leaving the door open for Cleveland once again. Jake Westbrook went for the Indians, and he was great through six. Then we rocked him.

The Indians went up 1-0 in the bottom of the fifth. Ronnie Belliard hit an infield single to short, then tagged to second on a fly ball from Ben Broussard. Casey Blake hit a single to right that was bobbled by Timo Perez, allowing Belliard to rocket around third and score easily. That, by the way, was the first hit in the last 25 at-bats with men in scoring position for the Indians. Choke, anyone?

We grabbed the lead in the seventh. Rowand led off with a single to right – I hope that can get him started, since he's been like ice lately. After Hambino popped out, "Producer" Blum laced a ball between first and second, putting men on first and third with one out. We got lucky when Pablo Ozuna chopped one sky-high off the plate; by the time Aaron Boone came up with it, Ozuna was standing on first and Rowand had crossed home.

Timo Perez lined out, and it looked as though Cleveland would escape with a 1-1 tie. But that would be overlooking the steadiest man on our team this year, Tad Iguchi.

Tad is an unsung hero, and perhaps the most underrated pickup of the offseason by the Sox. He's quiet, consistent, and a very smart ballplayer. On the second pitch from Westbrook, Tad got what he was looking for: a breaking ball, middle of the plate, down in the zone. Tad's a low-ball hitter, and he drove this one back, back, back to center field. There wasn't any place left for Grady Sizemore to go. He looked up, and the ball was over the fence. 4-1 Sox.

Though the Indians got two back in the bottom half of the inning (Say Hey, Luis Vizcaino), Politte and Jenks closed it out.

So here's the deal for the suddenly floundering Indians: their record going into the final game of the season is 93-68; New York's record is 95-66, and the Red Sox are 94-67. The Indians have to win their final game against us, then pray for the Yankees to beat the Red Sox. If the Red Sox win or if the Indians lose, Cleveland is out of it.

The Indians are on the brink.

Tomorrow, either we push them over the edge or Boston does.

I sure hope we're the ones.

October 2, 2005
DAD:

We did it.

Brandon McCarthy was magnificent for five innings, and when he gave up a pair of doubles for a run to start the sixth, Vizcaino shut the door until the eighth, when El Duque came out

290

of the pen and shut them out, too. Their biggest game of the year, and we held them to one run.

Meanwhile, Dye solo-homered for a run in the first and Crede singled home another in the second. But it was in the third that a play came that typifies this Sox team, and gave me a huge hint that people are underestimating the TEAM in this team.

Iguchi tripled to lead off, and Dye was walked, bringing up Konerko, who had 99 RBI for the season. He flied to medium-short center.

Now, with a 2-0 lead, and men on the corners, there is no reason whatsoever for the manager and third-base coach to send the runner from third; they'd be running themselves out of a possible big inning.

So what does Joey Cora, the third-base coach, do? *He yells to Iguchi to take off for home.*

Why?

Because Konerko has 99 RBI, that's why, and he might not get another chance to get his 100th. What does that tell you, especially when Ozzie hugs Konerko after Iguchi scores?

It tells you that Ozzie is a players' manager, that his players come first, because 100 RBI is a selling point for anyone, and *Konerko's contract is up at the end of the season.*

This gave me a really good feeling about the playoffs. Not only because it shows great team chemistry, but because in the cosmic scheme of things, it balances the scales from the last time the Sox should have won the World Series, 1919. That year, Charles Comiskey, the tight-fisted owner, benched Ed Cicotte when he reached 29 wins in order to avoid paying him a 30-win bonus. His less than philanthropic behavior stimulated the fix in the series, and we've been cursed ever since.

We have a different, better owner now, Jerry Reinsdorf, and something tells me that the Curse of Comiskey may be at an end, especially when I see what happened today.

So that's one reason I like our chances.

Reason #2 is our killer instinct. We didn't need this game, the Tribe did, but we nailed 'em anyway. I like that.

But reason #3 is the Big Reason.

Pitching.

We have the horses. The last time I saw horses like this was the chariot race in *Ben-Hur*, and although Ozzie looks nothing like Charlton Heston, he rides his horses every bit as well.

Our first series is against the World Champion Bosox?

Bring 'em on!

Part VI
The Hillary Step

October 3, 2005
DAD:

"Technique and ability alone do not get you to the top," said Junko Tabei, the first woman to climb Everest. "It is the willpower that is the most important. This willpower you cannot buy with money or be given by others . . . it rises from your heart."

Twenty-two years before her historic climb, back in 1953, Edmund Hillary and Tenzing Norgay became the first men to scale Mount Everest. In order to gain access to the summit, they had to ascend a slippery 40-ft. wall of rock and ice. It was the last obstacle they faced in order to make history.

That 40-ft. wall became known as the Hillary Step.

Now the White Sox are faced with their own Hillary Step, and if the character they've shown this year, especially in the last few weeks, is any indication, the willpower that Tabei spoke of should carry them to the summit.

I don't know about them, but for me, watching them, that good feeling she spoke of is rising in my heart.

October 3, 2005
BEN:

Okay, enough with the uplifting stuff. It's baseball time. Finally, after 162 games, the playoffs. I'm ready and raring to go. So here's my player-by-player breakdown. I called Dad after I wrote this and got his input on my judgment – his comments are included.

Starting Pitching: Curt Schilling went for the Red Sox in the last game of the season, which means we won't see him until Game 4, if there is a Game 4. That leaves the BoSox with a rotation of Matt Clement, David Wells, and Tim Wakefield.

Clement is a dud, Wells is old, overweight, and inconsistent, and Wakefield is hit or miss. Meanwhile, we have a solidly consistent rotation featuring Contreras, Buerhle, Garcia, and Garland. Advantage: Moderate, ChiSox.

DAD: Don't underestimate Schilling and Wakefield. If we lose one of the first two games, we could be in trouble.

Relief: The BoSox have nothing. I've been watching their games on NESN all season long, and they've had trouble there since day one. They have no closer, and their only consistent late-inning guy is Mike Timlin. They're relying on a rook named Jonathan Papelbon to get them through this series. Meanwhile, we have Politte, Cotts, Hermanson and Jenks. Yeah, we also have the Cuckoo Clock Brigade (Vizcaino and Marte), but I like our chances. Advantage: Heavy, ChiSox.

DAD: Yeah, their bullpen is terrible. I thought Foulke was mediocre when he was with the White Sox, and was shocked he was so good in last year's playoffs. I think he blew his arm out in last year's playoffs; I think he's done careerwise.

Catcher: This one is a toughie. Jason Varitek is probably the best catcher in the AL. He calls pitches well, he hits well, and he's a team leader. The good news is that Doug Mirabelli catches for Wakefield, so we won't see him in Game 3. A.J. is fantastic behind the plate, and he's a clutch hitter. If Varitek were catching all three of the first games, I'd take him, but as it stands, I'll take A.J. Advantage: Slight, ChiSox.

DAD: I love A.J., but I'll still take Varitek. Straight up, that is. I like A.J. on my team because of his incredible feistiness.

First base: Konerko vs. Kevin Millar/John Olerud. No contest here. Advantage: Enormous, ChiSox.

DAD: Duh.

Second base: We've got Tad, they've got Tony Graffanino. Graffanino is great, but he's a career backup. Tad can spray the ball, hit for power, and is strong in the field. He's also a calming presence hitting behind Scotty. Advantage: Slight, ChiSox.

DAD: I think we're about even here. Graffanino is as solid as can be.

Third base: Crede vs. Bill Mueller. Mueller's a former batting champion, but he hasn't hit as well this year. He's also unspectacular on defense. The question for Crede is which Crede will show up – end of the year Jedi Crede or beginning of the year "Trade For Randa" Crede? The good news is that Crede is streaky *and* clutch. Advantage: Moderate, ChiSox.

DAD: Crede's also a Gold Glover on the line. Crede for sure.

Shortstop: Edgar Renteria vs. "Long Juan Silver" Uribe. Renteria has had a miserable year, and has spent most of it hearing the boobirds at Fenway. He's got a ton of errors, and he's been spotty with the bat. Uribe's also spotty with the bat, but he's solid as a rock in the field, plus he has that cannon for an arm. Advantage: Moderate, ChiSox.

DAD: The way Uribe has hit at the end of the season, I'd say heavy advantage.

Left field: Ramirez vs. Podsednik. This is about as dissimilar as you're going to get. Ramirez is the best hitter in baseball outside of A-Rod and Albert Pujols. He's a total liability in the field, though he has a relatively accurate arm from short left to the plate. Scotty P. is the quintessential leadoff guy. He's our catalyst. He has a weak arm, but he covers a lot of ground. This is like comparing apples and oranges, but this one has to go to the BoSox. Advantage: Heavy, BoSox.

DAD: You should really compare Scotty and Johnny Damon, but okay.

Center field: Johnny Damon vs. Aaron Rowand. Damon is worshipped in Boston, and with good reason. He's weak defensively, but he's fantastic with the bat, and he's quick. Rowand is a hole in the lineup, but he covers a lot of ground when he's awake. Advantage: Heavy, BoSox.

DAD: Yup, Aaron still has to prove himself. But if we compare Scotty P. vs. Damon, I think it's a close call.

Right field: Dye vs. Trot Nixon. The Silent Assassin takes this one easily. Nixon has been injured much of the year, doesn't cover much ground, and though he's a hometown hero, he's been slow offensively since his return. Dye, meanwhile, has put up tremendous numbers. Advantage: Heavy, ChiSox.

DAD: Nixon is the X-factor. If he comes around, look out.

DH: Carl Everett vs. David Ortiz. Gimme a break. Advantage: Heavy, Ortiz.

DAD: Everett couldn't be much colder.

Bench: We've got Harris, Perez, Ozuna, Widger and Blum. They've got Youkalis, Olerud, Mirabelli, Kapler. They've got more power; we've got more versatility. Moderate advantage, Bosox.

DAD: Agreed.

Manager: Both are fantastic. Ozzie has kept this ballclub together, and Francona has kept his ballclub together despite massive injuries. Advantage: Toss-up.

DAD: I'll take Ozzie. Francona's had his day.

Intangibles: Boston is the defending champ. They're desperate to meet the Yanks in the ALCS. The Sox are in the playoffs for the first time since 2000, going for their first World Series ring since 1917. Advantage: Heavy, BoSox.

DAD: I like our chemistry. I'm not sure you can be Idiots two years running.

My prediction: BoSox in five.

DAD: ChiSox in five.

I hope Dad's right.

Dad and I have one problem. The playoffs hit right during the Jewish High Holiday season, which means that we're going to have to watch some of the games on tape. Jewish holidays usually last from evening to evening, rather than morning to evening, so that means we'll miss both day and night games, depending on when they're played. Sigh. But Dad and I have worked out an elaborate system, which should help: since I'm on the East Coast and he's on the West Coast, we should be able to catch more of the games between us than normal.

October 5, 2005
DAD:

There's always something strange about watching sporting events on tape after they've been played. There's a choice you have to make: do you deliberately keep yourself ignorant of the final score or do you want to know the outcome before you start watching? I don't really have a choice, having missed both games; if I watch without knowing the outcome my tension level will cause all flora and fauna within a ten-mile radius to wither away. Game Two is over already, since Rosh HaShanah just ended, and before I turn on the TV to watch the tapes of both games I want to know the scores.

It seems like it's taking forever for the computer to go online. Hurry it up, already!

There . . . okay . . . here we go . . .

Wow!

WOW!

We're up two games to none?

Unbelievable!

12-2 and 5-4!

I'm calling Ben. He must be walking on air.

DAD: Ben?

BEN: Dad, I'm really sick.

DAD: What's wrong?

BEN: I'm getting terrible chills.

DAD: Have you taken your temperature?

BEN: It's 102.4 degrees and I've already taken extra-strength Tylenol.

DAD: It sounds like the flu. Do you have any tea?

BEN: I'm taking it, Dad, but I'm so cold. I watched the game, but I'm so cold. I'm so sick.

DAD: You've got to stay hydrated. Just keep drinking and drinking. It's 10:30 there . . . can you try to go to sleep?

BEN: I've been trying, but I feel so sick.

DAD: Why don't you call me in fifteen minutes and let's see what's going on, okay?

BEN: Okay.

Twenty minutes later . . .

BEN: Dad?

DAD: What's going on?

BEN: I've been going to the bathroom every five minutes. It doesn't feel like the flu, either . . .

DAD: You've got to stay hydrated. Keep drinking, okay? Just keep calling me if you need me.

BEN: Okay . . .

I want to watch the games on the TV, but I can't concentrate. The whole joy I get out of baseball is sharing it with Ben, and if he's sick 3000 miles away from me, there's no way I can enjoy the games, even if we won.

My wife tells me to go ahead and watch, because what else can I do?

Typically, a weird detachment comes over you when you watch a game you know your team has won. But in this case, it's even weirder, because with so much at stake, all I can do is think about Ben.

I'm watching Game One. Contreras looks good. With Renteria on second and one out, Contreras strikes Ortiz out on a forkball that rolls off the table low and outside. Ortiz goes fishing, and then Ramirez grounds out to Crede.

Bottom of the first. Clement hits Scotty, who advances on Iguchi's perfect bunt, and after Dye gets hit, too, Scotty steals third. The Captain forces Dye at second, scoring Scotty. Everett singles Konerko to second, Rowand singles Konerko home, then Hambino launches a three-run HR to left center. 5-0. What a first inning!

Contreras has good stuff. He's got his forkball working, and the BoSox, even as a patient team, can't seem to hit him. In the third, Konerko rips a HR to left, 6-0.

Fourth inning. Trot Nixon somehow reaches out for the same pitch that Ortiz struck out on, and loops a single to right, and Varitek (as a tacit indication that Contreras is hard to hit) tries to bunt down the third base line for a hit. He succeeds, only

301

because Crede literally kicks the ball back over the first base line, allowing Nixon to go to third and Varitek to second. Contreras, as is his wont, wild-pitches Nixon home, Millar doubles Varitek home, and it's 5-2.

Nice that I know that two runs is all they got.

In the fourth, Hambino doubles into the right-field corner, and Uribe follows one batter later with a drive over the left-field fence, and it's 8-2.

In the sixth, Rowand walks off of Gonzales, who then hits Hambino. (That's a moral victory for the Bosox, after Hambino has already homered and doubled.) Uribe singles Rowand home, making it 9-2, and Scotty's up.

Scotty has exactly 0 (yes, zero) HRs this year, since he changed his whole approach, becoming a singles hitter and improving his on-base percentage. So what does he do? He turns on an inside pitch and cracks a rifle shot toward right.

Gone. Three-run HR. 12-2.

As if that's not enough, Hambino comes up in the eighth and whistles a shot over the right-field wall for his second HR. What a day he had.

What a day they *all* had.

Unbelievable.

Ben hasn't called, and I'm worried that if I call him, I'll wake him up. If he's battling the flu he'll need all the sleep he can get, so I have to hope he's sleeping. Might as well watch the 5-4 game.

First inning, and sure enough, Buehrle is slipping and sliding. Damon singles under Crede's glove (it looks as though Joe just didn't bend over to his right far enough, is his back bothering him?) and Renteria rips a 3-0 cookie down the left field line for a double, putting them on second and third. Buehrle slips past Ortiz, striking him out on a nasty two-seam fastball that dips low, but he can't slip past Manny, who lofts one over Scotty's head, scoring the runners. Yet Scotty plays the ball expertly, and what should have been a double is only a single. That matters, because Varitek forces Manny at second, and Nixon hits a tapper back to Buehrle. Could have been worse.

I am proud to say that the Sox fans have an electricity about them, just as they did in Game One. They're far more intense than I remember in 1983 or 2000. They smell a real chance for us to go all the way, and they're not leaving everything up to the players. The rise in noise during Ortiz's at bat was impressive.

Nothing much of note happens until the third; Wells has us off-balance. The only hard-hit ball is by the Captain, who launches a seeming HR that Damon flags down at the left-center field wall. Then, in their half of the third, Damon singles to left again. He and Konerko are laughing about something, and it seems as though neither guy is that tense. Amazing, considering that this game is so vital.

Renteria flies to Evel, and Ortiz is up. Buehrle gets ahead of him 0-2, on a fastball and great change-of-pace. Then Ortiz reaches out and flips one down the left-field line, and surprises everyone in the park by steaming around first and heading for second. He beats the throw, and now they've got two runners in scoring position. We walk Manny intentionally (duh), loading the bases, and Buehrle gets ahead of Varitek 0-2.

They've figured Buehrle out. Varitek, like Damon and Ortiz before him, goes the other way. Batting righty, he singles to right for one run. They've finally figured out that Buehrle lures batters into overswinging with his changes of speeds, and they're not gonna bite. They'll simply go the other way.

Nixon grounds one slowly to Konerko. With the bases loaded and Ortiz on third, he should go home first, but instead he turns and fires to second, for a possible 3-6-3 double play. It doesn't work, as Nixon beats the return throw, Ortiz scores, and it's 4-0.

Even though Mueller fans, we're in serious trouble, but I don't need my antacids, because I know we won. Still, I don't know *how*, so this should be interesting.

In the fourth, Evel robs Olerud with a tremendous running catch in center, Olerud responds in the bottom of the inning by robbing Scotty on a tough grounder down the first-base line. Tad singles on a sharply hit ball that ties up Mueller, and after J.D. flies out to center, Konerko launches *another* shot, but this time Damon robs him going straight back toward the center-field wall.

In their fifth, Evel does it again; he robs Renteria, catching the ball as he races toward the left-center field wall. There must be some fielding duel going on between Damon and Evel that I'm unaware of.

Then, in our half of the fifth . . . Everett singles to right. Evel lofts one that just touches inside the left field line, that should get Everett to third, but Joey Cora never hesitates; he windmills his arms and Everett flies for home. He scores, and just like that it's 4-1. Hambino, in his role as ultimate team player, takes a pitch and chops it toward Graffanino at second, advancing Rowand to third. Hambino claps his hands as he's thrown out; he's done his job, and he is roundly congratulated when he reaches the dugout.

Crede's up now, and he struck out the first time against Wells. On a 2-2 pitch, he swings at a ball at his ankles, and bounces it past Wells. Miraculously, it has eyes, and finds its way between Renteria and Graffanino into the outfield. Evel scores, thanks to Crede and Hambino's unselfish at-bat. It's 4-2, and Uribe is the tying run at the plate. Chris Berman, announcing for ESPN, says, "I do believe the decibel level is up."

You bet it is.

It's 0-2 on Uribe now, and after he fouls off a couple, the wild swinger on our team swings away, grounding a four-hopper double-play ball right at Graffanino. Graffanino reaches down to glove it –

And the ball rolls right through his legs to the outfield, a la Buckner.

Crede goes to third, Uribe is on first, and we've got the lead run at the plate in Scotty, with only one out. It's too bad about Graffanino (as he was once on our team), but Buckner's ball lost the game. It's only the fifth inning, so it ain't the same thing. I don't feel bad at all.

It's amazing how genuine compassion takes a hit when your team needs a break. Why, I'm downright bloodthirsty.

Wells recovers beautifully, though, getting Scotty to pop up to third. When Scotty reaches the dugout, he immediately heads for the locker room, and I'd bet something is gonna get yelled at or punched there. Two down.

It's Tad, now, and he's been pretty darn consistent all year . . .

He turns on a 1-1 pitch, and *creams* it. It's really crushed, and it soars over the left-field fence more beautifully than Jonathan Livingston Seagull ever dreamed of.

That's my partisan opinion. It's 5-4 now, which means no one scored the rest of the game. How in the world did we hold the Bosox scoreless for the last four innings?

Buehrle shut them down for the next two innings, and then it was Jenks.

In the eighth, he went three up and three down, and then in the ninth, after Olerud bounced back to the mound for one out, he faced Graffanino, who gave himself a shot at redemption by lining one over Uribe's head. Mercury raced over and cut the ball off, but Graffanino never wavered. He was going for two bases no matter what, and with Scotty's average arm, he beat the throw into second for a double.

Now, Damon. Ozzie refuses to play the percentages, here, bringing in a lefty to face Damon. He's going with the HEAT.

Jenks goes 3-2 on Damon. The next pitch, a *98* mph heater inside on the fists, causes Damon to pop the ball straight up thirty feet, and Hambino gloves it for the second out. Now, Renteria is up, with the major-league-leading RBI man, Ortiz, on deck.

Renterias swings at the first pitch, and grounds a simple grounder to Uribe, who throws him out by ten feet. Jenks made it look easy. How old is this kid?

What a game to win. And Ben hasn't called, so maybe that's going well, too. I don't know if I'll sleep, though with the excitement of the two victories and my concern for Ben. . . .

October 6, 2005
DAD:

Right again. I hardly slept. Ben's in the hospital. He called at 2:30 a.m. his time, saying his diarrhea was vicious and

306

constant, and he wound up going to the local infirmary, where they hydrated him, then sent him to the hospital. He's on an IV there, because even ginger ale goes right through him, and they've put him on antibiotics while they try to discover what is going on.

The doctor said that they have it under control, but when I talked to Ben he sounded frightened, because the fever hasn't abated. The Sox have the day off between games while they fly to Boston, and truthfully, that's about as secondary in my thoughts as it has ever been.

October 7, 2005
BEN:

Well, here I sit in the hospital. This is the first time in my life I've had to spend an extended period in a hospital, and it's just about all it's cracked up to be. Which is to say, it's awful. The nurses are nice, and the accommodations are okay, but I feel horrible all the time. My fever is still up, and I still can't keep anything in my body, so I'm on IV, which sucks. Meanwhile, the family is 3000 miles away. A few friends have shown up, but my guess is that the traffic will slow considerably tomorrow, because it's the Sabbath. Oh, well. Guess I'll have to read. And read. And read.

The good news is that we're up 2-0 and going for the sweep tonight. More bad news: I won't be able to watch the whole game, since Sabbath starts pretty early tonight. Dad and I have worked out a system, though. I can't pick up the phone after Sabbath starts, but Dad's going to call and let the phone ring a certain number of times. First, he'll leave the score of the White Sox in rings. Then he'll hang up, call again, and leave the score of the Red Sox in rings. If we're up 3-2, for example, he'll call once and ring three times, then call again and ring twice. He'll do that every half-inning until the end of the game. Good thing I have my own room – it would annoy the heck out of anyone else.

I've also made provision with the nurses, who will update me with the score and breaking news. I'm hoping this is a blowout so that I don't have to worry about what I can't see.

Okay, game time. Here we go.

Freddy Garcia, our road warrior, is going today. Tim Wakefield, their crafty knuckleballing vet, is going for them. Wakefield's unpredictable – he could be great, or he could be terrible. We should find out fast.

Wakefield starts off the game by hitting Scotty P. in the shoulder. Excellent. Yeah, so Scotty P. didn't make much of an effort to get out of the way. It's still a leadoff runner. A second later, Wakefield fires over to first, wide of John Olerud, and Scotty's standing on second. We had *better* get a run out of this. But wait a second – they're sending Scotty back to first. It seems Tad called time just before Wakefield threw to first. *Crap.* This bodes ill.

Wakefield is wild out there. He almost hits Tad, then throws outside, but that outside pitch puts Doug Mirabelli in perfect position to gun out a running Mercury at second. Instead of man on second, no outs, it's nobody on and one out. A second later, Wakefield drops a nasty knuckleball that Tad misses, striking out. Darn it, Tad. Then Dye strikes out, and things are looking very grim indeed. Dad calls after the half-inning.

DAD: Uh-oh.

BEN: That's what I'm thinking. I really don't want to see Schilling in this series.

Things start off badly for Freddy. He goes 3-2 on Johnny Damon, then walks him, and I'm beginning to feel even worse than I already do. But he comes back to pop up struggling Renteria, and maybe we'll get out of this. We put the shift on for David Ortiz (Rebecca calls him Shrek), and Ortiz tries to beat it by shooting a liner toward center. Unfortunately for him, Joe Crede is playing right on second. He leaps up, grabs the liner, comes down and finds Johnny Damon standing right there. He tags him, and we're out of the inning.

DAD: Maybe this won't be so bad after all. Garcia's got a good breaking ball.
BEN: Great call by Ozzie to keep working with the shift. Ortiz is a monster, but he isn't Ted Williams.

Wakefield starts the top of the second by striking out Konerko swinging on a *very* outside knuckler. But he hits Everett on another inside pitch, and we've got another baserunner. The problem is that so far, we're not getting any wood, let alone good wood. Aaron Rowand turns over his hands, grounds into a 5-4-3 DP, and that's the inning.

DAD: Didn't Rowand used to be able to hit?
BEN: If he turns his hands over any more, he'll break his wrist.

Garcia starts the inning with another walk. Okay, fair enough. Walking Manny isn't the worst thing that could happen.

And now we've got Trot Nixon, who hasn't recovered his swing. Ozzie is still putting on a minor shift; Uribe's playing behind second, and Crede's playing short. If Nixon could bunt, we might have some trouble here. Except he can't, and he strikes out on a low fastball. Bill Mueller spots the Sox shifting their outfielders toward right, and tries to go the other way with an outside fastball, but he drops a soft liner right into Uribe's glove. Ozzie's looking like a genius here.

Garcia is pounding Olerud inside, over and over. With the count 3-2, Garcia walks *him*, giving him three on the day. Garcia isn't going to last past the fifth at this rate. Mirabelli grounds to the right side after battling Garcia; Crede goes full out to his left for it. He grabs it, pushes to his knees, and guns to second for the force and the last out. *YES!*

DAD: Hope our relief is ready for some work.
BEN: A Jedi uses the Force for knowledge and defense, never for attack!

Top three. Now's the time to get us some runs, before Garcia wears down. Hambino gets a good piece of one and lines it to right – drop, baby, drop! – but it hangs up just long enough for Nixon to make a smooth sliding catch. Crede grounds one hard into the hole, and Renteria moves to his right, backhands it, leaps, throws … and beats Crede by a step. *Argh!!!* When the Red Sox play this kind of defense, it might be their night.

But Uribe counters that idea with a blast high off the Monster, and we have a man in scoring position, and Scotty P. coming up. And Scotty P. *delivers*, cutting an outside knuckler down the left field line. 1-0 ChiSox, and Scotty on second.

310

Steal, Scotty, steal! Nobody in the league is better at taking third than Mercury, and I'd love to see a squeeze here. But we don't need it – Tad bounces one up the middle, and Scotty scores. 2-0.

I'm starting to feel better already.

Wakefield gets out of the inning, but, as Hawk would say, we put a crooked number up on the board . . . yes!

DAD: How clutch is Scotty? How clutch?
BEN: I thought for sure we were dead in the water after that Renteria play. But Uribe really turned on that. Yarrr, he plundered that pitch, yarrr.
DAD: Feeling better?
BEN: Not really, but at least I'll be happy on the inside – that is, if I still have insides.

But Garcia gets it started bumpily again. Graffanino (who got a standing O from the Fenway crowd before the game) lines a single into left to lead off. But once again, Freddy recovers – Damon chops one to Garcia, who turns around and tosses to Uribe, who chucks to Konerko. Double play. I *love* our defense. A quick chopper to Crede from Renteria, and it's the fourth.

DAD: Beautiful.

Carl Everett crushes a ball foul down the right field line, then pops to Damon in center. Rowand, who has a good career batting record against Wake, waits, waits, waits on the knuckleball, then drives it over Ramirez's head for a double.

Oh, let's get some more.

311

Hambino grounds out, though, and Crede gets some of it, but not enough, and flies out to Damon. Another blown opportunity.

BEN: Methinks this is too close.

Good prediction. Ortiz takes the 1-1 pitch and drives it deep to center. The wind picks it up and carries it, all the way out of the park. 2-1, ChiSox. It didn't look like he got any of it, but he obviously got enough. "Freddy, Freddy, Freddy," I mutter.

Freddy doesn't hear me, and he throws an outside fastball that Manny Ramirez absolutely clobbers to right.

It's gone. This is horrible. The specter of Schilling looms large. We get out of the inning, but it's tied, 2-2.

DAD: When does Ozzie pull him?
BEN: I'm just happy Ortiz was leading off.

Top five, Wakefield is throwing beach ball BBs, ugly knuckleballs. We go down, 1-2-3.

DAD: Now he's settling in. What time is it there?
BEN: Just past 5:30. I can't believe I'm going to have to turn this off.
DAD: Don't worry, I'll ring you in Morse code.

Bottom five, and Garcia is working more smoothly now. Of course, it would hardly be possible to work less smoothly than he did last inning. Mirabelli grounds to third, Graffanino flies to left. Then Damon picks up where Ortiz and Ramirez left off, lining a double to right. Garcia goes 3-1 on Renteria – bear down, Freddy! – then walks him. Don Cooper comes out for a chat. The conversation must go something like this:

Cooper: "What are you doing?"

Garcia: "Just making sure Shapiro doesn't get too comfortable in the hospital."

Ortiz saves Garcia's rear, flying deep to center for the third out.

DAD: You might be lucky you don't have to watch the end of this game.

Dye leads off the top of the sixth with a walk. Then it's Captain Time; he picks on a slightly inside knuckleball, and muscles it over the Monster. 4-2, ChiSox. "You the man, Paulie!" I yell, startling the nurses. After Everett grounds to first, out comes Wakefield. Still, the Red Sox get out of the inning with no further damage. On the phone, Dad and I start quoting *L.A. Confidential*.

DAD: You sure Paulie's up to the task, Cap?

BEN: You'd be surprised what the lad is capable of.

Now it's borderline Sabbath time, and I'm desperately attempting to stop the sun, a la Joshua. Unfortunately, I'm not Joshua, so I'm failing. Ramirez makes me want to turn off the TV, smushing a fastball over the Monster for *another* bomb. 4-3 ChiSox. Ugly, ugly, ugly.

Ozzie motions to the bullpen. It's about time, Ozzie. Except he brings in *Marte*.

313

I'm about ready to get out of bed, crawl to Fenway, and strangle him.

Marte?!

Damaso "Mr. Hyde" Marte?!

Naturally, Marte gives up a single to Trot Nixon. He walks Bill Mueller.

And Ozzie doesn't pull him.

And he walks John Olerud.

Ozzie motions to the bullpen.

Bases loaded, no outs.

And it's time for Sabbath.

AAAAAAAAAAAAARRRRRRGH!!!!!!!!

DAD:

I'm picking it up from Ben here, who is now on radio silence.

I don't believe it. Bases loaded, Varitek up, El Duque in for the reprehensible Marte, every Sox fan probably with their heart in their throat, and Ben has to turn the game off *NOW?*

The Sabbath is inviolate. The old saying is "More than the Jews kept the Sabbath, the Sabbath kept the Jews," meaning, of course, that the keeping of the Sabbath was central to our identity as a people. There are occasions when the Sabbath may be violated, but those only occur when a human life is at stake. Ben's young, and even though he's in the hospital, he'll be okay, I hope, but this is still one heckuva time to shut off the TV.

Here we go. El Duque throws a curve that seems to catch the inside corner. Ball?

What?

Ozzie is screaming at Mark Wegner, the home plate umpire. The second pitch is right down the middle.

Ball.

Ozzie is SCREAMING at Wegner. He's a hairsbreadth from getting thrown out.

A 91 mph fastball . . . Varitek swings through it.

Another fastball, inside and letter-high . . . and Varitek pops it up. The Captain gloves it for the first BIG out.

Come *on* . . .

Graffanino up, looking for redemption, and he's hit the ball hard twice. Come on, double play, come *on!*

A strike, a ball, a foul to the side, another curve outside, 2-2.

Pay-off pitch . . . he fouls it off.

Another low curve outside. 3-2.

I can't stand it.

Another foul to the side.

Nurse: Your diastolic pressure is now 100, Mr. Shapiro.

Another foul.

Another foul.

Nurse: Diastolic now 110 and rising.

Hambino goes out to the mound. What are they saying to each other? Hambino probably told him something . . .

Here it comes, it's a curve over, knee-high, Graffanino reaches down to golf it –

And POPS it up!

Uribe has it for the second out.

There is *no* way we get out of this without them scoring, is there?

Damon up.

Quickly it's 2-1, all fastballs, and El Duque blows one by him for 2-2.

Next pitch, another fastball just outside, but Damon never budges, and it's 3-2.

It's a tremendous battle.

Please . . . let us win, just once?

Pop foul out of play.

Hambino goes to the mound. What will they throw, a fastball? A curve?

A curve, down and in, *way* down, it's a ball, but did Damon check his swing in time?

NO.

NO.

NO.

You're outta there!!!!!

The seventh, El Duque strikes out Renteria and Ortiz, and gets Manny to ground out to the Captain.

In the eighth, the Sox go down in order, but there's something definitely wrong with the Bosox. Millar, who seemed like the spiritual cheerleader last year, is sitting back in the dugout with his legs stretched out in front of him, one crossed over the other. How can he be so laid-back when they might be eliminated?

Because we want it more, that's why.

And it shows in the eighth, when the Captain robs Nixon of a base-hit, diving to his right. That pays off later when Olerud singles, because Varitek comes up with two out and a man on first instead of two men on and one in scoring position. Can El Duque get Varitek again?

Varitek fouls off a couple of two-strike pitches, then strikes out.

El Duque has four strikeouts in three innings, and given up zero runs. Maybe he *is* Satchel Paige.

Now it's the top of the ninth, and Timlin is in for them.

Hambino swings hard, and blasts one off the Monster . . . it's a double. I told you, Ben, he wins everywhere he goes. I knew he'd make the difference!

Crede up, and he lays an absolutely perfect bunt down the first-base line that moves A.J. over.

A Jedi may use his weapon for Small Ball, apparently.

But Ozzie does *not* pinch-run for A.J. even though he's reeeeeealy slow. I guess he figures this game may go extra innings and he wants A.J out there no matter what. I agree.

Uribe up, and the first pitch is a quasi-pitch out, with Varitek checking to see if A.J. is looking to come home on a squeeze. He's not, and it's 1-0.

A swinging foul back, and it's 1-1.

Hambino bluffs coming home on the next pitch, which is outside, and it's 2-1.

The next pitch, and Hambino takes off like a freight train, Uribe squares to bunt, and lays it down along the first-base line! Hambino beats the back-handed throw from Timlin to Varitek, wildly waving his arms in the safe sign after he gets up from his slide, the ball gets away, Uribe is safe at first, and we're up, 5-3!

Oh, Ben, if you could have seen it!

Wait, he can see it later on tape. But still, seeing it live...

Timlin tries to pick Uribe off and throws it away. Uribe on second. We're riding high. Scotty moves Uribe over with a bouncer to second. Two out, and Uribe on third. Tad's up. Let's get some more.

But he strikes out.

Whos gonna pitch the ninth? El Duque? He's already thrown three innings . . .

It's Jenks. Good.

Graffanino up, and he bounces to Crede, who guns to the Captain. One out.

Two more, guys . . .

Damon up, and he can't catch Jenks's fastball. It's quickly 0-2.

Ball. 1-2.

A Monster curveball. I mean, Koufax would've been proud. Damon flails at it for strike three.

One more . . . Renteria.

A strike.

A simple grounder to Iguchi, appropriately enough, since he killed them in Game Two, and he throws Renteria out by ten feet.

It's over, and we have knocked off the World Champions. Who's next?

October 11, 2005
BEN:

Before the game tonight, I think it's worthwhile to give an ALCS breakdown. Of course, my last team vs. team breakdown was so successful that I called the Red Sox in five, but if at first you don't succeed, try, try again.

Starting pitching: They've got Byrd, Washburn, Lackey, and Santana. We got lucky here, since their ace, Bartolo Colon, was injured in the Yankees series and likely won't be able to go until late in the series if he goes at all. Byrd is a junkball pitcher, the kind that gives us trouble. Washburn is solid all around. Lackey is their real ace, a clutch power-pitcher. And Ervin Santana shut us down the regular season. We've got our Four Horses of the Apocalypse. Advantage: Moderate, Sox.

Relief: They've got a terrific bullpen, probably the best in the league. With Scot Shields, Brendan Donnelly, Kelvim Escobar, Kevin Gregg, and closer Frankie Rodriguez, the Angels are spectacular in the late innings. With Marte on the outs, we've got Cotts, Politte, Jenks, and Hermanson. Advantage: Moderate, Angels.

Catcher: A.J. vs. Bengie Molina. Molina has had a breakout year at the plate, and throws out runners at a tremendous pace. A.J. has all the intangibles, and his fiery leadership has played a major role in getting us here. He also calls pitches better than anyone in the game. Advantage: Slight, Sox.

First base: Konerko vs. Darin Erstad. Erstad was a great center fielder and is excellent defensively. He's also a very good hitter. Too bad for him, his Sox counterpart is perhaps the best first baseman in the American League. Advantage: Moderate, Sox.

Second base: Iguchi vs. Adam Kennedy. Kennedy is decent in the field, and hits well for average, but doesn't have much pop. Iguchi is as solid as they come. Advantage: Slight, Sox.

Third base: Joe Crede vs. Chone Figgins. Figgins is smooth defensively and a terrific basestealer. He actually led the AL in stolen bases after a late season run (Scotty only played 129 games; Figgins played 158). Crede is Gold Glove caliber, and very streaky. Advantage: Toss up.

Shortstop: Uribe vs. Cabrera. This is the battle of the streaky hitting, tremendous fielding shortstops. Uribe has more power, but Cabrera has been here before – last year, with the Red Sox. Advantage: Slight, Angels.

Left field: Scotty P. vs. Garrett Anderson. Anderson is a perennial MVP candidate. Scotty is our jump-starter.
Advantage: Moderate, Angels.

Center field: Rowand vs. Steve Finley. This will be perhaps the only series all year in which Rowand gets the better of his counterpart. Finley has been miserable all season long. Advantage: Heavy, Sox.

Right field: Dye vs. Vladimir Guerrero. Vladdy is another perennial MVP candidate for the Angels, and he's a good arm in right. Dye is having a great year, but he's not Guerrero. Advantage: Moderate, Angels.

DH: Everett vs. Juan Rivera. Nobody has heard of Rivera, but he's put up good numbers in limited time (106 games, .271 BA, 15 HR, 59 RBI). Meanwhile, Everett has gone cold. Advantage: Toss up.

Bench: Our bench versus, Jose Molina, Kotchman, DaVanon, Itzuris, Quinlan, and Josh Paul. Not a particularly strong bench. Advantage, White Sox.

Managing: Mike Scioscia took the Angels to the 2002 World Series and won it. Ozzie has turned this team around. Advantage: Toss up.

Intangibles: We're on a roll. The Angels just got finished with the Yankees. We're getting the breaks. The Angels just lost their number one starter. Advantage: Heavy, Sox.

My prediction: Sox in six.

DAD: Sox in seven.

I think I'm losing that lifelong Sox fan pessimism. I hope that doesn't jinx us.

October 11, 2005
BEN:

320

All the pre-game talk is about the weary, weary Angels and the rusty, rusty White Sox. The Angels played in New York on Sunday, Anaheim on Monday, and are playing in Chicago tonight. Meanwhile, the Sox haven't played since last Friday, October 7. It's pretty clear that the media wants to make this a David vs. Goliath situation, with the Sox as Goliath.

I don't buy it. It's time for the Angels to suck it up. Three games in three days? Big freaking deal. The White Sox played 22 games in a row down the stretch without a day off. As for flying, ask basketball players about how tough that is. They play a different team every night. You're playing baseball for a living. Shut up and stop whining about the travel inconvenience.

Meanwhile, we have a problem – when we face junkball pitchers, we lose. I'm not so sure that the Angels pitching Paul Byrd instead of Bartolo Colon is a disadvantage for them. Contreras is going for us, and remembering how he fared when our family went to the game a few months back, that means that he should be excellent. Now if only he can keep avoiding a Secret Inning.

It's game time. Let's get going!

Contreras starts off beautifully. He drops a nasty forkball on Chone Figgins to strike him out swinging. He throws an outside breaking ball that Cabrera tries to poke into right, but pokes into the glove of Konerko instead. Guerrero swings and misses at a 55-ft. forkball, then grounds toward the hole on the next pitch. Uribe gets a good jump, moves to his right, backhands it, throws across his body from the outfield grass … and nails Guerrero at first. Yarrrrr! Quick note about Guerrero – he's really stepping in the bucket on a lot of his swings. We should start setting him up outside and wait for him to strike himself out.

DAD: Contreras looks great.
BEN: So much for rust – Uribe looks fresh as a daisy.

In the bottom half, Scotty P. pops to short to lead it off. Byrd saws Tad off on an inside slider, and Erstad is there for the pop. On the first pitch, Dye sees something he likes and lines it hard to right. Drop, drop! It doesn't, and Juan Rivera catches it.

In the second, Contreras leaves a low inside fastball over the plate for Anderson, and he turns on it and rifles it into the right field seats. That was a no-doubter. 1-0, Angels. My stomach is starting to rumble again. Bengie Molina grounds out to short, and Erstad chops to Konerko, who steps on first for the third out.

BEN: Ok, that wasn't a Secret Inning.
DAD: More like a Secret Pitch.

In our half, Figgins makes a nice pick of a hard-hit Konerko grounder to his left for out number one. We're getting good wood, and it's only a matter of time before they start falling in. Another groundout from Everett, and it's two down. Byrd is beginning to annoy me, not only because he's shutting us down, but also because he's the twitchiest pitcher I've ever seen. He adjusts his cap three times after every pitch, tugs at his sleeves, taps his feet. He's like an ad for *Rain Man*. And the Rain Man gets Rowand to fly to left to end the inning.

Contreras is looking weak out there, giving up a single to Steve Finley. Adam Kennedy singles to left, and we're in trouble. Bear down, Jose! Figgins bunts the runners over, and we have serious trouble. Cabrera chops a ball down the third base line, Crede charges . . . but he has no chance at a play at home, and throws to first – too late to catch anyone. First and third, one out, 2-0 Angels, and Guerrero at the plate. I can't believe this.

Guerrero chops one to Contreras; he has a play at home, but if we turn the DP fast, we can get out of here alive. Contreras throws to Iguchi, but Cabrera comes into second high, and Iguchi throws the ball 20 ft. over Paulie's head at first. That'll score another. 3-0.

Anderson grounds one hard toward second, but Iguchi is playing deep and throws him out for the third out.

DAD: Secret inning? Secret Game.
BEN: So much for no rust.

Cabrera makes a pretty play on a Pierzynski grounder for the first out in the bottom half of the third. Erstad stretches for the low throw. Great defense all around. You have to give the Angels credit – they look like we should out there. Joe Buck and Tim McCarver get into a lengthy conversation about Paul Byrd's "craftiness," and I'm about ready to puke.

Except that Byrd hangs one over the plate to Joe Crede. And Crede busts out the whoopin' stick and sends the ball soaring deep to left, well over the wall. 3-1. "The last of the Jedi will you be!" I shout.

Uribe follows with a smoked liner into left, and I'm starting to get *really* excited, but the ball hangs up long enough for Garrett Anderson to make the play. Scotty P. singles to center. Iguchi singles up the middle. Are we going to get some more here?

But Dye pops it up to the right side. "Get out of play!" I yell. It doesn't. Erstad comes down with it and we're done.

Contreras is settling in. Watch out, Angels. Bengie Molina flies to center, Erstad pops to Crede, Rivera grounds up the middle and Uribe throws him out. That's Contreras' first 1-2-3 inning since the first.

Konerko leads off by grounding softly to second. Not exactly the start we needed. But Everett singles up the middle, and now the stadium is rocking. Rowand grounds to Erstad, unassisted for out number two, moving Everett to second. The crowd quiets for a second, but gets back up as Hambino steps to the plate. He works the count to 3-2, and the crowd is on its feet. Crede is on deck. Byrd has to throw one down the pipe.

He does.

Pierzynski goes down and drives it into right for a single, and it's 3-2.

Here come the Sox.

Crede's up.

Use the Force, Joe.

Except he swings at an outside pitch, and strikes out.

DAD: Crap.

Things are moving fast now. Finley goes down on strikes. Kennedy grounds to second. Figgins breaks his bat, and grounds to Konerko at first.

BEN: Where was Contreras earlier?

Uribe flares one into left to start the bottom of the fifth, but it holds up too long and Anderson gets there. Meanwhile, the announcers are interviewing Bud Black, the Angels' pitching coach. What, Scoscia can't be bothered? Obnoxious. Byrd walks Scotty P., and this could be the big break.

Go, Scotty, go!

Byrd's thinking the same thing, and he throws over. Safe. Pitchout, and Scotty's out at second. Maybe Scioscia is too busy planning plays like that.

Iguchi gets a good piece of one to left. It's going . . . back, back, back . . . caught on the track by Anderson.

DAD: This just keeps getting worse and worse.

Contreras is still going strong, though, in the top of the sixth. He gets Cabrera to ground to Crede; Joe sucks it up and fires to first for the out. Vladdy grounds to Uribe. Two down. He strikes out Anderson, and Contreras has put down 10 straight Angels.

BEN: If he keep pitching like this, we can take this one.

But Byrd pops Dye out; Dye was trying to bunt. What? We're a run down, and Dye is trying to bunt his way on? Weird. Konerko and Everett both get the bat on the ball, but fly out to deep center. I'm really starting to dislike this ballgame.

DAD: What was Dye thinking? He was about as successful as Rowand has been.

325

It's already the top of the seventh, and Contreras is still rolling. Molina lines out softly to Uribe. Erstad lines softly to center, but Aaron is playing back, sprints in, and dives . . . but doesn't come up with the ball. On the 1-0 pitch, Erstad takes off for second; A.J. bounces the throw to second, and Iguchi somehow keeps it from trickling into center field. Contreras bounces back by inducing a Rivera pop-up and a Finley strikeout to get out of the jam.

BEN: His stuff is electric. We had better win this game for him.

DAD: We had better win this game for *us*.

Aaron takes one for the team to get the bottom of the seventh started. Good to know he can get on base *somehow*. Here comes A.J. Scoscia comes out for a chat with Byrd, and that's it for the "crafty" junkballer. In comes flamethrower Scot Shields.

Hambino promptly grounds to second base. Kennedy flips high to Cabrera, though, and Rowand is able to break up the DP even though he's forced at second.

Crede steps in. And on the first pitch, A.J. is *going*. What the heck? Sending A.J. is like sending a bull moose to second. Of course, Molina nails him at second, and it's two down and no out. We've run our way out of the inning. Crede skies a flyout to right, and we're into the eighth.

BEN: Hambino, where are you going? Come back, Hambino!

DAD: Cue music from *Shane*.

The first Angels batter, Kennedy, reaches for an eye-high fastball and chops it to Contreras for the first out. We get lucky when Figgins grounds a ball hard down the first base line – it hits the base. Konerko makes a great play, reaching behind him and knocking the ball down with his bare hand, but he can't get Figgins. At least the speedy 3B isn't on second.

At least not for a second. Figgins takes off for second, we pitch out, and we still miss him. A.J. double-clutched it, and almost threw it into center. This isn't Hambino's game.

Orlando Cabrera grounds to short, Uribe grabs it, throws from on the outfield grass, and nails him easily. Two down.
One more, Jose.

Vladdy's up. Work him outside. Work him outside.

A.J. sets up outside again, but Contreras misses, out over the plate. Vladdy gets almost all of it. This ball is crunched, a sure goner.

But for some reason, the wind is on our side, and the ball is dropping too fast.

Dropping, right into Aaron's glove for out number three.

DAD: Were you praying? I sure was.
BEN: I've never seen a ball die like that. Can you pray for lottery numbers next time?

Here we go now. Uribe starts off with a broken bat infield single that Adam Kennedy throws away. Uribe surely could have taken second, but everyone's a bit tentative after last inning.

Scotty's trying to bunt. Get it down, Scotty.

He doesn't. He fouls off two consecutive fastballs. This is just bad execution. Of all people, Scotty should know how to

327

bunt. On the next pitch, Shields racks Scotty up on an outside curveball. I thought it was outside, anyway, but Scotty seemed to know it was a strike and immediately went back to the bench.

Okay, Tad.

No, Tad, no! He fists a flare right to Cabrera. Shields is really throwing bullets.

Dye singles to right, and we're back in business. Uribe, acting like a moron, almost gets thrown out at second after making a wide turn. Men on first and second, two down.

But Paulie pops up to center, and we get nothing.

BEN: Paulie. I don't want to see him again. Make that first thing on your list, understand?
DAD: Okay, boss. Have we heard from Luca Brasi?
BEN: He sleeps with the fishes.

Top of the ninth. Contreras is still in there. He's throwing a phenomenal game. He gets Garrett Anderson to fly harmlessly to left. But Molina singles up the middle, and here comes Ozzie. That looks like it for the big righty. Here comes Neal Cotts.

Erstad hits a slow roller that Uribe picks and flips to Iguchi at second, but we don't have time to get the double play. One more out, Neal.

He gets it, jamming Rivera and popping him up to Iguchi.

DAD: Just one run. Time for some Ozzie Ball.
BEN: Uh-oh, Rodriguez is coming in.

328

Here we go. Everett nubs one off the end of his bat. It bounces once in front of Figgins, then catches him short, bouncing off his glove. Figgins has no play and just eats it.

Oh, baby.

In comes Ozuna to run for Everett. And now it's up to Aaron to lay down a bunt.

Dad's nightmare.

With good reason. He fouls off his first bunt attempt, still attempting to bunt down at the ball on an angle.

But he gets the bunt down. Figgins is playing in—maybe 15 feet from the plate. He charges it, and Ozuna is cut down at second. We just gave up an out for nothing. Why in the world can't Rowand bunt down the FIRST BASE LINE?

Hambino gets a good piece of the first pitch, but lines it right into the glove of Rivera, who is playing deep. We're down to our last out.

Jedi.

Do it, Jedi.

Except Rodriguez gets him swinging on a big curve, and we're down 1-0 in the ALCS.

I'm done writing. I'm depressed. I'm going to go take a shower, then sleep on my dorm mattress, which I fondly call The Rack. It'll be an improvement over watching that debacle.

Well, tomorrow is another day.

October 13, 2005
DAD:

It sure was. Ben wrote about Game One Tuesday night after the game, and now it's Thursday night. I didn't see Game Two because it fell on the eve of Yom Kippur. The twenty-five hour fast of Yom Kippur ended an hour ago, and after drinking and eating something to get my strength I'm watching the tape of Game Two. This time I have no idea of the result, and I told Ben I wouldn't call him first to get the result. If the Sox lost they're in serious trouble.

The announcers are playing up the strep throat Jarrod Washburn had over the weekend, and here we go again. First they were whining about the Angels' "rough" playoff schedule, and now this? When my kids have had strep they get an antiobiotic and two days later they're fine. Come on, give me a break.

Buehrle better pitch his best game of the year tonight. The first inning he looks good; first strikes on all three batters, three up, three down. Good.

Let's get started early, boys. Scotty hits it right back to Washburn, who floats it – over Erstad's head! Two bases for Scotty, and that's a good start, all right. Iguchi lays one down, and Washburn throws it in the dirt to Erstad, who makes an excellent pickup, but now Scotty's on third. If the Assassin hits it anywhere but third, Mercury will score, because the infield is back.

Dye does, hitting a shot to Cabrera's left that he makes the play on, gunning out Dye at first, but Scotty scores. An unearned run and I'll take it. The Captain singles, but Everett grounds out to short.

Second inning. Bengie Molina pops out to Dye, and Anderson's up. Buehrle has two strikes on him, then fans him on a wide curve ball as Hambino guns the ball to third.

Wait a minute . . . what? The home plate ump says it was as foul tip? I'm watching the replay, and though the ball bounced before it hit the glove, no way does Anderson tip it. Why doesn't the ump consult the third-base ump? That's standard. Ozzie comes out to protest for a moment, but only for a moment; I guess he doesn't want to destroy Buehrle's rhythm. It turns out that the ump blowing the call doesn't matter, because Buehrle throws a change-of-pace that totally fools Anderson, striking him out anyway. Quinlan fans, and Buehrle has thrown a first-pitch strike to all six batters. Six up, six down.

Rowand's leading off now. He launches a shot toward the right field corner, and no way Guerrero's gonna get it. Weirdly, Guerrero takes his time picking it up; he must figure it's a sure double, and there's no way Evel's gonna challenge Guerrero's arm and go for third.

Except he *does*. He flies toward third, and Guerrero, showing off his cannon, fires the ball far over the head of the cut-off man and the ball bounces across the left-field line while Rowand slides into third. Joey Cora, seeing the ball bounce away, flails at Evel to get up and run, and he does. Meanwhile, Quinlan has caught up to the ball, and he needs to peg it from foul territory back to the other side, the first-base side, of the plate so he doesn't hit Evel. Throw it away, come on . . .

Nope. It's a good throw, and Evel is out by a foot. It was a bad decision by Cora, because with nobody out a man on third has an excellent chance of scoring. Crap. Hambino fans, and Crede flies to Guerrero, and we blew a chance.

Buehrle sails through the third, even though a one-out error by Uribe puts Jose Molina on base. Kennedy grounds into a 4-6-3 double play, and that looked easy. Buehrle has thrown a first-pitch strike to 9 consecutive hitters.

We get a one-out single from Scotty in the third, but can do nothing with it. Washburn is pitching well. So much for the "strep-throat" weakness.

In the fourth, after knocking Figgins's ball down so Uribe can throw him out, Buehrle finally throws a first-pitch ball. Cabrera then gets their first hit, a double to left. Figures. Crede makes a very nice 5-3 putout on an in-between hop, though Cabrera moves to third with two out. Buehrle, strangely, lets a pitch get away, and hits Bengie Molina, which is dangerous with Anderson on deck. But Buehrle gets ahead of him 1-2, and Anderson grounds out to Crede.

So far, Buehrle *is* pitching his best game of the year. We do nothing with Washburn in our half, and we go to the fifth.

Buehrle throws a pitch for a ball to Quinlan. The very next pitch, Quinlan hits it over the left-field fence. Quinlan? Are you kidding me? If we have to get beaten, it should be by Guerrero or Anderson, but Quinlan? First his throw, and now this. It's no consolation that he's from St. Paul, Minnesota, where I was born.

I wonder if my relatives there paid him off?

Erstad singles, and I hope Buehrle's not losing steam. He gets two quick outs, but then somehow Hambino lets a pitch glance off his glove, and the lead run's now on second. Figgins hits a line drive to right . . . Dye is running in . . . the ball is dipping . . . can he get there in time?

Yes! And one run is all they get. Still, it's 1-1 now.

Hambino, leading off for us, walks, and after Crede flies to center, Uribe singles Hambino to second. Scotty lofts a pop fly down the left-field line . . . it's foul. He follows by popping out to Figgins. Two outs for Iguchi, who goes 2-2 before Washburn hits him, loading the bases with two out. That's it for Washburn.

Brandon Donnelly comes in, Mr. Herky-Jerky, and he strikes out Dye on three pitches. We're just not executing, and I have a sick feeling that it's going to cost us again, like the first game.

Cabrera singles to open the sixth, and Vlad is up. Will they ask him to bunt? He hasn't been hitting a lick.

Nope. He's swinging away, and it serves them right. He grounds to Uribe, and 6-4-3, we have two out. Bengie Molina fans.

Konerko leads off in our sixth against Scot Shields. He goes 3-2, then checks his swing on a low outside curveball, and the ump calls him out. I've never seen Konerko react like that. He waves at the ump, then throws his bat toward the dugout. He's really angry, and the pro that he is, I have to think the ump blew the call again. Everett and Evel go down quietly, and to the seventh we go.

Buehrle, utterly unfazed by the pressure, goes three up, three down. Forget his best game of the year, he's pitching the best game of his *life*.

Kelvin Escobar comes in for them. Hambino goes down quickly, but Crede creams one to left for a double. Uribe lines one toward left field, straight at Anderson, who throws a strike to second. For some crazy reason, Crede has taken off, doesn't get back in time, and he's doubled off. Unbelievable. First Rowand, and now this?

I'm beginning to have Jerry Dybzinski baserunning hallucinations from 1983.

Buehrle allows Jose Molina to single, leading off, and is Ozzie going to pull him?

No. Kennedy's a left handed hitter, so perhaps that's it. Jeff Devanon runs for Molina, so they'll have a new catcher in our half of the eighth, probably Josh Paul. Kennedy bunts Devanon to second, and is Ozzie gonna pull Buehrle now?

No, he's staying with him. Figgins is up, and Buehrle induces him to ground out 6-3, moving Devanon to third with two out. Now Cabrera's up. I hate to see this; he was a great clutch hitter last year in the playoffs with the Bosox.

Buehrle goes 2-0.

A strike, then a ball, and it's 3-1. A hitter's pitch is coming. I don't know if I can watch this . . .

He crushes it toward left. Run, Mercury! Fly!

Scotty takes off like a shot toward the wall --- he's watching the ball all the way --- he reaches back with his left arm as he nears the wall to know where it is --- he throws his glove up ---

And snares it just before he hits the wall for the third out. Whew.

That should fire us up.

So Escobar strikes out the side in the eighth. No fire at all – from our side.

Buehrle's *still* out there in the ninth. The guy is Mr. Freeze tonight; icicles in his blood. Guerrero flies to Dye, Molina pops to Iguchi, and Anderson, appropriately enough, pops to Buehrle.

Here we go. Can we score here and end it for Buehrle? If ever a guy deserved the win, he does tonight.

Escobar's still in there, for his third inning, which seems a mite strange, but Scioscia's as smart as any manager in baseball, so I guess he knows what he's doing.

Yup. Everett grounds out to Erstad, Rowand strikes out, and Hambino is our last hope to win this now.

Hambino's fighting hard, though, running the count full.

Here's the pay-off pitch . . .

He strikes out on what should have been ball four in the dirt. Crap.

Wait . . . wait . . . he's running to first?

The ball was rolled out to the mound and Hambino's running toward first?

Now the ump is calling him safe at first. Did Paul drop the ball or something? He never tagged him...

Whoa . . . the Angels are going nuts. The replay is unclear, although McCarver is adamant, saying Paul caught the ball. Of course, this is I've-never-been-wrong-about-anything McCarver, so I'm not paying attention.

Scioscia is not letting go. This is turning into a rain-delay, for crying out loud. Interesting how Ozzie, earlier in the game, protested for a moment and then let go because he didn't want to ice his pitcher. What does Scioscia hope to gain?

Turns out that the ump thinks the ball hit the dirt before Paul caught it, meaning that Paul had to tag Hambino out. He didn't, the call stands, and now Ozuna is running for Hambino. Typical Hambino, never taking anything for granted.

And the Jedi is up. Crede takes a strike, and it looks as though he wants to give Ozuna a chance to steal before he swings at anything.

The next pitch is down the middle. Crede is motionless, taking the pitch again, but Ozuna is flying, with a *great* jump, and Paul doesn't even make a throw.

But, still, even though Ozuna is on second, it's 0-2 on the Jedi.

Escobar will probably waste a pitch here . . .

He doesn't! He doesn't! And the Jedi uses the Force and wallops it toward the left-field fence! It's off the wall, and Ozuna is gonna score and we are gonna win!

I'm calling Ben *now*.

DAD: Did you see the game? Can you believe the game Crede had?

BEN: The Force is strong with him. By the way, before I forget, I got an e-mail from the hospital. The reason I was so sick last week was that I had salmonella.

DAD: That's serious, I think.

BEN: Apparently I had a serious case, and it could affect me for a long time. There are some problems that could crop up.

DAD: What does the doctor want you to do?

BEN: He wants to put me on Cipro and see if that knocks this thing out of my system for good. He said the salmonella should be asymptomatic by this point, but I'm not sure precisely what that means, since I still feel pretty crappy. The game helped, though. I'm going to try and get some sleep.

DAD: So I'll talk to you tomorrow?

BEN: Sounds good.

DAD: All we have to do is win one of the three in Anaheim to bring it back to Chicago, so maybe on Saturday night we'll be in reasonable shape. Garland hasn't pitched in how long?

BEN: Roughly two weeks.

DAD: Hope he doesn't look too rusty out there…

October 15, 2005
BEN:

Shabbat just ended, and I don't know a better way to open the new sin-free year than with a White Sox tape. I'm really ticked I didn't get to watch Game 3 live, but I kept myself ignorant of the outcome. I've calculated, and I should have *just* enough time to watch Game 3 on tape before Game 4 starts. The start time for Game 4 is 8 PM ET, which means it won't get underway until 8:20 or so. That gives me about an hour and a half to watch Game 3 sans commercials. I have no idea how long the game went, but we'll find out.

I pop in the tape.

Let's get going.

Game Three

It's Garland for us, Lackey for them. Lackey's their real ace; he's a moose, and he's clutch. Garland hasn't pitched for a very long time, so he's a mystery. I don't have too much time to mull over the matchup though, if I want to finish the tape before the start of Game 4.

Scotty P. has been ice-cold the first two games, but he turns on an 0-2 pitch from Lackey and smacks it into right for a single. Iguchi bunts Scotty to second, since Ozzie is worried about Mercury's recent stealing troubles. Dye follows with a rocket into the right field gap, and Scotty's home. 1-0. It's about time we started off fast.

Lackey's pitching on full rest, but he's hanging his breaking pitches. Captain Konerko smokes a ball foul, then goes 3-2 on Lackey. Lackey comes at him with another hanger, and this time Konerko jumps on it. It is *gone*, an absolute no-doubter. 3-0.

I like this game.

Everett grounds out and Rowand flies to right, but we're off to the kind of hot start we've needed all series long.

Now we just need Garland to get rolling. Garland is pitching on *12 days rest*, which is unheard of. Some are worried, but I think this is good news; he looked tired down the stretch. The problem with rest is that Garland is a sinkerball pitcher, and if he's too strong, he starts to elevate the ball.

He walks the leadoff man, Figgins. Not a good sign. But his fastball is working, and he blows away Orlando Cabrera.

He throws another heavy fastball on the inside corner, and Guerrero is jammed. He chops it up the middle . . . right to Iguchi, who steps on second and fires to first to end the inning.

I like this game a lot.

Hambino leads off the second by breaking his bat and grounding out to first. Lackey's fastball is working, but Jedi Joe fouls off pitch after pitch. Finally, he grounds to third for the second out.

The announcers can't shut up about that call on Pierzynski in Game 2, though they briefly mention the fact that it was great hitting by the Jedi that won that game, not the bad call by Doug Eddings. It's beginning to annoy me; let's just play the game already.

The Sox are making Lackey throw a lot of pitches. Uribe's taken a bunch, and finally he singles to right. The problem with working Lackey is the Angels' bullpen. I just hope Scoscia sticks with his horse too long.

Scotty nubs one to the pitcher for out number three.

Garland starts off the second inning by striking Anderson out swinging. He pops Bengie Molina up to Rowand for the second out, bringing up Erstad. But Erstad doubles into the right-field corner, and he takes off. Dye picks it up, guns it to Iguchi, and Iguchi guns it to third. For some strange reason,

Erstad is determined to get three bags. He's out by five feet, and that's the inning.

Oh, I love this game.

With two outs, I don't understand that move by Erstad. You're down three runs and will score on a single anyway. It's just bizarre.

Iguchi starts the third with a sharp single to left on a 3-2 pitch. Lackey has thrown 39 pitches through two innings, and we're working him some more. Dye takes him to 3-2 *again*, then walks. Lackey could be gone by the fifth at this rate.

But he throws a fastball right by Paulie, and Lackey looks like he's back in business.

Not so fast, says Carl Everett, who loops one into left, and it's 4-0. Lackey goes full on Evel, who crushes a fastball, and I'm out of my chair, but it's right at Cabrera, who catches it and doubles off Dye to end the inning.

Oh well, it's still 4-0.

Garland is going strong, and he gets Rivera to ground to out to Paulie. Garland saws off Finley, but Finley muscles a liner toward center. Garland leaps, knocks it to Uribe, who is charging across the infield, and Uribe fires to first for the out. That's a bizarre 1-6-3 putout. Heads-up play by the resident pirate.

Garland's throwing a lot of fastballs tonight. He gets Kennedy on a soft liner to Uribe, and we're into the fourth.

Hambino goes down on strikes; he's having a tough series thus far, even despite his Olivier act in Game 2. Crede flies out to right. Uribe pops to second. We're taking less pitches now, which doesn't make me happy. We don't want Lackey settling in.

The good news is that Garland is lights out. He pops Figgins up to Iguchi, and punches out Cabrera. Guerrero hits a ball hard off of Garland's shoe and ends up on first, but keeping Guerrero on the infield is an accomplishment. Anderson grounds softly to third, and that's the inning.

So far, so great.

In the fifth, Pods grounds sharply to Figgins for the first out; Figgins was playing in for the bunt, and displayed some nice reflexes there. Iguchi hits Lackey hard, and laces a liner to the warning track in right center for a double.

I'm thinking we'll get a run here, but Dye is blown away by an outside fastball.

Good thing the next batter is Konerko, who smashes a liner into center for a single, scoring Iguchi easily from second. 5-0. Konerko takes second on the throw home. Everett flies out to end the inning.

Where were our bats the first two games? Lackey's their horse. I'm so confused. In a happy way, that is.

Garland starts off hot again, throwing a nice cutting fastball to Molina, who bloops it just over Garland's head. Uribe charges across again, and cuts Molina down at first. Uribe's great with that charging play – he fires to first so smoothly.

Garland strikes out Erstad on a sinker. He follows by freezing Rivera on a breaking ball. He might be pitching the best game he's pitched all year. And this for a guy who won 18 this year. This is dominance.

Top of the sixth. Lackey's gone. This is unreal. Lackey, on full rest, and he's gone after five. Now we face Kevin Gregg, a guy with a weird delivery. It works on Rowand, who grounds to Figgins at third. Gregg goes full on Hambino before inducing a groundout to short. Crede flies to Guerrero, who catches the ball in foul ground, and then we're into the bottom half.

Keep it going, Big Jon.

Garland pops up Finley to third, but surrenders a base-hit to left from Adam Kennedy. Buck, Piniella, and McCarver are talking up Garland, remembering that he's had three complete game shutouts this year. This performance is topping them all, I think.

Figgins flies to Scotty, who comes flying in from left to make the putout in left-center territory. I love speed. Carlos Lee misses that ball by about three miles.

Cabrera's battling Garland. Finally, Garland leaves a ball out over the plate, and Cabrera bashes it to left.

High, deep, gone. 5-2.

It's not a crisis yet, but I don't like it.

Guerrero strikes out to end the inning.

Let's get a couple back, guys.

Uribe strikes out looking. Scotty goes down swinging on a high fastball. Iguchi strikes out on a low breaking ball. This isn't a recipe for success. Bring back Lackey, please!

Recover out there, Big Jon. Cotts and Politte are up in the bullpen in case something goes wrong. Garland's velocity is still high; he's been throwing 94 and 95 mph all night. Anderson hits a hard grounder destined for center field, but Garland (who is an excellent defensive pitcher) stabs at it and comes up with it, then tosses to first for the out. Molina goes down swinging on high heat. Erstad chops to Crede, who flings to Konerko for the third out.

We're into the eighth, two innings from a 2-1 ALCS lead.

Dye walks on four pitches, and we may be in business here. Gregg is clearly worried about Dye on first, and he keeps throwing over there. It distracts him, and he throws an inside fastball to Konerko, who inside-outs it and bangs it to right for a single. Men on first and third, no outs.

Ooooh, I'm getting greedy.

Gregg comes out, and Brendan Donnelly comes in. This guy looks like he's doing the robot every time he throws a pitch. Everett goes down swinging, and it's the player I least like to see up there: Rowand. Naturally, Rowand fists it toward second base; Cabrera cuts over, catches it, steps on second, and fires to first for the DP.

That was ugly.

But we've still got Big Jon. It's the top of the eighth and he's still out there. Jeff Davanon pinch hits, and Garland jams him. He grounds to Iguchi at second, breaking his bat in the process. One out. Finley lines the ball hard, right at Dye in right. Two down. Kennedy grounds to Garland on the mound, and the inning is over.

Jon Garland. Unbelievable.

Hambino leads off and salivates at the second pitch he sees, a fastball over the meat of the plate. He drives it off the right-field wall, so hard that he has no time to take second. Man on first, no outs. Crede skies one to Anderson in left, and there's one down. Uribe strikes out, and it's Scotty time.

He comes through, singling hard up the middle. Iguchi moves with an outside pitch, and grounds it down the right field line – just foul. He strikes out, though, and we go to the bottom of the ninth.

The big question: do we take out Garland?

Ozzie says no. The big righty is still out there. Figgins pops one to short left, and Scotty P. takes off running. At the last minute, he makes a basket catch. Garland's pounding the outside corner on Cabrera; he isn't going to make the same mistake with him this time. The count goes full. Finally, he throws a fastball down the pipe. Cabrera hits it on the screws to center – right at Rowand.

One more out, big guy. Garland throws an outside fastball to Guerrero. Guerrero opens his hips, steps in the bucket, and lines it hard ... right to Jermaine Dye.

We're up 2-1.

Game Four

And there's nothing better than watching a playoff doubleheader, especially one where we win both halves of it.

We have that shot right now.

Freddy Garcia goes for us tonight, trying to keep the streak of complete games going. Ervin Santana goes for them; he shut us down earlier this season. This could be a real pitcher's duel. The good news for us is that our bullpen is rested more than Rip Van Winkle – they've pitched a combined 2/3 of an inning, and that was in Game 1.

Unfortunately, I can't call Dad between innings because he's still on Pacific Time, meaning that Shabbat won't be over for him until about 10:30 PM my time.

Let's get started.

Santana starts Scotty off 0-2, but Scotty works him for a walk. Santana's throwing with speed (96 mph), but he can't hit the strike zone with his off-speed stuff. Santana drills Tad in the elbow with an inside fastball, and we have two on with no out.

Oh, baby. Come on, Jermaine.

The announcers are astonished that Santana is so wild. He's missing the zone repeatedly. But Dye finds a pitch he likes and smacks it to Finley in deep center. Both runners tag, and both are safe. Second and third, one out.

Come on, Paulie.

Halfway through the at-bat, Fox shows a replay of Konerko's 2-run dinger last night. A few pitches later, on a 3-2 count, Santana throws a slider that doesn't slide, and Paulie hammers it. It's back, back, back . . . gone! 3-0 Sox, and I'm humming, "Na na na na, na na na na, he-ey-ey, goodbye."

Everett takes Santana 3-2 before flying softly to Guerrero in right, and Rowand strikes out (as usual), but the damage is done.

It's Freddy time.

Freddy punches out Figgins on a low fastball. Cabrera grounds to Crede on the first pitch. Guerrero grounds to shortstop on the second pitch, making him 1-13 for the ALCS.

This is shaping up to be a great, great evening.

Pierzynski gets to 3-2 before popping to left, and Santana has thrown well over forty pitches in just 1 1/3 innings. Crede goes after the first pitch and pops to Kennedy at second base. Not smart hitting – make Santana work.

Santana goes 3-2 to Uribe, too, and then walks him. As good as Garcia was, Santana's been twice as bad. Podsednik grounds to Cabrera, though, and Santana's out of the inning.

Bottom of the second. Garcia gets Anderson to pop to right. Then the announcers go to Chris Meyers, who explains that Garcia's wife gave birth after Game 2. I love the fact that we have so many new fathers on the team: Garcia, Konerko, Crede, and even the much-maligned Hambino, among many others. As Hawk puts it, we are the Good Guys.

Erstad walks, and the Angels have a baserunner. It's been awhile. Casey Kotchman is batting DH tonight, and Garcia goes 2-0 on him. A.J. comes out for a chat, and that settles the big fella; Garcia gets Kotchman to chop one down the third base line. Garcia leaps off the mound and barehands it, but he's falling away from first base. He flings the ball wide of Konerko, and all the sudden the Angels have men on second and third with only one out.

Freddy, don't do this. Please, don't do this. We *need* this game.

Molina reaches out and pokes one to center. Rowand can't get there, and it's 3-1. Luckily, the Angels' third base coach holds up Kotchman, because Rowand double-clutches the ball and heaves it into the ground. Kotchman would have scored easily, but we're still in trouble. Now it's first and third with only one out. Maybe I should have taped this game, too.

Finley grounds to Iguchi, though, and Iguchi and Uribe put together a nifty 4-6-3 DP.

Wait a second. Finley is screaming about *something*. After Fox gets back from break, they show the replay. Looks like Finley hit A.J.'s glove on the swing, which is catcher's interference. That would have awarded first base to Finley and kept the inning alive.

Finley still could have kept the inning alive, but he stupidly turned to scream at the home-plate ump as he ran to first. He would have beaten out the throw easily had he put his head down and argued later; instead, he was thrown out by half a step. Scoscia's fighting mad at the umps and he has a right to be, but perhaps he should be even more angry at Finley, who could have had an RBI groundout and brought the Angels within one.

I get an IM from one of my friends after that play.

DANI: Did you pay off the umps?

345

BEN: Yup, before Game 2. When I pay people off, they stay paid off.

Iguchi pops to Kennedy to start the third. Dye grounds to Cabrera, but he fires high and Dye is safe. Cabrera only made seven errors the entire year – the Angels look rattled. Konerko flies to Finley in right center, but on the second pitch to Everett, Dye takes off for second and makes it easily.

And Everett takes advantage like he did at the beginning of the year, grounding the ball through the middle and scoring Dye. 4-1, Sox.

"Yes, yes!" I scream at the TV.

Everett makes a wide turn at first, though, and he gets caught in a run-down to end the inning. "No, no!" I scream at the TV.

Meanwhile, Fox keeps showing the replay of the Finley/A.J. interference non-call over and over. Does Hambino have to be in the middle of every play? This is getting ridiculous.

Garcia's back on track. He strikes out Kennedy on a nasty breaking ball. He strikes out Figgins swinging, Figgins' 11th strikeout of the postseason. He gets Cabrera to line out to Scotty P. He's looking great. Guess it only took a little catcher's interference to get him going again.

Rowand starts the fourth by grounding to short, as usual. Hambino decides to add insult to injury, and takes out his club. He takes a fat fastball and rocks it to deep center. Gone. "You're killing them, A.J.!" I shout.

5-1, Sox. And the Angels' fans are stunned. McCarver calls it the "hardest hit ball of this series," and he's right. That ball was hit right on the screws.

Crede goes down looking and Uribe pops to first, but this game is quickly getting out of hand.

Eeeeexcellent.

Once more, Guerrero grounds to shortstop leading off the bottom of the fourth. Anderson flares to left center, just over Uribe's head. Don't open the door now, Freddy.

He doesn't. Erstad pops to Uribe, and things are looking up.

But Casey Kotchman, the no-name DH, blasts a double to left-center, beyond the reach of Aaron, and Anderson scores to make it 5-2. Bullpen activity, Ozzie?

Molina grounds to short. But for some reason, Crede is cutting over, and he's right in Long Juan's way. He ducks at the last instant, Uribe throws over Crede's head to first, and we nail Molina. Phew.

Top five, and Santana is still out there, which is somewhat surprising. This game isn't out of reach yet for the Angels, but Ervin can put it out of reach with another bad inning.

He walks Scotty P., and Bud Black goes to hang out with Santana as Scot Shields warms up. Santana's not long for this game. He's throwing over to first repeatedly, probably to give Shields time in the bullpen. Finally he throws a pitch, and Iguchi flies to deep center. Finley's there, though.

And out comes Santana. Shields throws over to first a couple times, then catches Scotty P. off guard and Scotty is tagged out . . . but the first-base ump calls him safe.

DANI: You weren't kidding, were you?

BEN: Would I kid about the White Sox?

On the next pitch, Scotty steals second. My evil plan is working. Shields saws off Dye, and the ball ends up in the mitt of Adam Kennedy, who flips to first for the out; Scotty P. stayed on second for some strange reason. The Angels walk Konerko to set up the force.

Everett is the Everett of old, singling through the left side and scoring Scotty. 6-2. I smell victory.

Rowand grounds to short (as usual), and that's the inning.

Garcia, who has had a nice long rest during this game, comes out rusty, going 3-2 on Finley before inducing a fly-out to Rowand in right-center.

It's time for the Ozzie interview. He says he didn't see the Hambino non-call (yeah, right) and says that he just wants six or seven innings out of Garcia. Odds are that he'll get it.

Kennedy grounds out to short. Figgins tries to bunt his way on, and he's down 0-2 yet again. He works it to 2-2, then flies to Podsednik. Garcia is breezing his way through the Angels tonight.

It's getting close to the end of Shabbat on the West Coast. Dad should be calling soon, and I'll update him.

I love Hambino. He goes down on strikes, but he's ticked. He's ticked with a 6-2 lead, after he already hit a HR this game. He's great.

Crede follows with a single to left. Uribe pops to center, and Crede tries to steal second but gets gunned out. It's ok – I like to have him running with Scotty up there and two outs. At least Mercury leads off next inning.

Cabrera gets good wood leading off the bottom of the sixth, but it's a lined shot right at Crede, who sucks it in. Garcia's starting to get hit, so I hope Ozzie's got the quick hook. Guerrero, who has ceased to worry me, grounds toward the hole, but Jedi Joe dives for it, then throws him out easily. Our infield is great – if Crede had missed the ball, Uribe was right there to make the play behind him.

Anderson goes down swinging on a 55-ft. curveball, and we're into the seventh. Ozzie's got his six from Garcia – how deep will Garcia go?

Shields is out for the Angels, and Donnelly is in. If our bullpen is underworked, you have to think that the Angels' is overworked. Scotty walks for the third time tonight, and Scoscia has to be upset. His pitchers can't seem to find the plate, his hitters can't seem to find their bats, and the umps can't seem to find their glasses.

Muhahahaha.

Iguchi goes down on strikes. But Podsednik steals second, and we have another runner in scoring position. Fox shows the replay again, and it looks like the Angels might have nabbed Scotty. Another bad call?

Let me clear my throat. Okay. I'm ready. Muhahahahaha!

After a lifetime of calls going the other way, this is beautiful.

Dye flies to Guerrero, and Scotty tags and moves to third. Guerrero shows off his cannon, but can't nab Mercury. Come on, wild pitch. But instead, Konerko grounds out to Cabrera to end the threat.

Garcia's back out there, and he's as cold as the other side of the pillow. Erstad pops to Iguchi at second. How many pop-ups has Garcia induced tonight? Kotchman flies softly to Scotty P. in foul territory.

McCarver's commenting on the absence of the Angels' annoying Rally Monkey, a mascot that supposedly puts the curse of the simian on opposing teams. Buck explains that it only comes out if the Angels are down three runs or less. "He has a good agent," says Buck.

Molina chops to Crede, and we're into the eighth.

It's ridiculous how smooth this is. As a Sox fan, I'm suspicious.

Donnelly's gone, and Esteban Yan is in. Meanwhile, Marte's getting his throwing in down in the bullpen – no chance he sees any action. Buck cracks me up: "The other guys down in the bullpen are doing some online shopping, getting an early jump on holiday cards." This is truly unbelievable. Our relievers have pitched 2/3 of an inning, out of 34 innings total thus far. And Garcia ain't done yet.

Everett walks, and we're not done yet. Rowand's up, which I guess means a double-play groundout. But he shocks me by lining a ball down the left-field line for a double, and we've got men on second and third and no outs. Hambino strikes out on a dirtball, and Molina reaches up and tags him. The crowd roars, remembering the supposed injustice of Game 2.

Insert evil laugh here.

Crede smashes a grounder down the third-base line. Figgins dives but can't come up with it, and it's 8-2, Sox.

Oh, it's good to be a Sox fan.

So good.

So fine.

I've got-a you. Da, da, da, da, da!

I feel good. Da, da, da, da, da, da, da.

Okay, that's enough of that. Time to call Dad.

BEN: Dad, we're whooping them tonight 8-2, and we won last night, 5-2.

DAD: Are you serious?

350

BEN: Yup. Tonight, Garcia's throwing a gem, the Angels can't do anything right, and God has struck the umpires blind.

DAD: I *knew* my atonement was good this year.

BEN: God's making it easy for me not to start off the year on the wrong foot. I'm not cursing or throwing things. I made a deal with Him this year – let the Sox win it, and I won't yell at them.

DAD: We'll see how long *that* lasts. I'm heading for the TV.

Uribe grounds into a double play, but it doesn't matter. Garcia is cruising. Finley singles, but we're up six runs. Kennedy grounds to Crede, and Crede tosses to Iguchi, who tosses to Konerko for the DP. But for some reason, the umps call Finley safe at second, saying Iguchi didn't touch the bag. As McCarver correctly points out, umps call this a DP all the time – it's a "neighborhood play."

Whatever. We're up six runs.

I can't remember the last time I've felt so mellow.

Figgins flies to left, and the announcers are mentioning that the last time three pitchers have thrown consecutive complete games was 1973 with the Mets.

Cabrera pops to center, and bring on the ninth.

The announcers are great tonight. As they go to break, they show the "neighborhood play" and pipe in "Mr. Rogers' Neighborhood." It is, indeed, a wonderful day in the neighborhood.

Scotty P. leads off with a triple into the right-field gap after Vladdy misses the cutoff man (which is routine for him). Scotty's had a heck of a series, and this is his crowning

351

achievement. He's been on base four times, and he has two steals (one questionable).

Tad goes down on strikes (he's still in the Neighborhood of Make-Believe). Dye pops out to right, Konerko flies to right, and we're going to blow a leadoff triple. Grr.

Oh, wait. The score is 8-2.

Now let's put down the Rally Monkey.

Guerrero grounds up the middle, Uribe cuts over, fields it, and fires to first for the out. Good play. Anderson strikes out, and Pierzynski tags him just to make sure. Erstad's the last man. Garcia almost has him, but Erstad singles to right. Guillen goes to the mound to hang out with Freddy. What is he, joking? One out away with a six-run lead?

Kotchman gets a good piece of one and shoots it toward Iguchi, but Tad picks it up, flips to first, and we're up 3-1.

One game away from the Series.

BEN: Dad, can you believe this?

DAD: Papa would have loved it. I'm sure he's enjoying it right now.

October 16, 2005
DAD:

Dear Dad:

One game away from the Series. I know you're watching this, too. Remember when I asked you why we were White Sox fans when I was little, and you said because of Bill Veeck? You'd like Jerry Reinsdorf, too, Dad. Even though he owns the Bulls, and they won six titles with Jordan, he's said winning the Series with the Sox would top all of that, because he's first and foremost a baseball fan. And he's really generous with his employees, too. You'd like him a lot.

You'd love the way the Sox players pull for each other, too. When Paul Konerko was being praised for his three-run homers the last two games, he immediately gave credit to Scotty and Tad. He said, "Our wins go hand in hand with those guys at the top. They get on base, Pod's stealing some bases, Iguchi's moving him over. We've won games without those guys but we've won our best games when those guys are clicking." And Scotty said, when asked how he is so successful once he's on base, "You watch Paul Konerko swing the bat." They're a real team, Dad. They check their egos at the door. I hope they win tonight for you, Dad. You never got to see them win the Series, but maybe if we get there, you can put in a good word with the Man Upstairs.

It's Contreras against Byrd, a rematch of Game One, but this time, I'm not really nervous, just expectant. On the Fox broadscast, Lou Piniella says that when the Angels lost last night they looked like a beaten team. Apparently they called a rare team meeting, and Scioscia reminded them that they're only three games away from the Series.

I don't see the fire in them that the Bosox had last year, though. Most of the Angels were there when they won the Series in 2002, and they just aren't that hungry. *We* look hungry, and just as the Bosox played for their fans last year, our Sox seem to be on the same mission this year.

We're 5-0 in the playoffs when we score first, so I hope we get out to a quick start tonight. It rained this afternoon, and I'm hoping the gloomy skies bode ill for the local team.

DAD: Are you ready to rumble?

353

BEN: (Growls)

DAD: Yup, you're ready.

Scotty, who is batting .357 in the series and had a great game last night, takes Byrd to 2-2, then fans. Okay . . . it's early. I'm a lot more tolerant of our mistakes when we have a 3-1 series lead. Tad gets hit by Byrd in the side, though, and that's a good sign. If Byrd doesn't have his control, he'll be toast. J.D flares one toward left. Rivera, in the lineup for his hitting, can't run that well. It drops in front of him, and we have runners on first and second for the Captain. Another three-run HR, Paulie?

He gets good wood on it, going deep the other way, but it's playable, and Guerrero hauls it in. Tad tags, and Guerrero's cannon finally hits the cut-off man, Cabrera, who turns and guns to third, but too late – Tad's safe. Erstad has to hold J.D on, now, leaving a hole for Everett, but he doesn't capitalize, grounding out to Cabrera. I hope that doesn't haunt us later. . . .

Contreras looks strong. Figgins lifts an easy fly to Evel, and Cabrera doesn't even try to swing when he comes up next, just tries bunting, and Jose makes a very nice running grab as Cabrera pops it in the air down the third base line.

Now it's Anderson, and I'm glad no one's on base so he can only touch up Jose this time for one run if he hits it out. He hangs tough, fouling off pitches, and finally shoots a single to left. That's a moral victory, I think.

Bringing up Guerrero, which doesn't scare me at all. I think we have his number; he's only got one hit in the series. Sure enough, he pops to Dye in short right, and they're gone. I think Guerrero is so befuddled, he's no threat from here on in unless he gets a couple of lucky hits.

Rowand leads off in the second. There's a long fly down the right-field line . . . it's tailing foul . . . stay fair, darn it! . . . and it does, just barely inside the line before it bounces and spins toward the right and over the stands in foul territory for a ground rule double. Cool, man on second and Hambino up. He'll move him over. I have total confidence in the man.

Yup. He manages to get his bat way up for a high pitch and bunt the ball straight down, sending Evel to third. A.J. is just fundamentally sound. That's all. He plays baseball the way it should be played.

One out for Crede. Can the Jedi do it again? Byrd goes 2-0 on him, then delivers.

Craaaa --- ck!

Deep sacrifice fly to center, and there's no doubt: we have drawn first blood again. 1-0 Sox.

We're in the money, we're in the money . . .

Careful, David, remember which team you're rooting for...

BEN: I think we should move Crede up in the lineup.
DAD: To what?
BEN: President.

Uribe grounds out, 5-3, but we have the lead.

Oh, look . . . that's a great sign. Thanks, Dad, for putting in a good word. It's starting to rain. Normally I'd worry about the game being rained out, but somehow it feels more like the hopes of the Angels are being rained on.

Sure enough, they go down easily in the second, one-two-three, and maybe Piniella was right; maybe they are a beaten team.

355

But in our half of the third, we don't touch Byrd, either, and that's a sign I *don't* like. Especially now, because Rivera just laced one into left leading off for them in the third. Scotty runs over to get it, but the footing is uncertain, and Rivera is smart. He knows Scotty won't have solid footing, and Rivera steams for second and makes it.

Uribe is dancing over to keep Rivera close. There's a daylight play (if the pitcher sees daylight between the shortstop, who has run to second base, and the runner who is taking a lead, he throws there to try to pick him off) and Jose throws it away into center field. Rivera's on third with nobody out. Crap. Can Jose hold them off?

No. Kennedy lines a 1-1 pitch to center for a base hit, and we're tied, 1-1.

Now Figgins tries to move Kennedy over with a bunt, and does, 5-3, and the Angels have the lead run on second. Cabrera's up. Uh-oh.

But Jose gets him to ground out 6-3, holding the runner. Good. Now don't do anything fancy, Jose . . .

Hambino misses catching a tough pitch, and Kennedy takes third on a passed ball. Now what? Anderson is up, with Guerrero on deck. Don't *pitch* to Anderson, for cryin' out loud. Don't let him beat you.

Jose doesn't; he's careful, and walks Anderson, bringing up Guerrero with men on first and third. He gets a strike, then throws a split-finger that Guerrero beats on the ground to Uribe, who forces Anderson at second. Good; we're still tied 1-1.

BEN: Whatever we're doing with Guerrero, don't change it.

DAD: I'll call Don Cooper right away.

356

But we still aren't getting to Byrd. Captain hits it hard again, but Rivera catches it in left. Everett singles to center, but Rowand hits a liner that Kennedy soars to catch, and Hambino flies out to left.

Before the Angels' fourth, Bud Black is interviewed. It's between innings. Does Scioscia take himself (and his guidance of his team) so seriously that he won't talk between innings?

It doesn't help them. Erstad grounds out on a great play by Konerko, who is definitely the most underrated first baseman in baseball defensively. Bengie Molina lines out to Uribe. Kotchman walks, but then Crede absolutely robs Rivera with a leaping catch on a line shot to his right. I think he's been studying *Return of the Jedi*; that leap was just like Luke's in the final battle.

In our half of the fifth, I'm praying for a run, because if we can get through the fifth, it'll be an official game. (I know, I know, they'll never call a playoff game early, but I can hope, can't I?)

Crede grounds out 5-3, but Uribe hits one down the left-field line, and he's going for two – Rivera comes up with it quickly, guns it to second, but Uribe makes a *great* slide, coming in to second from the outfield side, and beats the throw. A great, great slide.

Scotty up now. He goes 2-2, then fouls off, fouls off, fouls off, gets a ball making it 3-2, then walks. A great at-bat. Now, if Tad can hit a 'tweener . . . nope. Tad pops one to left for the second out, leaving it up to Dye.

On the first pitch, the Silent Assassin roars. Yes! He didn't use a silencer with that one! He lines one to left-center, scoring Uribe, and when Rivera hits the cut-off man Cabrera,

Cabrera uncharacteristically hesitates before turning to throw to second. A break for us, and Dye beats the throw. Runners at second and third, and we're up, 2-1.

BEN: The Silent Assassin leaves no trail.

That's it for Byrd. Scot Shields is in, *very* early. Scioscia's not letting this game get out of hand. But he has to face the Captain, who has hit the ball hard twice. And he does again . . . it's a deep shot to left . . .but Rivera hauls it in.

If there's justice, one ball Konerko hits tonight will fall in. But we are up, 2-1, so I'm not complaining.

Their half of the fifth, now. Kennedy is working Contreras hard. He grounds one hard down the line to Crede's right, and Joe grabs it but there's no way to gun out Kennedy, who's safe at first. Figgins is up, but he hasn't done anything to scare me yet.

He does now. He pulls a pitch toward the right-field fence, and is it gonna clear it? . . . no. But it takes one bounce toward the fence, and some jerk reaches out and grabs it from the stands. Ground-rule double, and Kennedy will have to stop at third. Okay.

But here comes Scioscia, and he's red in the face, and he's imploring the umps to let Kennedy score. It's a judgement call for the umps, but hey, the fan is an Angels fan in their park. Why should they be rewarded? We'll never know whether J.D. could have hit the cutoff man to throw Kennedy out at the plate.

BEN: Don't let him talk you into it, blue.
DAD: Don't be surprised if he does, I smell a make-up call here.

Sure enough. They're giving Kennedy the plate. It's 2-2. Now the question is going to be why didn't they give Figgins third base. After the way the media keeps harping on the Game 2 A.J. call, maybe the umps are bending over backward the other way now. Figgins, on second, could steal third anyway.

After all that, Cabrera is up. He hits it up the middle, a high bouncer – grab it, Tad! – he does, can he throw from up there? In one motion he leaps, catches, and throws, and Cabrera is out at first. Figgins is at third, but Tad saved a run.

Anderson goes 2-1, and we are saved by Hambino blocking the 0-1 pitch, which is a 55 foot splitter. But on the 2-1 pitch Anderson nails it to deep right. It's a sacrifice fly, and they're up, 3-2. Guerrero's up. Big deal. He grounds out 4-3 to end the inning.

BEN: Well, at least the Angels fans can't moan about Figgins not getting the extra base now that he's scored.

It's the sixth, now, and we're running out of innings. We have to get something started; I don't want the Angels to win this game and get their hopes back. Everett hits a shot down the first-base line, but Erstad, a great defensive first-baseman, gloves it for the first out. Rowand bounces out 4-3, and Hambino strikes out. Uh-oh.

In their half of the sixth, Contreras is looking hittable. Not good, not good at all. Erstad flies to J.D. but Bengie Molina hits a line shot to Scotty, and Kotchman lines to Tad. Three hard-hit balls. No runs, but that's foreboding. We have got to score, and soon.

But we're getting a break: Shields has gone an inning and a third, and now we get Escobar for our half of the seventh. Phew!

BEN: I'd rather face Escobar any day.
DAD: Let's get some runs, now!
BEN: Look who's leading off.

It's Crede. He's been so quietly reliable, driving in our only run tonight, maybe he can get something started –
Thunder.
He *thunders* it to left. There is no doubt; no doubt at all. It's a massive home run, and before I can get a word out, my fifteen-year-old, Rebecca, screams, "The Force is with him!"
And this ain't no movie, either.
Uribe fans, but Scotty walks. On a 1-0 pitch to Tad, they pitch out, but Mercury has the wings on his feet again, and he makes it anyway, putting the lead run on second.

DAD: One must not interfere with the God of Speed.
BEN: Even the God of Speed needs a base hit to score.

But Tad and J.D strike out.
Still, the Jedi has pulled us even, 3-3.
Contreras, smelling a chance again, has recovered. Three up, three down in the seventh. Escobar is even tougher; he strikes out Konerko and Everett, making it five out of the last six batters he's fanned.
Now Evel is up, another strikeout, I'm betting, or a grounder to short. But he hangs tough, going to 3-2, then watches a pitch *just* outside and steals a walk from Escobar.

360

There are two out, and it's up to A.J. Okay, Hambino, you can do it!

Crap. He bounces one slowly up the first base line, and Escobar is going to field it and tag him. Escobar grabs the ball with his bare hand, and tags Hambino as he runs by. For some reason, he throws the ball to first, but Erstad can't field it. It doesn't matter; the ump has already called Hambino out. Wait a minute – the whole Sox team just leaped out of the dugout – now they're calling Hambino *safe*. Scioscia is out, and this time he's really going crazy.

Here's the replay . . . AHA! Escobar tagged Hambino with his *glove* as he went by, and the ball was in his bare hand.

BEN: We gotcha!
DAD: Didn't Scioscia see the play?

Scioscia won't let go, and now the crowd is booing. Why don't they simply show the play on the scoreboard? That would end the controversy. They won't; perhaps the rules forbid it.

The Angels fans are beating their Thunderstix so loudly it's almost deafening. Escobar is leaving and we get Frankie Rodriguez. Terrific. He's tough. But –on the other hand, we have our hero of the night up now –you guessed it – the Jedi Knight.

First and second, two out, tied 3-3, he can't do it *again*, can he?

Low curveball away. 1-0.
High pitch called a strike. 1-1.
55 foot curveball, no swing, 2-1.
High curve, strike, 2-2.

Low outside fastball – hold up, Joe! – he does – 3-2. The runners will be off with the pitch.

BEN: Can it get more tense?
DAD: Maybe have a guillotine over Crede's head?

Rodriguez is throwing so hard that his whole body is falling off the mound and turned toward first base. That's not sound fundamentally --- it leaves him out of position.

Here it comes . . . the 3-2 pitch . . .

Crede swings. He bounces it right up the middle, past Rodriguez, who can't field it because he's fallen off the mound again. The ball bounces right over second base . . . Kennedy dives to keep it from going into the outfield . . . Evel is running hard . . . Kennedy is on his knees on the outfield grass with the ball . . . Evel has rounded third and is flying for home . . . Kennedy, on his knees, hurls it home with everything he's got …

Evel beats the throw! We're up 4-3, and the Jedi has done it again!

BEN: If they do another Star Wars movie, this guy has *got* to play Luke.

Escobar, shaken, walks Uribe on four pitches.

Scotty is up with the bases loaded. Mercury runs the count to 3-2, and the three balls were curves that either went 55 feet or above his head, while the two strikes were fastballs, so . . .

BEN: I'm thinking fastball.
DAD: Me, too.

Wrong. It's a beautiful curveball that freezes Scotty for the third out.

BEN/DAD: Ohhhhhh . . .

Now, their eighth. Cabrera grounds to Uribe, and we're only five outs away. Anderson steps in. We've got Jenks and Cotts warming up, but Ozzie's sticking with Contreras, who seems to be getting *stronger*. Anderson looks almost helpless up there. On a 2-2 pitch, he flies to Scotty.

Four outs away . . .

Guerrero, who is now one for his last nineteen, is at the plate.

DAD: Remember the hot dog act he pulled in their last series against us?

BEN: You mean when he stood admiring his HR and then had to run because it wasn't gone?

DAD: Yeah. I hope he whiffs; it would serve him right.

The crowd is expectant, and sounds a little angry. Contrera jams Guerrero, who weakly grounds to Tad. We're three outs away, and now they're booing Guerrero, the reigning MVP.

DAD: This is delicious.

BEN: We still could use an insurance run – don't get too excited yet.

Rodriguez is overthrowing big-time. I guess he's not as confident when he doesn't have the lead. Tad works the count to 3-2, then walks. The Assassin steps in.

On the 2-1 pitch, Tad breaks for second. The throw from Molina is to the right of second base . . . the ball, Kennedy, and Tad all arrive at the same time . . . Kennedy catches the ball and swipes at Tad all in the same motion, and Tad's out. No – the ball is loose, and Tad's safe! Dye walks on the next pitch; there's no way they're going to throw something Dye can hit with first base open.

BEN: Maybe Konerko's going to hit his three-run homer now. He's been hitting the ball hard all night.

Curve   outside.   1-0.
Curve high, inside. 2-0.
Low outside . . . he swings, and drives it deep toward right. Guerrero's on his horse, but it's over his head, off the wall. Tad's across the plate, but with nobody out, Cora holds Dye at third, and the Captain delivers a double.

DAD: You called it! You called it!
BEN: I called a homer, Dad.
DAD: Who's counting?

Everett clumps to the plate. He's persistent, fouling off pitch after pitch, but he finally strikes out.

DAD: Crap.

Rowand's turn. Will they walk him to load the bases? There's only one out, and that would set up a double play . . .

No, they're pitching to him. He hits it fairly deep to right, and Guerrero's poised to catch it and throw home. Cora's aggressive, I think he'll send Dye . . .

He does! Dye's off and Guerrero unleashes the cannon . . . the throw's a rocket, but it's up the third-base line, and Dye scores easily. Paulie tries for third on the throw home, and Molina throws him out for the third out, but Dye has already scored, and we're up 6-3!

BEN: Evel comes through!
DAD: They are toast! Toast!

Three outs away, now. It's still Jose on the mound, and if he finishes it'll be our fourth straight complete game.

Erstad gets down 0-2, then chops a high bouncer toward the middle. Tad makes a quick jump, grab and throw, and that's one out.

REBECCA: Sit down, Daddy! We can't see! Stop pacing!

Bengie Molina is up, and Contreras dazzles him, too. Molina's down 1-2, then lines easily to Rowand.

BEN: Can it be this easy?

Casey Kotchman is their last hope.
A foul off to the right.

365

A sharp grounder to first, and the Captain gloves it, steps on first, and runs to Contreras and leaps into his arms. Mercury is running in from left, grinning like a kid along with Evel from center and Dye in right, Hambino has taken off his mask and is screaming to the skies, the players are mobbing each other in the middle of the infield, and Ozzie . . .

Ozzie is calmly walking in front of the dugout, watching the pile of Sox in the middle of the field. He waves to someone in the stands, but he's letting the players have their moment.

Is he the best manager I've ever seen? Of course he is. Don't anyone, *anyone* argue that with me right now.

> **BEN:** Dad? Dad? Are you there?
> **DAD:** I'm here.
> **BEN:** Do you believe this?
> **DAD:** Just . . . one . . . more . . . step.

October 17, 2005
DAD:

I want Houston, but Ben wants St. Louis. He's concerned about the Houston pitching, with Oswalt, Clemens and Pettite and their stellar bullpen; I'm concerned about various factors should we play St. Louis.

1. They were in the Series last year, so they'll have the experience, and the motivation that comes with being soundly defeated the year before.

2. Houston, which got off to a horrible start this year, may be just a touch grateful to have gotten this far, and may relax just enough to give our will to win an edge.

3. St. Louis has better hitting; Pujols alone is enough to scare you.

366

4. LaRussa may have an axe to grind, since he was once our manager, even though he has stayed close friends with Jerry Reinsdorf.

5. St. Louis has a great history in the World Series; they've been in it 16 times, and their fans, who are arguably the best in baseball, will be on their toes every second.

If the Sox weren't in the Series, I wouldn't mind the Cardinals winning it, even though I always pull for the American league, because I have a sneaking fondness for the Cardinals. Partly it's because they are the Cubs' hated rivals, but mostly it's because of one man who was the classiest baseball player I ever heard of. . . .

August 1970

"It's straight ahead, Butch," my father said, as we drove down the street in Cooperstown.

I was fourteen, but I felt like a little kid. I had memorized the batting averages of all the players in the Hall of Fame, and most of the pitchers' stats, too, and now we were actually going there. Our family had driven across the country to visit New York City, and my father had made sure that we would go upstate, too.

As we neared our destination, I looked for an enormous structure that I was sure would dominate the landscape. I was disappointed that the building turned out to be a rather small one, but I hid my disappointment as all of us followed my father inside. Five minutes later, I was in the room where the plaques with the statistics and name of each player were displayed. Babe Ruth, Lou Gehrig, Christy Mathewson, Ty Cobb . . . I searched for the Sox in the Hall. Ed Walsh, Luke Appling, Ted Lyons, Ray Schalk, Red Faber . . . all the ancient Sox who had populated the team's early years. Then I noticed my father standing in front of a very new plaque.

Curious, I walked over to him, and saw the name: Stan Musial, who had been elected the year before. Musial had topped the .300 mark 17 times and won seven National League batting titles, in addition to holding virtually every national League hitting record. My Dad had purchased a record album for me years before that featured Stan the Man's advice on hitting, and I knew it by memory, so I wasn't surprised that my father was standing there, but he was lost in thought, and I wondered why.

"Great hitter, Dad," I said.

"One of the best, Butch," he said, "but that's not the best thing about him."

"He was a good guy?"

"One of the best. Did you ever hear the story about Musial and the cab driver?"

"No. . . ." I marveled again at my father's never-ending capacity for storing information.

He looked at the plaque. "One day, Musial was taking a taxi in New York to the ball game, and one of the players riding with him, noticing the driver was Jewish, started to use a mock Jewish accent, making fun of the driver. Musial told him to knock it off, and when they got to the park, Musial made sure he paid the driver himself, then told the player that he didn't ever want to ride with him again."

"I didn't know that about him," I said.

"True story, Butch. He's a Hall-of Fame guy, as well as a player. That's why I was standing here so long." He pointed across the room. "Want to go see Babe Ruth's bat?"

"Is it okay if I stand here for just another second, Dad? Just out of respect?"

"Sure, Butch," he said, putting his arm around my shoulders. At that moment, baseball and honor came together.

October 17, 2005

So I hope for Houston, but out of respect for Stan the Man, I can't root in good conscience against the Cardinals.

October 20, 2005
BEN:

Well, Dad got what he wanted: we face the Houston Astros in the World Series. Plus, in a lucky break, I'll be home for the Series, since it's fly-out week, when Harvard 2Ls interview at various law firms around the country.

Time for the breakdown, with Dad's commentary.

Starting pitching: We've got the Four Horsemen of the Apocalypse coming off of what may be the best staff postseason performance of all time. They've got Clemens, Pettite, Oswalt, and Backe. Advantage: Toss up.

DAD: I like our starters. Clemens has never impressed me in the playoffs, and Oswalt is untested. Pettite's the key.

Relief pitching: They've got Chad Qualls, Russ Springer, Mike Gallo, and Dan Wheeler. Gallo's the only lefty, and Qualls and Wheeler are similar in style (sinkerballers). They do, however, have the best closer in the National League: Brad Lidge. Pujols lit him up, but I wouldn't count on our lineup to do the same thing. Meanwhile, we've got Politte, Cotts, Hermanson, Hernandez and Jenks. None of them have pitched for awhile, so at least we'll be rested. Advantage: Slight, White Sox.

DAD: I'm not that high on their bullpen. I'd say moderate advantage, Sox.

Catcher: A.J. vs. Brad Ausmus. Ausmus is a solid ballplayer and an excellent defensive catcher. He simply doesn't have A.J.'s fire – or power. Advantage: Slight, Sox.

First base: Mike Lamb/Jeff Bagwell vs. Paul Konerko. No contest here. Advantage: Heavy, Sox.

Second base: Tad Iguchi vs. Craig Biggio. Biggio's playing in his first Series; he's a good defensive ballplayer, and versatile as they come (he's played catcher and outfield). He's also an excellent hitter with above average speed. Tad's coming off a good series in Anaheim, but give the veteran advantage to the Astros. Advantage: Moderate, Astros.

Third base: Joe Crede vs. Morgan Ensberg. Ensberg's had a career year. He's a good defensive third basemen with a blossoming power bat. Crede's having a postseason for the ages, doing it all. I'll take Jedi Joe. Advantage: Slight, Sox.

Shortstop: Juan Uribe vs. Adam Everett. The battle of the no-hit, good glove shortstops falls in the Sox's favor here. Uribe's got a better arm, and he has the ability to hit one out of the park. Advantage: Slight, Sox.

Left field: Scotty P. vs. Lance Berkman. Scotty's been fantastic, but Berkman is one of the top five hitters in the game. He's passable defensively, and look for double switches late in ballgames, with Berkman moving to first. Advantage: Moderate, Astros.

DAD: This is another mismatch. Compare Scotty to Tavares and we come away smelling like a rose.

Center field: Rowand vs. Tavares. Rowand's got a good glove, but he's erratic with the use of the three B's: his bat, baserunning and bunting. Tavares is the probable National

League rookie of the year. He has tremendous speed, and he's a good slap hitter with no power. Advantage: Moderate, Astros.

DAD: Aaron needs to show what he can do in the spotlight.

Right field: J.D. vs. Jason Lane. Lane is an underrated outfielder with decent pop. J.D. has recovered to post excellent numbers. Advantage: Moderate, Sox.

DAD: Dye will be more consistent than Lane.

Bench: We've got Ozuna, Harris, Perez, Widger, and Blum. They've got Lamb/Bagwell, Vizcaino, Bruntlett, Burke, and Orlando Palmiero. That's a tremendous bench, with lots of versatility. Advantage: Heavy, Astros.

Managers: Phil Garner is a longtime vet who helped this team recover from a brutal early-season start. Ozzie has been the best manager in baseball since Spring Training. Ozzie manages like a National Leaguer, so that removes any advantage Garner might have had. Advantage: Moderate, Sox.

DAD: Garner's had to do a heck of a job just to keep the Rocket happy. Clemens has that amazing ERA and that mediocre record. Run support was terrible.

Intangibles: The Sox are on a roll, having gone 10-1 since the Cleveland series ending the regular season. The Astros are coming off tough series with the Braves and Cards. We're battling an 88 year history of failure; they're battling a 45-year history of failure. Our curse is better, and our record is better.

Advantage: Heavy, Sox.

DAD: Plus the Sox have the prayers of at least a couple of religious people in this household.

World Series Game One
October 22, 2005

371

Game-time temperature is 55 degrees, and it's *cold*. They announce the starting lineups, and Joe Buck refers to Hambino as A.J. "Controversy" Pierzynski.

BEN: Like that, Dad?
DAD: Muhahahaha!

Contreras looks a bit iffy out there. He's throwing a low curveball, but somehow gets Biggio to chop one toward short on a 3-2 count. Crede cuts in front of Uribe, gloves and fires for the out.

Willy Tavares, the Astros' rookie sensation, is trying to get down a bunt, but Contreras is throwing a heavy, *heavy* splitter.

DAD: Look at the action on that.

Finally, Tavares tries to golf it toward center but only pops it to Uribe behind second. Contreras' forkball is falling off the table, and he goes 2-2 before freezing Berkman with an off-speed pitch for the strikeout.

BEN: Picking up right where he left off.

Clemens deals in the bottom of the first. His velocity is a bit low – 92-93 mph rather than 94-95 – but he gets Scotty to ground to short. Iguchi follows with a groundout to third base, and Clemens is looking strong.

Former St. Louis Cardinal Tim McCarver is explaining the difference between a splitter (Clemens) and a forkball (Contreras); he says looking for that difference is "cutting hairs."

DAD: Uh, I believe that's splitting hairs, Tim.

BEN: He's still reeling from the shock of Houston beating St. Louis, Dad.

A second later, Buck corrects McCarver. At least *someone's* awake in the booth.

Dye is having a great at-bat. He works his way back from an 0-2 hole to get the count to 3-2, fouling off a couple along the way. On the ninth pitch of the at-bat, Clemens throws him an outside fastball.

He goes with it.

Back, back, back . . . gone. 1-0, White Sox, in the *first game of the World Series.*

BEN: He's so strong, he can just muscle it out of here.

DAD: Don't wake me up.

Hambino's going berserk in the dugout, as usual. Ozzie doesn't even move.

Konerko, the reigning ALCS MVP, grounds out 6-3, but we're winning.

Top two. Contreras deals, and Ensberg is first-pitch swinging, flying out to Dye in right. Contreras deals to Lamb, ball one. Then, *boom.* He leaves one over the plate, and Lamb, the Astros' first baseman, gets all of it. Rowand is on his horse, but this one is gone, straightaway center field.

DAD: That's a bazooka. That lead didn't last long.

BEN: Please, God, not the return of the Secret Inning. Not now.

Jeff Bagwell, DHing tonight, takes one for the team on the shoulder. To his credit, he tried to get out of the way. On the 1-1 pitch, Jason Lane rips one foul down the left field line.

DAD: Contreras is getting hit.
BEN: At least our bullpen is rested.

Contreras comes back to force a grounder from Lane, a perfect DP ball to Uribe, who flips to Tad. Tad makes a beautiful turn and rifles to Konerko to get out of the inning.

Carl Everett leads off the bottom of the second with a bouncer up the middle for a single.

BEN: Good piece of hitting.

On the 2-1 pitch, Ozzie sends Everett. Rowand comes through, bouncing through the hole vacated by the second baseman, Biggio. First and third, no outs.

DAD: He's a much better hitter when he's not bunting.

Pierzynski grounds to Lamb at first, who looks Everett back, then guns to second, but Rowand makes a great takeout slide, preventing the DP. Everett, holds, then takes off and scores on the play, and we're back on top, 2-1.

DAD: Rowand's a better slider when he's not bunting.

McCarver makes a nice point – Everett was far enough off of third to take home on the throw to second, but close enough to make it back to third if Lamb had decided to throw to third.

BEN: Everett's a better runner when Rowand isn't bunting. Seriously, though, my man Rowand came through big time.

DAD: Agreed.

Crede breaks his bat and grounds softly to third for the second out, but Hambino moves to second. McCarver and Buck comment that they voted for Crede for ALCS MVP.

DAD: He really should have won, but there's a good argument for Captain.

BEN: Agreed. But they should not have underestimated the power of the force.

Uribe turns on one and laces it to left center for a double, and Hambino scores, and it's 3-1.

DAD: Boy, does that missed DP look bad for the Astros now.

BEN: Clemens is looking very human.

Scotty's making Clemens work, taking him 3-2 and fouling off a bunch of pitches. After a long battle, Clemens strikes him out on high heat.

BEN: Good inning.

The Astros pick up where they left off in the top of the third. Brad Ausmus, their catcher, lines a single to right. Adam Everett is their number nine hitter, and for some reason he isn't bunting. He's quickly down 0-2.

DAD: Now he's in trouble.

Everett nubs weakly to Contreras. Contreras double-clutches and then throws to Uribe, and Uribe can't fire in time to Konerko, so we only get one out. Biggio is sweeping at the ball and goes down 0-2, but somehow floats one into center, and it drops in front of Rowand. Tavares drops a nice bunt, but Contreras is off the mound like a cat and guns him out at first. Still, he advances the runners to second and third. Lance Berkman's up.

DAD: Yuch. Why can't it be Vladimir Guerrero?

Like clockwork, Berkman lines a ball into the right field corner, and we're knotted at 3-3.

BEN: Jose just can't leave well enough alone.

Ensberg grounds hard to short, and we're into the bottom of the third.

Clemens is out. What's going on here? Some guy named Wandy Rodriguez is in for the Astros. From Clemens to this?

Iguchi loops a ball toward second, and Biggio races in, scoops it in on the bounce, and rifles to first for the out. As Dye walks, the announcers state that Clemens is gone due to soreness in his left hamstring. Konerko follows the walk with a single to right, and there are two on with only one out. Everett strikes out on a nasty curveball, bringing up Rowand.

Can he do it again? Nope. Rowand turns over his hands and grounds to third, and the Astros get the force at second.

DAD: He should've bunted.

Contreras starts off the fourth with a nasty forkball strikeout of Mike Lamb. Bagwell flies to left – it looks scary, but it's not hit that hard. Lane pops to Dye in right, and Contreras is settling down.

Hambino grounds quickly to first for out number one. The announcers are interviewing Jim Hickey, the Astros' pitching coach, as Jedi Joe bats. Rodriguez throws Crede an outside fastball, and Crede whips the bat off his shoulder.

BEN: Get out, get out, get out . . .
DAD: Holy crap!
BEN: So be it, Jedi.

It's 4-3, Sox, and the stadium is *rocking*. The ball ended up in the left-field bleachers, and as Joe touches home and heads for the dugout, J.D. is laughing like, "Who *is* this guy?"

Uribe walks, and Rodriguez is beginning to look like A Fish Called Wandy. Scotty P. singles up the middle, Uribe stops at second, and we have two on with one out. But Iguchi grounds into a 4-6-3 DP, and the inning is over.

Ausmus pops to Dye to begin the fifth. Adam Everett chops one down the third base line, and Crede reaches over into foul territory to grab it, then chucks to first for the out. Biggio grounds to Crede's left; Crede sucks it up and throws to first.

DAD: He's a vacuum out there.

Dye walks on four pitches. Konerko drills the 3-1 offering up the middle for a single. The crowd is really into it. Everett lays down a beautiful bunt to move over the runners.

DAD: What other team has its DH lay it down there?

Rodriguez issues an intentional walk to Rowand, loading the bases. It's Hambino time. If he can get a hit and bring in an insurance run, Crede's up next and we could blow this thing wide open.

But Pierzynski grounds into a 3-6-1 DP to end the inning.

BEN: Grr. Good play by Wandy.

And so the sixth. Willy Tavares rockets a double into the left-center gap to lead it off. Berkman's up. He grounds *hard*, but it's right at Paulie, who scoops it up and touches first. Tavares takes third on the play, though, and a sac fly will tie it.

Ensberg smokes the ball down the third base line. It takes one bounce, and Crede goes down to a knee, backhands the ball, holds the runner, and throws to first for the out.

DAD: That's a do-or-die play. He has only one shot at that – stabbing it. Great reflexes.

Contreras seems determined to let in the tying run, and he almost throws a wild pitch on the 2-1. Hambino makes a tremendous block, saving him – at least for the moment. A second later, Lamb smacks the ball right at Iguchi, and that's out number three.

BEN: Hope Ozzie has the bullpen up. Contreras is getting killed out there. He's just getting lucky that everything is hit right at our guys.

On the 1-1 pitch, Joe Crede, leading it off for the Sox, hits a monster shot toward the left field foul pole. It swerves foul at the last moment. Dad and I groan. Crede pops to Biggio for the first out.

Uribe walks, and we've got another shot. Wandy comes out, and Chad Qualls comes in for the Astros. Scotty shoots one toward the right side, but it's right at Biggio, who flicks to Adam Everett for the fielder's choice. No chance to double up Scotty with his speed.

On the 1-0 pitch to Tad, Scotty takes off for second. He's got the swipe easily, and the ball gets away from Ausmus as well. Unfortunately, Scotty is sliding, so he can't see the passed ball and he has to stay at second. It doesn't matter, because Tad strikes out to end the inning.

DAD: Where's Tad? He seems a little lost out there.

Bagwell leads off for the Astros, and Contreras plunks him.

DAD: Wait a second, he's got to try to avoid that pitch. He stepped right into it.

The umps don't call it, and he stays at first; for some reason, Ozzie isn't saying anything. Jason Lane pops to Konerko at first. Why wasn't he bunting? Contreras plunks Ausmus, and there are two on.

BEN: Where's the bullpen? Where's the bullpen?!

McCarver is quite correctly pointing out that Contreras is dropping down as he throws, almost throwing sidearm. That means that his pitches tail in toward right-handed batters.

Adam Everett hits a slow roller to short. Uribe fires it to Iguchi, and Tad makes a nice turn and throw, but the ball was hit too slowly for the double play, and the inning remains alive. Men on first and third, two down.

Biggio rifles a shot down the third-base line, but Crede's there *again*. He lays out, picks it, and fires to first for the third out.

BEN: A Jedi must have the deepest commitment, the most serious mind.

Dye chops to short, and Everett rushes the throw, firing low. Mike Lamb can't pick it, and it bounces away. Dye is safe at first. Marte's up in the bullpen.

BEN: Oh, no. Not him, Ozzie. Anyone but him.

DAD: Maybe he's a decoy. Maybe Ozzie's trying to fool Garner somehow.

BEN: What, by calling in the entire cast from *One Flew Over The Cuckoo's Nest*?

Jenks joins Marte in the bullpen, and my disquiet is quelled. Meanwhile, Dye has a short lead off first as Konerko bats. The count is 1-2, and Dye takes off for second. Only one problem: Qualls hasn't thrown to the plate yet. Qualls doesn't see him, but Ausmus alerts Qualls to the situation. Qualls turns and throws over to Biggio at second, and Dye's in a rundown. Biggio throws to first, but he held the ball too long, and Dye slides back into first safely.

DAD: That's bizarre. And really out of character for Dye. He doesn't make silly baserunning plays like that.
BEN: He must have been fooled. Qualls has a great move to first.

Konerko pokes a fly deep to right, but it's hauled in. Everett follows by flying to left, and that leadoff walk looks like it will come to naught. It does; Qualls strikes out Rowand easily.

BEN: Ozzie's not going to stick with Contreras, is he?
DAD: It's been so long since he's called the bullpen, maybe he's forgotten the phone number.

Ozzie sticks with Contreras in the eighth. And Tavares creams a ball to left-center, about 380 feet. It drops in for a double.

That's it for Jose. In comes Neal Cotts. We didn't even see him warming up – Ozzie *did* fool everyone. The last time the Sox bullpen saw action was 11 days ago, Game 1 of the ALCS. How will they respond?

The good news: Berkman's batting righty, not lefty. He's a switch-hitter, so they've turned him around to face Cotts. It doesn't matter. He singles to left, but he hits the ball so hard that Tavares, on second, doesn't have time to make it home and he stops at third.

First and third, no outs. 4-3 Sox. How are we going to get out of this?

Cotts goes to 2-2 on Ensberg, their cleanup hitter, and the crowd is on its feet, pleading for a strikeout.

And Cotts obliges, blowing Ensberg away on a high fastball.

Cotts goes 2-2 on Lamb, who hit that longball in the second. McCarver points out that Cotts is coming with nothing but fastballs – he's thrown 11 straight at this point. Lamb has to be sitting dead red.

It doesn't matter. Cotts strikes him out on an outside fastball.

DAD: That proves it's location that matters. He was moving it inside high, then outside low, then inside, then outside. The hitter can't get comfortable.

Ozzie comes out of the dugout and signals for the bullpen. He does so, hilariously, by spreading his arms to their full length horizontally and bouncing his hands up and down (indicating girth), then taking his right hand and motioning above his head (indicating height).

That's right. It's time for Big Bobby Jenks. All 6'3" and 270 lbs. of him.

Despite the enormous tension that Dad and I are experiencing, we almost fall off the couch laughing.

It's Bagwell, the old vet, vs. Bobby Jenks, the young cannon.

First pitch. Chest high, 99. Bagwell swings, but he's in a different time zone.

Second pitch. Chest high, 100. Bagwell swings, fouling it off. He's getting closer, but he's not quite there.

Third pitch. Jenks almost throws it to the screen, but Hambino leaps to his feet and flings his glove up to snare it. Burke takes second on the pitch without a throw from A.J. The go-ahead run is now in scoring position.

Fourth pitch. 100 mph, and this one almost sails to the screen. It's 2-2.

DAD: I think he's warmed up.

Fifth pitch. 100. Bagwell manages to foul it off to the right.

Sixth pitch. 100. On the outside corner, at the knees. Bagwell swings.

Good night.

BEN: Hasta la vista, baby. He had no chance on that one. Sit down.

That's the inning.

Russ Springer is in to pitch for the Astros in the bottom of the eighth. Pierzynski greets him with a single into right. Iguchi's now the only member of our lineup without a hit.

Crede flies to right. Uribe flies to left. On the 1-2 pitch to Scotty, Pierzynski strolls off of first base, pauses between first and second for a cigarette, sees that Springer hasn't yet thrown the ball to the plate, reads the newspaper, watches Springer throw to the plate, then lumbers the rest of the way to second. There's not even a throw.

DAD: Interesting way to steal a base. The man is a total original.

BEN: We need an insurance run. Come on, Scotty . . . come on, Scotty . . .

The count goes full. Here's the pitch . . .
Scotty P. crushes a ball into the right-center gap.
Nobody's going to get there.
Come on, A.J. . . .
Pierzynski rolls around third and scores.
Come on, Scotty . . .
Scotty makes it to third himself, easily, for a triple.

DAD: *YES!!!*

Tad flies to right to end the inning, but it doesn't matter. We're going to win Game 1 of the World Series.

BEN: Jenks with a two-run lead? You can put this on the board . . . yes!

Jenks is back out there, now. Jason Lane is the batter.
First pitch, 96. Strike one.
Second pitch, 97, fouled toward right. Dye runs over, slides, but can't come up with it. 0-2.
Third pitch. Yellow hammer. Nasty curve. Off the table. 84. K.
Next?

Brad Ausmus grounds weakly to short on the second pitch. One more out to go.

The entire stadium is rocking. They're on their feet.

We're on our feet.

Adam Everett is up. The first two pitches are strikes, both 96. Jenks is obviously tiring.

Muhahaha.

Third pitch. 98, outside corner. Everett swings, gets nothing but air.

White Sox win. White Sox win. White Sox win!

Jenks struck out three of the final four batters. He *destroyed* them. I'm watching Ozzie's face and he's laughing. It looks like *he's* saying, "Muhahaha."

Dad and I high-five and almost break our wrists.

Game 2 tomorrow night.

We can't wait.

Game   Two
October 23, 2005

It's really coming down out there. It's 45 degrees. It's horrible weather.

Let's play some baseball.

Andy Pettite is going for the Astros. He's a great big-game pitcher going back to his days as a Yankee. We've got Buehrle, Mr. Slip N' Slide, and considering the weather, that may not be a good thing.

Buehrle starts off with a strike, then gets Biggio to fly softly to center field. Another first pitch strike to Tavares, and then Tavares tries to bunt his way on. He puts it down toward Buehrle, who leaps off the mound and tosses to first for the easy out. The fans come to their feet as Buehrle goes 1-2 on

Berkman, batting right. Buehrle racks him up on an outside fastball.

DAD: He froze him on that one.
BEN: He looks great.

Pettite scowls out from beneath the bill of his cap as he goes 3-2 on Scotty, who, as usual, is battling hard. Finally, Scotty lines a shot toward right field, but Jason Lane is on his horse and he stabs the ball just before it hits the ground.

DAD: Scotty's keyed in in a major way.
BEN: I like him even better than Carlos Lee.

Iguchi goes down swinging as Pettite works him outside, then inside. Dye gets our first hit of the night with a seeing-eye single just past Adam Everett. Konerko tries to stave off a strikeout, but Pettite finally nails him with a fastball on the outside corner. Pitchers' duel?

Guess not. First pitch from Buehrle in the top of the second, Ensberg smacks it to deep left. It's gone, and the Astros are up 1-0.

DAD: With Pettite pitching, this could get ugly.

Bagwell bounces slowly to third. Crede charges, guns to first, and gets the out. Jason Lane follows with a single over the shortstop, and Buehrle's looking far too human out there. Chris Burke lofts one softly to right, and it has a chance to drop. But J.D. is on the move and makes the catch look easy. On the 1-1 pitch to Ausmus, Lane takes off for second. He gets a surprisingly good jump, and the throw from A.J. isn't even close.

Ausmus dribbles one down the third base line, and Crede has no play. He lets it roll, hoping it will roll into foul ground, but the infield is wet from all the rain, and it sits in the mud. With one strike and two outs, Adam Everett feebly attempts to bunt, but misses the ball. On the next pitch, Buehrle fans him.

DAD: Buehrle's leaving everything up in the zone.

Pettite's cruising. Everett fans on a cut fastball low and inside. Rowand hits a hard grounder about six inches to Ensberg's left, but Ensberg isn't Crede and doesn't get in front of the ball, instead doing what Dad calls the "matador act," waving at the ball as it goes by.

Pierzynski goes the other way, lining a ball toward the left-field wall. A good left fielder would have a bead on it, but Burke is a former infielder, and he runs straight back and to his right, missing the ball as it clangs off the fence. Rowand, however, is running like a dope, and he ends up on second. He waited, then tried to tag on a fly that wasn't caught.

BEN: No way he should be on second. He should have been standing at least halfway between first and second the whole time, and when that ball hit the fence he should have taken off for third.

McCarver echoes the point a second later, but Crede saves Rowand, coming through again. He bloops a Texas Leaguer just beyond first base, tying the ballgame at 1-1 as Rowand comes around to score. A.J. winds up on third.

BEN: The Force is strong with this one.

Uribe lofts an easy pop fly into short right. Biggio goes back for it, throws up his glove – and the ball glances off of it and drops in. A.J. scores easily, but the Astros get the force at second base (Crede couldn't be running on that). We're up 2-1, and suddenly there's more oxygen in the room again.

On the first pitch to Scotty, Uribe takes off for second and makes it. It doesn't matter though, because Scotty grounds to Berkman at first to end the inning.

DAD: That play by Biggio has to kill Garner. Garner used to play second.

Biggio grounds to Crede to start the third. Willy Tavares (who is just killing us this series) triples to the right field corner, and the air is starting to get thin again. Berkman sac flies to center, Tavares scores, and we're tied again, 2-2.

DAD: If we could just get Berkman out of the lineup, we'd be fine.

Buehrle freezes Ensberg on a 3-2 curveball, and the Sox are batting again in the bottom of the third. Iguchi leads off with a single to left (his first hit of the Series). Dye turns on the 1-0 pitch and hits it 9,675,439.2 miles to left – foul. Dye breaks his bat a couple pitches later, bouncing to Berkman at first. Berkman tags the bag; he has no play at second. Konerko grounds 4-3, advancing Tad to third, but Everett shoots a hard grounder to Ensberg's left. This time, Ensberg comes up with it and throws Carl out to end the inning. Oh, well.

Buehrle is still going high in the zone. Bagwell hits a breaking ball hard to Iguchi's left; Iguchi goes back and spears the ball on the short hop, tossing to first for the out. Lane grounds to Konerko, who sucks it up for out number two.

Chris Meyers is talking about Bill Murray, the terrible actor (his performance in *The Razor's Edge* was so wooden it set the new standard for Grade A lumber) and diehard Cubs fan. Meyers says he asked Murray if he'd done anything since *Ghostbusters*, and Murray hung up on him.

DAD: Ah, taunting a Cubs fan while we're in the World Series. Does it get any better than that?

BEN: It's the little things in life.

Buehrle saws off Burke, who grounds to Konerko, and we're into the bottom of the fourth. Dad and I are sensing momentum building.

Maybe not. Rowand pops to shallow right. Down goes A.J. on a nasty curve. Crede drives the 1-1 inside cutter just the way Dye did before, a million miles and foul. He grounds to Everett to end the inning.

Ausmus starts off the fifth by smoking a grounder down the third-base line. Crede dives, but can only stab at the ball, which bounces off his glove as Ausmus chugs his way to second base. Everett tries to lay down a bunt, but fouls it off his leg. With one strike, he swings away – a dumb baseball move. With two strikes, he whiffs.

389

DAD: What is Garner thinking? That's stupid. So what if everyone knows the bunt is coming with one strike? Everett's batting about .021. Lay it down.

BEN: I like Phil Garner.

Biggio breaks his bat and hits a mini-pop to Iguchi at second. Iguchi plays it off the bounce, and fires to first to nip Biggio. Tavares grounds softly toward short. If anyone's going to make a play, it has to be Crede, but it gets past him. Uribe catches it and throws to first, but Tavares is too speedy for that.

Men on first and third, two outs, Berkman up. Berkman lacerates a change-up down the left-field line, a double. Ausmus and Tavares both score, and the Astros are up 4-2. Dad was warned after the surgery to be careful about twisting, turning, etc., but he slams his fist into the couch and I can see him biting his lip.

Ensberg lines softly to Uribe to end the Astros' half, but they're up, and Pettite's got the lead, and all the world is crap.

Somewhere, Bill Murray is laughing.

Sick bastard.

Uribe leads off the bottom of the fifth with a double down the left field line. McCarver says, "The ball *just* gets by Morgan."

DAD: How come McCarver's on a first name basis with the Astros, but every White Sox player is only referred to by last name? His National League allegiances are showing.

Scotty flies to center, but Uribe doesn't tag because Tavares has a good arm. Pettite snares Iguchi's comebacker, then turns toward Uribe, who is wandering off of second. He catches him in a rundown, and throws him out at second. Pettite picks Iguchi off of first, and the inning's over.

BEN: This is freaking awful. They're running themselves out of the ballgame.

Bagwell lines to Crede for the first out of the sixth. Buehrle is still out there for some reason. Lane strikes out on a high fastball, and they're showing the replay of the Iguchi pickoff.

DAD: That's a balk, and Pettite only gets away with it because he's a vet. He has to step toward first. He doesn't. There's no way for a runner to read that.

Burke flies to Scotty, and we're into the bottom half. We're at the meat of the order, so if we're going to do some damage, now is the time. Dye leads off with an easy fly to Jason Lane. The rain is really falling now, and McCarver is composing an Ode to Andy Pettite, speaking flowingly of the lefty's "penetrating" eyes.

Konerko ignores Pettite's penetrating eyes and drives the ball deep to right, but Lane is there. Everett keeps the inning alive with a soft single into left. Rowand drives the ball to left for a double, and it's second and third with two outs. Apparently the Sox aren't as enamored as McCarver.

All of a sudden, the crowd is electric. But Pettite pops up A.J. to short, and the inning is over.

DAD: Where's the hemlock?

BEN: I'm not sure, but I have a fork, and I believe there's an electrical outlet behind the couch.

Ausmus flies to center to start the seventh. Adam Everett slashes a liner headed for the left field corner, but Crede goes Superman, diving horizontally to snare it. The whole play takes perhaps a millisecond. Buehrle catches Biggio looking with a fastball on the outside corner.

Pettite's out, Dan Wheeler's in (yet another bearded white guy for the Astros – this is like the Unabomber Official Team). Thank goodness. Crede pops to third for the first out. Uribe crushes an 89-mph fastball off the left-center wall, and he's on second. Scotty strikes out; only he and Paulie don't have hits tonight. We need them both.

Iguchi walks, and it's up to J.D. Wheeler throws a ball in the dirt for ball one. He goes low again for ball two.

DAD: All I ask is a three-run homer for the lead.
BEN: And a pony.

Strike one on the corner. The count is 2-1. Up and in, and it's 3-1.
Pay-off pitch.
Dye fouls it off, and the count is full.
Another pay-off pitch.
Dye fouls it off again.
Let's try this again.

DAD: I don't know how much more of this I can take. That electrical socket looks good right about now.

392

Here's the pitch.

And it hits him in the hand.

Dye walks to first, the umpire signals HBP, and we've got bases loaded. Garner's coming out to argue with the ump, though. What's going on? Fox shows the replay. The ball hit the barrel of Dye's bat. It would have been just a foul tip. The ump missed the call.

This controversy is getting monotonous. A.J. is sitting in the dugout whistling to himself.

And the Captain is at the plate.

Bases loaded, two outs, second game of the World Series.

Wheeler is coming out, replaced by Chad Qualls – you guessed it, a white guy with a beard.

He's ready.

Here comes the first pitch.

It's fat.

It's juicy.

Paulie's eyes open wide.

He cranks, he swings ...

That ball is HAMMERED.

It's deep into the left-field seats.

A grand slam. In the World Series.

We're up 6-4.

Dad and I are jumping around the room, slapping each other high five, head-butting (well, okay, not head-butting). High five, low five, high ten, low ten, up high, down low, too slow. The fireworks from the scoreboard are beautiful in the night sky.

We're gonna win this ballgame and go into Houston up 2-0 in the World Freaking Series.

Of course, we still have two innings to play. But soon we'll be into Jenks time.

Everett singles while Paulie takes a curtain call at the top step of the dugout. Everett takes off on a 1-2 pitch and is thrown out by three feet to end the inning.

Who cares?

Cliff Politte comes in for us. Dad can't even remember what he looks like, it's been so long since he pitched. Tavares flies to Dye in right. Five outs from glory. He racks up Berkman on a fastball down the middle. Just four more outs.

Meanwhile, Joe Buck and McCarver are going on and on and on about the A.J. play back in the Angels series. Can we get over this already?

DAD: Let's get one thing straight. None of those calls mean anything if the team doesn't capitalize on them. There are tons of calls that go wrong all the time, but if the team doesn't take advantage, nobody remembers.

Ensberg grounds to Uribe at short, and we're three outs away from a 2-0 lead in the Series.

Qualls is back out there for the Astros. Rowand nubs one down to third. Ensberg charges and fires low, but Berkman scoops it for the first out. Hambino comes to the plate as some white guy with a beard named Mike Gallo comes out of the bullpen. McCarver refers to Gallo as Mike as Dad fumes to my right.

DAD: Thanks, *Tim*.

Hambino grounds 4-3. Crede grounds 5-3. Whatever. It's Jenks time.

First batter is Bagwell. 97 mph strike. 95 mph strike, fouled off. A curveball in the dirt. 1-2. 98, on the outside corner; Bagwell's lucky to foul it off. Jenks fires in, but Bagwell is equal to the task this time and lofts one into short center, where it drops just in front of Rowand.

No worries.

Jason Lane. 95, strike. 97, strike. 96, high and inside, but Lane can't hold up. Two outs away from a 2-0 lead.

Chris Burke. 93, too high. Ball one. 96, on the outside corner, but called a ball. 95, on the outside corner, but called a ball. They're really squeezing Jenks tonight. Jenks throws a ball right across the letters, on the heart of the plate. The ump calls ball four, and Don Cooper is immediately out of the dugout to chat with Jenks.

DAD: Is this a makeup for Dye?

Ausmus up. 95, strike one. McCarver is saying something about Jenks throwing a wild pitch; you can hear the hope in his voice. Ausmus checks his swing on the next pitch but it works for the Astros; the ball bounces to Konerko at first, who fields it and steps on the bag for the second out. The Astros now have the tying runs on second and third base.

Joe Buck is surprised that Garner has called on Jose Vizcaino, the former Yankee, to hit. He's a contact hitter, and that's the best they can do against Jenks anyway.

Jenks throws heat on the outside corner, but Vizcaino flips the ball over Uribe's head and into left. Bagwell scores easily. Scotty comes up throwing, but the throw is on the first-base side of the plate, and Burke slides in under the tag with the tying run. The Astros have tied it, 6-6.

DAD/BEN: &%#!*&#%!!!!

Jenks is out, Cotts is in. Vizcaino's on second with the go-ahead run. Mike Lamb is pinch-hitting. Cotts goes 2-2 to Lamb before Lamb flies to left.

DAD: Catch it with two hands, Scotty!

He does. That's been about the only thing to go right this inning.

Jenks is sitting disconsolate in the dugout. We're sitting disconsolate on the couch in Los Angeles. Vizcaino has turned the world to crap again.

Brad Lidge is in for the Astros. He's the best closer in the National League. The last time he pitched, Albert Pujols hit the longest home run I've ever seen. Apparently, when the Astros were flying to St. Louis for the next game, the pilot announced that a baseball had just flown in front of the plane, joking about the length of that shot.

Maybe J.D. or Paulie can get hold of one, but it's not likely. This guy is dynamite.

McCarver is gushing about the "remarkable hit" by Vizcaino.

Lidge is throwing bullets – 96, 97. Uribe gets around on it, but flies out to left center.

Scotty's up.

DAD: We need a baserunner. Work him for a walk, Scotty.

BEN: He's still the only player on our team without a hit.

Meanwhile, Buck and McCarver are going *on* and *on* and *on* about the brilliance of Vizcaino.

BUCK: Tim, you and I have seen him . . . he has bounced around and always been a very good part-time player wherever he's been.

Ball one, outside.

McCARVER: Absolutely.

BUCK: But to me he was not the obvious choice in the top of this ninth.

McCARVER: No, but the right one.

BUCK: But the right one.

Ball   two,   low.
Strike, inside corner.
Now McCarver and Buck are talking about Lidge again.

BUCK: Do you, sir, buy into the theory that people said with regard to Lidge that it would have been nice to get Lidge in the game in game six in St. Louis in the NLCS to get that taste out of his mouth from the Pujols home run?

McCARVER: I don't think that taste is there –
as Lidge delivers, a bullet over the plate – Scotty swings –

BUCK: Podsednik hits one to deep right-center field . . . back at the wall . . . this ball is *GONE!* Podsednik goes deep! His second home run of the postseason, and the White Sox win it 7-6!

Bedlam.

Scotty's pumping his fist as he rounds the bags. The Sox are charging out of the dugout to mob him at home plate. Dad and I are yelling and screaming and shouting and laughing. My sisters are yelling and screaming. Chicago is yelling and screaming.

BUCK: Lidge has a new taste.
McCARVER: The taste might be there now. Scott Podsednik had *no* home runs this season. *None.*

The fireworks are exploding. The fans are going insane on this rainy, dreary, wonderful Chicago night.

McCARVER: (forlornly) Unbelievable.
BUCK: Over 500 regular season at-bats for Podsednik and not one home run . . . he homers to end Game Two of the World Series.
McCARVER: (forlornly) How do these things happen?
DAD: Because God is a White Sox fan – *Tim.*

This is the most exciting ballgame I've ever seen.

BEN: Dad, I'm going to ask you a stupid question. Is this the greatest moment in baseball history?
DAD: It's the greatest moment in *human* history.

We're laughing hysterically.

They're showing the replay now with the shot of the dugout. They've got a microphone on Evel, who is standing next to Brian Anderson as the ball is hit.

ANDERSON: Oh my God . . . oh my God . . .
ROWAND: No way . . . no way . . . no, no way . . . YAAAAAAAAA!!!!!

Buck is signing off the broadcast.
BUCK: Shock and awe here on the South Side. Podsednik with a blast to right center field . . . the White Sox win it in the ninth, 7-6.

Papa's enjoying this, that's for sure.

October 26, 2005
DAD:
Ben and I are hermetically sealed from the outside world. Because of the two holidays of Shemini Atzeres and Simchas Torah, which started Tuesday night and just ended tonight, we couldn't watch Games Three and Four, and we're watching the tapes now. Because the rest of the world knows what happened, we have conversed with no one, turned the answering machine off, and since we don't use the phone on holidays or Shabbat, we know nothing of what's happened.

Except for what Boggle has told us. During the holiday, Dad and I brought out the Boggle game, shook it up, and laughingly decided to look for a sign from Upstairs as to what was happening in Game Three.

We shook it once . . . looked . . . nothing.
A second time . . . nothing.

399

Finally, on the third attempt, we struck gold. Amazingly enough, clearly (though circuitously) spelled out was Joe Crede's full name. (Of course, the odds against A.J. Pierzynski's name being spelled out were astronomical.)

So we enter the land of Game Three with hope. We can skip all the commercials, so watching the two games should take about three hours. We should be done about ten p.m.

Game Three

All the pre-game talk on TV is about two things: The retractable roof in Houston, which has been ordered open by Bud Selig, and Roy Oswalt. It's Roy Oswalt this, Roy Oswalt that, and Jon Garland must wonder if the announcers know he's pitching. Apparently the Astros are fussing about their lack of supposed home field advantage, since their record lately has been considerably better when the roof is closed.

BEN: Funny, I thought baseball was meant to be played outside.
DAD: You didn't grow up in Houston.

Our favorite bit of news, though, is the fact that the inestimably classy Jerry Reinsdorf brought a group of roughly 250 people comprised of White Sox employees and their families (yes, you heard that right, 250 people) and flew them to Houston for the Series, as well as giving them the week off. This guy treats the whole organization like they're his family. If ever an owner deserved a ring, it's Reinsdorf.

Well, let's see if he'll get it . . . here we go.

Oswalt throws bullets, usually 97 mph, Jenks style, and Scotty can't catch up to them, swinging late and fouling pitches off. Then Oswalt freezes him with a perfect 72 mph curve for strike three.

BEN: Forget it, Scotty, if he's throwing 97, and he can throw *that*, just forget it.

Tad takes an outside 1-0 fastball and singles to right, though.

DAD: Tell the announcers that Oswalt is human after all.

But Dye bounces into an easy 6-4-3 double play.

BEN: Maybe not.

In their half, Biggio immediately doubles into the gap, but Taveras pops up a bunt attempt to Crede, leaving it up to Berkman. Sure enough, he singles down the left-field line, scoring Biggio, and is that all Oswalt will need? Maybe that's all he'll get: Ensberg hits into a 6-4-3 double play, but the Astros have grabbed the lead, 1-0.

Konerko starts the second with a double into the left-field corner and Hambino walks, but they get a break – Rowand lines it directly to Everett at short, and he doubles up Konerko by an eyelash. Crede walks, but Uribe, jammed, pops to first, and we're still trailing.

In the second, Garland gets Lamb to fly to center, but then Lane pops a foul over the first-base stands. Konerko is ready to glove it, but a fan gets his glove up higher and snares it. Buck and McCarver go to great lengths to assert that the fan has a right to the ball.

DAD: Where were they when Steve Bartman needed them?

Reprieved, Lane draws a walk on a pitch that looked very much like a strike. Garland quietly asks the ump where the pitch was, but to no avail. Ausmus gets the ump off the hook by bouncing one directly toward second base, where Uribe grabs it, steps on second, and fires to first for the double play.

Garland, leading off our third, is taunted by Oswalt with a two-strike curve for strike three. Scotty can't catch up again, grounding to third, and Tad grounds right back to Oswalt.

BEN: That was quick.

The Astros come up in their half of the third, and we need to stay close. Adam Everett dribbles one toward short, but Uribe can't make the throw quickly enough. With Oswalt up, Ozzie smells a hit-and-run, pitches out, and we've got Everett caught halfway to second as Hambino guns it to Uribe.

Uribe misfires, though, and plunks Everett in the back as he scampers safely back to first.

BEN: Look at Ozzie; he's not happy.

Given another chance, Oswalt lays down a perfect bunt to advance Everett to second. On the first pitch to Biggio, he takes an outside pitch the other way, singling to right to score Everett, 2-0, Astros. Garland recovers with a sinking fastball to strike out Taveras for the second out, but Berkman keeps the inning alive, singling to right with Biggio easily making third.

402

DAD: Why don't we just walk Berkman intentionally every time he's up there? He's killing us.

Ensberg looking to push their lead, singles hard to left, we're down 3-0 to Oswalt, and there are *still* runners on first and second. Lane strikes out to end the innng, but our task may be like climbing Everest with 1000 lbs on your back.

Dye leads off the fourth by launching one deep to left-center, but the fleet Taveras runs it down. Then Taveras runs the other way, racing in to catch Konerko's soft fly to center. Buck and McCarver are raving about Oswalt because he is throwing much more off-speed stuff than his last start, and how versatile he is.

BEN: But he's throwing the soft stuff for a reason; his fastball must not be up to par, which means we should have a shot at him before this is over.

Hambino is hanging tough, fouling off pitch after pitch and finally drawing a walk. Rowand rolls one toward third, and Ensberg races in, barehands, and throws and Rowand is out by ten feet. We're done again.

DAD: We'd better not wait too long; he's making us look like jelly out there.

We may be toast. Lane takes a cockeyed swing that looks like he's swinging a sword, but the ball flies deep to center, and hits the wall just above the cockeyed yellow line of demarcation that serves to distinguish a HR for a ball in play. It's 4-0, Astros.

BEN: This is like pulling off a scab one piece at a time. If Garland had given up the four runs all at once, he'd be gone, but they're spreading out the damage just enough so Ozzie leaves him in there.

Ausmus grounds back to Garland, Everett grounds to Uribe, and Oswalt back to Garland, and Garland lives to fight another day. (Not that his presence is any panacea at this point.) Crede leads off for us in the fifth.

BEN: Get us started, Jedi.

And he does, blasting one over the right-field fence, making it 4-1.

BEN: The game of Boggle reveals the Force's inner workings. Clearly this gane must be kept out of the hands of the Empire.

Now McCarver is saying that after watching multiple replays of the Lane HR, the ball was not a home run, and was really in play instead.

DAD: Will the announcers give that blown call the same attention they've given the calls that went our way? We might be down only 3-1, and against Oswalt that extra run is huge.

Uribe singles to left, though, and we're starting to wake up. The crowd is silent. As Oswalt pitches to Garland, Ozzie yells to Angel Hernandez, the third-base ump, that Oswalt is not making the required pause before delivering the pitch, and he's right. Oswalt is *not* stopping, but they're not calling it. Garland strikes out swinging after attempting to bunt, and there's one down. Scotty's up, and he hasn't been able to handle Oswalt tonight.

But Scotty singles to right, and we have runners on first and second, with the tying run to the plate in Iguchi. This may be the only chance we get, so we'd better take advantage *now*.

Tad singles up the middle! And Uribe scores, flying, and Scotty's on second.

BEN: Yes! He was due.

We've cut the lead in half, and it's 4-2. The 2-2 pitch to Dye grazes his uniform but no call. Dye forces the count full, then fouls off pitches until Oswalt throws a slider outside. Somehow Dye reaches waaaayyyy out and flips the ball softly to center where it lands in front of Taveras. Scotty scores, it's 4-3, and now Tad's on second, Dye at first, and if the Captain drives them in, we'd have an amazing comeback and be ahead.

DAD: He's the guy you want up there . . .

Konerko flies to center for the second out, though, and is disgusted with himself. Leaving it all up to Hambino.

DAD: Who else? Who else has been in the center of everything throughout the playoffs? Who else could seize the lead role in this drama? Can he?

He *wallops* it. The ball soars deep to right-center, and hits the wall, two feet short of a HR, and Tad and Dye score easily, while Hambino stands out at second, triumphantly out of breath. It's 5-4 Sox, we have gotten six hits off of Oswalt in this inning, and suddenly Garland has outpitched him?

BEN: Un-freaking-believable!

Now Rowand walks, and we have batted around. Crede gets drilled in the ribs, and suddenly the game takes an ugly turn. Crede says something out toward the mound as he goes to first, and Carl Everett is up at the top step of the dugout yelling at Garner, who starts yelling back.

DAD: Look at that look on Garner's face.

It isn't very pleasant. In fact, it looks downright ugly.
Uribe, up next, hits one deep down the right-field line, and Buck says, "If that stays fair it's a ton of trouble."

BEN: So much for impartiality.

It goes foul, and Buck can relax now, especially because Uribe flies to right to end one long, wonderful inning. We're up 5-4.
What a nice feeling to be on top. Biggio grounds to Crede for one easy out, Taveras pops to Iguchi for a second easy

out, and even Berkman makes it relatively easy for us, lofting one that Evel catches on an easy run in left-center.

Into the sixth. Garland grounds to Everett and Scotty grounds out 4-3, but Tad gets on when Ensberg does the matador again. This time, he actually touches it and it glances off his left wrist, so he gets an error. We don't take advantage, though as Dye flies to center.

In their half, Ensberg strikes out on a classic Garland sinker.

BEN: I think he's found his rhythm.

Lamb pops to Uribe and Lane grounds deep in the hole to Uribe, who guns him out.

DAD: My, that was easy.

The seventh. Konerko walks on four pitches, and it's good-bye Oswalt.

BEN: So much for the pre-game show hype.

Springer is in now, and he shuts us down completely. Hambino pops up back to Springer, Rowand strikes out and Crede grounds out 4-3. We're up 5-4 as the Houston crowd takes the seventh inning stretch.

The Astros send up Ausmus, who walks, and when Everett bunts directly in front of the plate, Hambino thinks for a moment about going to second, but Ausmus has a good jump, so Hambino takes the out at first. The crowd is alive, now, especially since Bagwell is going to pinch-hit. Garland runs the count full, then throws a change-up, and Bagwell pops up to Konerko for the second out. Now it's Biggio, and Garland throws him two changes in a row, then a couple of 55-foot curveballs, then finally fires a 94 mph heater for strike three and they don't get anything.

BEN: Two to go, Dad.

DAD: Ozzie should bring in Jenks after we bat. I'll risk him going two innings here.

In our half of the eighth, Wheeler comes in. Uribe flies to right. Everett bats for Garland and singles to right, and Willie Harris makes a rare appearance to run for him. Harris takes off, and Ausmus has a bad grip, so his throw is very high, and Harris stands on second.

BEN: Bring him in, Scotty . . .

But Scotty flies to left, and Tad grounds out to third, and we're still hanging on by a thread, 5-4.

BEN: Garland was all guts. He deserves the win.

Politte is in for the bottom of the eighth. He pops up Tavares on a 1-0 high fastball, and we're five outs from a 3-0 World Series lead. Lidge is getting warmed up for the Astros, and Cotts and Hermanson are getting warmed up for us.

DAD: I know Jenks blew the save in Game 2, but I'm not sure why Ozzie would go to anyone else in the ninth, if we keep the lead.

Politte goes 3-2 on Berkman, then fans him with an outside fastball. Four outs away now. Great pitching by Politte – he pounded Berkman inside, then went outside for the strikeout. But Ensberg is able to work Politte for a walk.

Ozzie motions for Cotts; he wants a lefty to face Mike Lamb. Cotts walks Lamb on five pitches.

BEN: So much for that strategy.

Ozzie motions for the shorter, skinnier righty – Hermanson. It's a bizarre move; why not bring in Jenks now?

It turns out to be a rotten move; Hermanson doesn't locate, and leaves a breaking ball over the inside half of the plate. Lane turns on it and drives it down the left field line. Ensberg comes around to score, and we're all tied up, 5-5. The Sox get a break, though – the ball doesn't bounce all the way down the line. Instead, it caroms off the corner of a seating area intruding into the playing field, and bounces right to Uribe, who is able to hold Lamb at third.

BEN: Where was Jenks?

The crowd is going berserk as Ausmus steps to the plate. Hermanson takes care of him, though, on an inside breaking ball, and we're into the ninth.

DAD: A little late . . .

Wheeler is still in for the Astros. Dye chops softly to short, and Everett makes a nice running play to pick it and nab

409

Dye at first. Wheeler hits Konerko on an inside slider, though, and the Sox have an opportunity.

Out goes Wheeler, in comes Gallo. The count goes 2-2 on A.J. and the crowd is on its feet, begging for a K. Instead, Hambino grounds softly to second, advancing Konerko to scoring position with two outs.

Out comes Gallo, in comes Lidge.

BEN: Hey, Tim, you think he has that taste in his mouth?

Earlier in the year, Rowand was our two-out RBI machine, but he's had a tough time of it lately. The trend continues; he strikes out on 57-ft. breaking ball. A bad at-bat, and a bad inning.

BEN: Guess not.

Bottom of the ninth. It's a tie ballgame, so the Magical Mr. El Duque is in; Widger comes in in place of Pierzynski. Everett immediately pops to Uribe in foul ground. Chris Burke, who entered the game in the eighth in left field, walks on four pitches (mostly because El Duque doesn't feel comfortable without men on base). For some weird reason, Garner comes out to talk to Burke. Whatever he says doesn't work, because Burke almost gets picked off. On the next pickoff attempt, however, the ball gets away from Konerko and Burke ends up on second, putting the winning run in scoring position.

On the first pitch to Biggio, Burke gets a tremendous jump and steals third. A sac fly will win it for the Astros. Hernandez walks Biggio to set up the double play, and it's up to the rook, Tavares.

DAD: I can't stand this . . .
BEN: He did it against the Red Sox, Dad.

Hernandez puts him down on strikes, coming sidearm on a slow off-speed pitch that fools Tavares. But Hernandez still has to go through Berkman. For some odd reason, Ozzie doesn't elect to intentionally walk Berkman to get to Ensberg. Meanwhile, homeplate ump Jerry Lane is calling an exceedingly tight zone. It doesn't matter, as El Duque walks him anyway. The bases are loaded, two out, Ensberg up, and the crowd – is going insane.

El Duque runs the count to 2-2 on Ensberg as the crowd noise is thunderous. The game is on the line.

BEN: Dad, you can breathe. Take a breath!

Here's the pitch –
It's an inside curveball, and Ensberg strikes out.
We're into the tenth.

DAD: Ahhhhhh . . .

Lidge is still in there for Houston, and he's sawing his way through the lineup. Crede taps a grounder to second for the first out. Uribe flails at an outside curveball and goes down swinging. Widger goes down swinging as well, and the momentum is all with Houston.

El Duque still enjoys pitching with runners on base, so he walks the leadoff man, Orlando Palmiero, on four pitches.

411

Hernandez's shoulder is tightening, and our bullpen options are thin, at best: we're down to Marte, Vizcaino, and Jenks. Marte and Vizcaino are warming up, and it's Vizcaino who comes in now.

Lane is batting, and he pops up to Widger in foul territory to start things off right for our non-crazy low man on the totem pole.

DAD: Why didn't Lane bunt over the runner?

Palmiero gets a monster jump on the 1-1 pitch, but Ausmus pops up to Rowand for the second out. Garner reacts like a loon, picking up a chair and smacking it down on the ground as he yells.

BEN: Way to loosen up your team, Phil.

Everett gets the count to 3-2, then walks, and the Astros have two on with two out, and they can win it again right here. But Chris Burke bounces back to Vizcaino, who throws to first to end the inning.

The marathon continues in the top of the eleventh. Chad Qualls (Konerko's victim in Game 2) is in now. After Qualls throws what looks like strike three to Podsednik on an inside fastball (it's called a ball), Scotty singles through the right side. Iguchi is showing bunt, but can't get it down and fouls one off for strike two. On the 1-2 pitch, Scotty takes off for second. It's a pitchout, but Scotty's too fast and he slides in safely. We've got a man in scoring position with no outs.

BEN: Any kind of a hit . . . *any kind* . . .

But Tad flies to right, and Scotty fakes tagging up. Lane throws the ball over third base, but the ball doesn't trickle away.

BEN: Why wasn't Scotty tagging there?

Qualls quickly goes 0-2 on Dye, and this is looking like another blown opportunity. Dye strikes out, and this is *really* looking like another blown opportunity. The Astros opt to intentionally walk Konerko, and Timo Perez is preparing to pinch hit. He grounds to Berkman at first, and into the bottom half we go.

DAD: No comment.

Jenks is in. McCarver points out that Jenks is hittable low in the zone, but virtually unhittable when he elevates the cheese. Meanwhile, the annoying buzzing sound effect piped in by the stadium signals the at-bat of Craig Biggio. Buck mentions that Ozzie sought out Jenks after the Game 2 win to comfort him.

DAD: That's what a great manager does – he doesn't throw chairs.

Jenks is *on* tonight. He's bringing the high smoke. He goes 3-2 on Biggio, then strikes him out swinging on a nasty curveball outside. But instead of bringing the heat to Tavares, he goes to the curve on 1-2 and hits Tavares in the head.

The ever-dangerous Berkman steps to the plate, and Jenks is throwing high, afraid of leaving anything out over the plate. Sure enough, he walks Berkman, and there are two on with one out. The count runs full on Ensberg, but then Ensberg pops up to short left. Uribe is waving off Scotty, and ranges deep into left field to pull in out number two. That out seems to settle Jenks, who begins throwing 99 mph BBs. He puts Palmiero in a 1-2 hole, then breaks his bat on a comebacker for the third out.

And we're into the twelfth. Rowand leads off against Qualls and strikes out. He has been a bust in the Series, especially in Game 2 – Ozzie pointed out that Bagwell's Game 2, ninth-inning single never should have fallen in front of him. Jedi Joe Crede softly lines a one-hopper to short for the second out. Uribe breaks his bat and pops to short.

BEN: How long can this last?

Jenks remains on the mound. Lane pops to Podsednik; Ausmus Ks on 97-mph heat; Everett slashes at a 96-mph heater and comes up empty for the third out. Finally, a quick inning from the Sox bullpen.

Chris Meyers points out that the Astros have shaven their unkempt beards and gone with goatees, trying to change their luck. So far, so good for them.

Widger is swinging for the fences in the top of the thirteenth, but somehow works Qualls for a leadoff walk. Scotty P. tries to get down a bunt, but blows it; the bunt attempt bounces foul, then spins fair. Ausmus, alert, leaps out from behind the plate, fires to second for the force. Scotty, who thought the bunt was foul, doesn't even leave the box, and he's thrown out at first for the DP. Score that one 2-4-3.

BEN: Ugly.

Tad strikes out on a breaking ball in the dirt, and that's it for the Sox thirteenth.

Ozzie pulls a double switch, bringing in Damaso "Nuttier Than a Christmas Fruitcake" Marte to pitch and Geoff Blum at second to sub for Tad. Marte goes 3-2 on Jose Vizcaino before walking him to lead off the inning, and Ozzie is pacing worriedly in the dugout. But he comes back to strike out Biggio on the 2-2 pitch, firing on the inside corner for a called strike three. He strikes out Willy Tavares on an identical inside fastball for the second out.

BEN: Where has this guy been all year?

Marte even gets Berkman to chop to Uribe, who flips to Blum at second for the force.

On to the fourteenth. Will this game ever end? The length of the game almost sucks away the tension. Almost.

Ezequiel Astacio is on the mound, and Jose Vizcaino is playing second for Biggio.

J.D. leads off with a liner into right for a single. The crowd goes quiet. Konerko drills a ball down the third base line. Ensberg somehow slides and picks it at third, fires to second, and Vizcaino fires to first for the DP. It's brilliant defense, and the crowd is reinvigorated. Astacio only has to get Geoff "The Producer" Blum now, who came in in the thirteenth on the double switch. He goes to 2-0 on Blum, then throws one practically on the ground at Blum's feet.

But the former Astro swings down (how he found room for that swing I'll never know) and laces the pitch and drives it deep . . . deep . . . and *gone* into the right field seats.

415

DAD: Geoff Blum?
BEN: What the heck?

All the air is sucked out of the ballpark. Phil Garner, ever in control of his emotions, grabs a chair, swings it over his head, and bashes it against the ground.

Rowand follows by chopping a swinging bunt down the third base line, and he's safe at first. The wheels are falling off the Astros' train.

Buehrle is up in the Sox bullpen, and McCarver points out that the longer the Sox take at bat, the longer Buehrle gets to warm up, which is important since he's a starter.

Crede follows with *another* swinging bunt, and he, too, is safe. Free-swinging Juan Uribe walks to load the bases as the bizarre inning continues. Now it's up to Widger.

And Astacio walks him. 7-5 Sox.

Astacio's done. Wandy Rodriguez comes in.

Finally, Scotty P. strikes out to end our half.

BEN: Three outs to go.
DAD: Ben, Marte's pitching.
BEN: Good point.

But Marte strikes out Ensberg.

BEN: What the hell is going on in this game?

Marte reverts to form by walking Orlando Palmiero. But Jason Lane pops to Blum, and there are two outs.

Ausmus grounds hard to Uribe. This should end it.

But Uribe bobbles it, and the game remains alive.

DAD/BEN:
Aaaaaaaaaarrrrrrrrrgggggggggghhhhhhhhhhhh . . .

First and third, two outs.
In comes Mark Buehrle, our . . . *closer?*
Adam Everett, who went 0-3 against Buehrle in Game 2, pops up the 1-1 pitch to short. This time, Uribe's there . . . and that's the ballgame.

DAD/BEN: You can put it on the board . . . yes!

It's almost midnight, and the girls have gone to bed because it's a school night.
There's no way we're going to sleep *now*.

Game Four
It's do-or-die for the Astros. Who would have thought we'd take Clemens, Pettitte, and Oswalt, and they'd have to rely on Brandon Backe to save them? Freddy's going for us, and there's no reason to believe he won't be strong. Facing an 0-3 deficit, Backe has to have the weight of the world on his shoulders, while the Sox should be loose as a goose.

Backe starts off like *he's* loose as a goose. Scotty works the count to 3-2, just like he has all series. Finally he flies out the other way to Berkman in left for the first out.

417

DAD: Scotty's reaching again, just like he did at the beginning of Game 3. When he catches up to Backe's stuff, he'll start pulling the ball.

Tad pokes an outside fastball to right for the second out. He's had a miserable series. Fox shows a graphic stating that Backe was traded for Blum a couple of years ago, in 2003. Another subplot.

BEN: And somehow, that deal ends up helping the Sox. God loves us.

Dye slashes a double the other way, into the right field gap. He thought about taking third, but didn't want to run his way out of the inning.
Backe goes full on Konerko, and the crowd is on its feet. Backe throws another outside fastball, and Paulie tries to go the other way like Dye did, but nubs it back to the pitcher for the third out.

DAD: Did you see the sign in the background flashing: "NOISE"? The crowd needs to be told this?

Big Freddy starts off poorly, surrendering a single through the left side to Biggio, who must be going berserk.

BEN: His only World Series appearance, and his team hasn't won a game.
DAD: Yeah, I feel sorry for the guy. He's supposed to be a good fellow.

Tavares lays down a poor bunt, but he gets it down to advance Biggio to second. But Freddy goes 1-2 on Berkman, then fans him on a breaking ball that falls off the table.

BEN: That's the same pitch he threw on 1-1. Berkman just can't find it.

DAD: Trying to hit that pitch is like trying to eat soup with a fork.

Ensberg can't handle Garcia, either, and he check swings a grounder to Garcia, who throws to first to end the inning.

Hambino leads off the second and puts the hurt on Backe by lining hard off of Backe's right shoulder. That knocks the ball down, and Backe throws to first for the out.

BEN: That'll sting in the morning.

Rowand chops to third, and Backe is cruising.
Meanwhile, Fox goes to Chris Meyers, who talks about his conversations with Phil Garner and Hambino, respectively. Garner apparently told Meyers that his guys know what to do, they've been down before, the usual baloney. A.J., on the other hand, said that the Sox had to stomp them, crush them, pull their hearts out, eat their livers with fava beans, etc.

DAD: I was right all along about him. I love that guy.

Crede pops softly to right, and Backe's brilliance continues.

In the bottom half, Garcia leaves a fastball up in the zone, and Mike Lamb jumps on it, driving it off the top of the right field wall. Dye makes a tremendous throw into second, but Lamb beats it.

Jason Lane steps to the plate.

DAD: Why isn't Lane bunting? Ausmus is batting next, and there are no outs.

Dad's right. Lane isn't showing bunt; he's swinging away. What's going through Garner's head? A bunt would put Lamb in sac fly position. Garcia throws a tight curve at 86 mph on the outside corner, and Lane goes down on strikes. A minute later, Ausmus joins him on the bench after freezing on a 2-2 inside curveball. Adam Everett lines a one-hopper to Crede, who fires to first to end the inning.

BEN: Garcia's starting to groove.

Uribe leads off the third, and flies quickly to center. Garcia follows suit. Scotty, however, rips a ball into the right field gap. As he leaves the batter's box, wings suddenly sprout from his heels and I could swear that someone has pushed fast forward on the TV. He's flying – *flying* – around the bases, and he decides to take third. He just makes it, his helmet flying off as he dives in, head first.

DAD: That is old school. Capital O, capital S.

Iguchi is first-pitch swinging, though, and he grounds to short to solve Backe's problem.

DAD: Iguchi has to at least wait and see if Backe throws a wild pitch. That's impatient.

BEN: Other than Scotty, the whole team looks impatient.

DAD: It only took Scotty two at-bats to catch up to Backe.

Garcia strikes out Backe on four pitches. Biggio one hops to Crede, who guns him out. Tavares chops toward short, but Crede cuts it off and fires to first. It's a good thing he did, because Uribe wouldn't have been able to nab Tavares, not with his speed.

BEN: Finally, here's the pitchers' duel we've all been waiting for.

DAD: I'm just glad it happened when the series was 3-0 Sox.

Dye starts the fourth by ripping a 1-0 offering into left for a single. He's now two for two. Up in the bleachers, somewhere, there's a fan holding a sign that reads "I'm Cold – Close the Roof."

BEN: There is no escape. Don't make me destroy you.

DAD: So you've turned to the Dark Side, now?

BEN: You don't know the power of the Dark Side.

Backe strikes out Konerko, however, and he's pitching the game of his life. Hambino battles Backe, fouling off pitch after pitch, until finally Backe throws him a nasty 58-ft. inside curveball. Hambino swings, and he's gone. Aaron fans, and Backe strikes out the side.

421

DAD: Who *is* this guy?

Garcia isn't sailing as smoothly as Backe, and he walks Berkman on five pitches. Ensberg's up, and McCarver shows the wide variety of stances Ensberg has used during the Series. McCarver's openly rooting for "Morgan," but Ensberg goes down swinging. Lamb grounds to Iguchi, who throws to second for the force.

Lane grounds to short, and Uribe throws to second to force Lamb and end the inning. The crowd is beginning to boo.

To the fifth we go. Backe picks up where he left off, striking out Crede on an outside curve. He strikes out Uribe the same way, and he's struck out five in a row. This is getting ridiculous. The Series record is six in a row, but Garcia breaks *that* up, grounding hard to third for the last out.

DAD: Garcia *was* always known as a contact hitter.

Garcia, who seems to have consistent trouble with leadoff batters, gives up a single to Brad Ausmus, who pokes the ball into center.

Adam Everett rips the ball toward third, and Ausmus is going on the pitch. Somehow, Crede gloves it and fires to second in time for the force. Iguchi is standing on the third-base side of the bag, then turns and rifles to first for the double play. Beautiful.

Backe's frustrated, and he swinging for the fences. He bounces to third; Crede bobbles it, recovers, and throws a frozen rope to first for the third out.

BEN: Crede's everywhere.

Backe's still going strong, and he induces a groundout to short from Scotty. Tad shows bunt, hits a slow roller past Backe, and Everett charges across the middle, barehands the ball, and flings to first as he runs. It's a great play, and Backe is rightly fired up. Dye strikes out on an outside fastball.

DAD: This guy is unreal.

Biggio tries bunting in the bottom of the sixth, but A.J. leaps out from behind the plate and guns to first. Tavares singles to right, though. Garcia's rattled. He walks Berkman on four pitches, putting two runners on with one out.

Garcia makes a mistake up and in, and Ensberg punishes the pitch deep to left, but the ball lands foul. Garner sends the runners on 3-2, but Ensberg strikes out on a high inside fastball – it would have been ball four.

Second and third, two outs. Mike Lamb bats. Garcia goes 2-0 on Lamb, then walks him intentionally to fill the bases for Jason Lane.

Ozzie's fidgeting in the dugout. The crowd is on their feet. Garcia quickly goes 0-2 on Lane.

DAD: Look at Buehrle. For the first time all season, he's silent and watching the game intensely.
BEN: If Slip N' Slide's tense, everybody's tense.
DAD: You're tense? Why?

Garcia throws a 55-ft. fastball that takes a weird hop, but A.J. makes the block. No surprise there – he led all A.L. catchers in fielding percentage.

Lane fouls one off. Garcia comes up and in, and Lane, swinging from the heels, strikes out.

BEN: He wasn't looking for a base-hit there.

Top of the seventh. Konerko flies out to left, A.J. grounds out to first. Backe goes 2-1 on Rowand, and Fox announces that Backe has now retired 11 in a row. On the next pitch, Evel singles to center. Crede's up. He's been the hero all series. Can he pull the trigger one more time?

On a 1-1 pitch, he swings for a strike, and Ausmus guns behind Rowand at first, almost catching Rowand napping. On the next pitch, Crede crushes a ball toward the left field wall. It bounces high off the fence, and he ends up on second with a double.

DAD: Why didn't Rowand score?
BEN: Look at him. He hesitates between first and second for some reason. There are two outs!
DAD: What the heck?

Uribe doesn't ease Rowand's pain; instead, he fans to end the inning. Backe is bouncing off the field.

Garcia's still going strong in the bottom of the seventh. Ausmus flies softly to J.D. in right. Adam Everett lines softly into left, and Scotty charges hard, slides forward, takes up half the turf in the stadium, and catches it.

DAD: I hope he's not hurt!

BEN: He's fine. He just did a Manny Ramirez, except he caught the ball.

DAD: Replace your divot, Scotty.

Bagwell's batting for Backe.

DAD: This makes *no* sense. Do they really think Bagwell's going to knock one out?

BEN: I'm just glad to see Backe gone.

DAD: He isn't. He's distraught in the dugout.

Bagwell grounds to Iguchi, and that ends the seventh.

BEN: Way to waste Backe, there, Phil.

Lidge is in. Willie Harris pinch hits for Garcia. And, on the 2-2 pitch, he lines a single into left. Garner has to be doubting his Bagwell-for-Backe move now. Scotty lays down a beautiful sacrifice bunt, advancing Harris to second.

DAD: Look where he bunts that. The pitch is eye-high, and he gets it down. He literally catches the ball with the bat to deaden the impact. Fundamentals. Aaron, are you watching?

Everett pinch hits for Iguchi. He grounds to Biggio, advancing Harris to third. Now it's up to J.D. He's fooled on the first pitch, then takes a ball. On the 1-1 pitch, Dye hits a hard grounder up the middle.

No one's going to get there, and we're up 1-0!

DAD: That run was a true team effort. Single, sac bunt, groundout to the right side, single.

BEN: This might be the Series . . .

Konerko strikes out, and we're into the bottom of the eighth. Politte's in for Garcia, and Houston has the top of the lineup. On the 1-2 pitch, Biggio pops one foul. Hambino's after it and so is Jedi Joe; each thinks the other has it. It drops between them.

DAD: Bad omen.

It doesn't matter, as Biggio grounds out to short.

But it can't be that easy. Politte hits Tavares in the hand to put on their speedy rookie. Politte wildpitches Tavares to second, then intentionally walks Berkman. He goes 2-0 on Ensberg, and he can't find the plate.

Ensberg swings on a low fastball, and sends the ball out to Rowand in center, who drifts over and catches it. Tavares tags, and they have men on first and third with two outs.

Cotts is in, Politte is out. Garner is trying to recapture the magic of Game 2, batting Jose Vizcaino for Mike Lamb.

It doesn't work. Cotts goes 2-2 on Vizcaino, then breaks Vizcaino's bat. The ball rolls slowly out to short. Uribe will have to hurry . . . he backhands it, then throws a bazooka to first. The throw is low, but the Captain picks it, nabbing Vizcaino and ending the inning.

Lidge, trying to hold the Astros close, gets ahead of Hambino 1-2 to start the ninth. But then Hambino hooks a low pitch down the right-field foul line, and with speed not seen since

Orson Welles last saw a buffet line, chugs into second. We need a bunt here. Who's up?

It's Evel.

DAD: Not a chance. Have him swing away instead.

BEN: You have a point.

Sure enough, Rowand stabs at the first pitch, bunting it foul. Bunts the next pitch, which is at his eyes, foul, and then, surprisingly, makes a *third* attempt to bunt, and foul it goes for strike three. The camera catches Ozzie looking *very* angry; Rowand must have bunted the last time on his own.

Crede can drive A.J in now, but he strikes out swinging as Lidge really bears down. Uribe, the wildest swinger in the West, grounds to third on the first pitch, stranding Hambino, and setting up the usual scenario: Sox up by one run and their opponent with one last chance.

BEN: Three more outs, Dad. Three more outs.

DAD: This must be an alternate reality.

It's time for Jenks to close it out. The kid has to face Lane, Ausmus, and Everett.

First, Lane. Jenks is throwing nothing but heat. Every pitch is 95 mph or greater, and he runs the count to 3-2. Lane swings at the clincher, and flips a soft fly ball that manages to land five feet in front of a charging Evel. They have the lead-off man on.

DAD: Nope, this is definitely reality.

Ausmus bunts perfectly on the first pitch, and Konerko, charging, throws to Harris at first for the out, but Lane is at second.

BEN: You survived 45 years of this?

Burke pinch-hits for Everett.
First pitch, high, 1-0.
Second pitch, low outside, 2-0.
94 mph heater, called strike. 2-1.
96 mph heater, swinging strike, 2-2.
The next pitch, Burke swings and it's a foul fly. It's far past third base, heading for the area just before the left-field stands jut out toward left field. Crede is running hard, with his back to the plate, but he'll never make the play.

But Uribe is racing there, too, with a sharper angle, although his back is to the plate, too. Just as he reaches the stands, he throws his glove up to try to catch the ball and plunges head-first into the stands, disappearing from view.

The ump is right behind him. There is a pause, and then the ump dramatically throws his thumb up in the out sign.

DAD/BEN:
Yeeeeeeeeeeeeeeeeeeeeeeeeeeeeessssssssssssssssssssssssssssssss!

Everyone is stunned by the catch. McCarver and Buck are stunned. The crowd is stunned. The planets have slowed their orbits to see what happened.

BUCK: The White Sox continue to prove that they can win post-season games in so many different ways: with pitching,

428

with situational hitting, with moving runners along, great defense as we just saw from Uribe, and now they're one out away from the championship.

Orlando Palmiero stands in the batter's box. There is still a major threat, the man on second base, but somehow after Uribe's tremendous catch there doesn't seem to be any doubt in the cosmos that we are destined for victory.

Jenks delivers.

94 mph. high, ball one.

Jenks delivers again –

and Palmiero fouls it off. 1-1.

Jenks throws again –

fouled off. 1-2.

Jenks reaches back . . . fires . . .

Palmiero chops a high bouncer. Jenks jumps, but it's over his head. Palmiero can run, and he takes off like a scared rabbit. Uribe charges the mound hard . . . gloves the ball . . . grabs it with his right hand and throws . . .

Nirvana.

Heaven.

Good night, Houston.

Good morning, good morning, good everlasting, eternal, forever, bright sunny morning –

CHICAGO!

Konerko has the ball, as the throw beats Palmiero by an eyelash. Hambino charges the mound, and has the presence of mind to jump into the arms of Jenks instead of the other way around, the pileup in the middle of the field has begun, Ozzie has his two sons wrapped in a bear hug in the dugout, Konerko runs up to Dye and grabs him in a hug, Ozzie hugs Scotty . . .

They did it.

Epilogue

February 1, 2006
BEN:

It's been three months since Juan Uribe threw out Orlando Palmiero at first. It's been three months since Jerry Reinsdorf held aloft the World Series trophy. It's been three months since the Silent Assassin, Jermaine Dye, carried home his World Series MVP award. It's been three months since Dad and I danced around the room celebrating the first White Sox World Championship in our lifetimes.

A lot has changed in three months. Trader Kenny hasn't been sitting on his hands. Aaron Rowand, one of the most exuberant members of our World Series team, is gone. Jim Thome, the slugging but aging first baseman/designated hitter, is here. Orlando "El Duque" Hernandez, the hero of the ALDS, is gone. Javier Vasquez, another young gun and former Yankee, is here. Damaso "Head Case" Marte is gone. Rob Mackowiak, one of the best bench players in the game, is here. Carl Everett, our hot-and-cold DH, is gone. Paul "Captain" Konerko, the ALCS MVP and post-Series free agent, stays here (we signed him to big money). Frank Thomas, the mainstay of the Sox for the past decade, is gone. Jon Garland, who would have been a free agent after the 2006 season, stays here.

I began this journal by writing about the beautiful stasis of baseball: the leisurely pace of the game, the stability of its rules, the fan allegiances that span decades. But baseball is also a game of constant change, constant movement. Though we may wish that Orlando Palmiero's chopper over the mound would hang in the air forever, it always falls.

Time passes. Things change. Players leave the club, players join the club; people grow, people move on.

But moments never grow or change. They remain fixed in our memories. Baseball provides us those moments. It is we who make the memories.

And we make memories by sharing them.

Baseball is America's national pastime because Americans of all ages, races, and backgrounds share the same memories. We remember where we were when Kirk Gibson hit his home run in the 1988 World Series, or when Mazeroski hit his home run in 1960, or when Bobby Jenks threw the final pitch of the 2005 World Series.

Baseball is the pastime of fathers and sons because we share it together.

This magical season, I shared a book full of moments with Dad. Those are memories that will last beyond this season, or next season, or the season after that. Like the signed photo of Scotty P.'s home run swing in Game 2 that now hangs on our wall, I'll always be able to look at these memories and cherish them – and someday, build new memories with my son.

That's the wonderful thing about baseball: there's always next year.

And there will always be this year, too.

DAD:

Sometimes the Big Questions that we have as children turn out to be as important as the Big Questions we have as adults.

One of the Big Questions of my childhood has been answered.

Yes, David, you will actually see the White Sox will win a World Series.

Its twin, the initial question that had to be asked, was my query to my father as to why we were White Sox fans to begin with. In that question to my father, I wanted to know more than just which team to root for. Growing up in Chicago, we had a choice of baseball teams. The mere fact of rooting for the team on the other side of town implied that there was more to choosing a team than simple proximity.

Thus there was more to that question than I knew, for in the question was another, deeper question: why choose one thing over another? And because my father knew the value of fun in the life of a child, he gave me the proper answer. He knew that there are times in life when fun is the best medicine for a wounded spirit.

Baseball is fun. Rooting your team home is fun. Baseball has so many moments of pure zaniness, and fun, and, well, Not Taking Itself Too Seriously, that it is a palliative for the most wounded of spirits.

Ozzie describing Jenks' huge size as he calls for him from the bullpen . . . Buehrle slipping and sliding on the tarp before a game to entertain the fans . . . Hawk intoning pseudo-portentously, "He gone," as another opposing batter strikes out: these are the province of a sport that knows what people really need to take their minds off their cares and worries.

And we did have worries this year, Ben and I. It was hard for him to watch me in pain, and it was doubly hard for me to see my child suffering 3000 miles away from me. But the Sox pulled us through. There is no way I can ever express my gratitude to this team for what they offered us, and by extension, my family. And I'm sure there are many, many others who were inspired by this team to put aside their daily cares and woes and simply enjoy watching baseball be played the way it was meant to be played. They wound up dominating the season for one good reason: they were a team, with a capital T, and it showed from the start to the finish. They certainly bewildered, annoyed, excited, and seduced us into loving the game with all we had.

Just the other day, Ben and I, wearing our White Sox hats, were waiting for the girls as they went shopping. A fellow in his late thirties strolled by wearing a Yankees cap. As he walked by, he smirked a little, and said, "You guys really lucked out last year."

Ben and I looked at each other and grinned, thinking the same thought.

Loser.

Made in the USA
Middletown, DE
07 June 2017